How to
Start
a
Business
in
Massachusetts

Fifth Edition

How to
Start
a
Business
in
Massachusetts

Fifth Edition

Julia K. O'Neill

Mark Warda

Attorneys at Law

SPHINX® PUBLISHING
AN IMPRINT OF SOURCEBOOKS, INC.®
NAPERVILLE, ILLINOIS
www.SphinxLegal.com

Fifth Edition, 2008

Published by: **Sphinx® Publishing, A Division of Sourcebooks, Inc.®**

Naperville Office
P.O. Box 4410
Naperville, Illinois 60567-4410
630-961-3900
Fax: 630-961-2168
www.sourcebooks.com
www.SphinxLegal.com

This publication is designed to provide accurate and authoritative information in regard to the subject matter covered. It is sold with the understanding that the publisher is not engaged in rendering legal, accounting, or other professional service. If legal advice or other expert assistance is required, the services of a competent professional person should be sought.

From a Declaration of Principles Jointly Adopted by a Committee of the American Bar Association and a Committee of Publishers and Associations

This product is not a substitute for legal advice.

Disclaimer required by Texas statutes.

Library of Congress Cataloging-in-Publication Data

O'Neill, Julia K.
  Start a business in Massachusetts / by Julia K. O'Neill and Mark Warda. -- 5th ed.
    p. cm.
  Rev. ed. of: How to start a business in Massachusetts. 4th ed. 2004
  Includes index.
  ISBN 978-1-57248-622-5 (pbk. : alk. paper) 1. New business enterprises--Law and legislation--Massachusetts--Popular works. I. Warda, Mark. II. O'Neill, Julia K. How to start a business in Massachusetts. III. Title.

KFM2552.Z9O54 2008
346.744'065--dc22
                                        2007048103

Printed and bound in the United States of America.
SB 10 9 8 7 6 5 4 3 2 1

Contents

Using Self-Help Law Books xi

Introduction xv

Chapter 1: Deciding to Start a Business 1
    Know Your Strengths
    Know Your Business
    Sources for Further Guidance

Chapter 2: Choosing the Form of Your Business 9
    Proprietorship
    General Partnership
    Corporation
    Limited Partnership
    Limited Liability Company
    Limited Liability Partnership
    Massachusetts S Corporations versus Massachusetts LLCs
    Start-Up Procedures
    Required Contacts
    Business Comparison Chart
    Business Start-Up Checklist

Chapter 3: Your Business Name. 25
Name Searches
Fictitious Names
Corporate Names
Professional Corporations
The Word *Limited*
Domain Names
Trademarks
Massachusetts Classification of Goods
Massachusetts Classification of Services

Chapter 4: Preparing a Business Plan. 39
Advantages and Disadvantages of a Business Plan
Outline for Your Business Plan
Sample Business Plan

Chapter 5: Financing Your Business 53
Growing with Profits
Using Your Savings
Borrowing Money
Getting a Rich Partner
Selling Shares of Your Business
Using the Internet to Find Capital

Chapter 6: Locating Your Business. 61
Working Out of Your Home
Choosing a Retail Site
Choosing an Office, Manufacturing, or Warehouse Space
Leasing a Space
Buying a Space
Check Governmental Regulations

Chapter 7: Licensing Your Business. 67
Home Businesses
State-Regulated Professions
Federal Licenses

Chapter 8: Contract Laws 75
Traditional Contract Law
Statutory Contract Law
Preparing Your Contracts

Chapter 9: Insurance 81
Workers' Compensation
Unemployment Insurance
Liability Insurance
Hazard Insurance
Home Business Insurance
Automobile Insurance
Health Insurance
Employee Theft

Chapter 10: Health and Safety Laws 87
OSHA
EPA
FDA
Hazardous Material Transportation
CPSC
Additional Regulations
Smoking

Chapter 11: Employment and Labor Laws 95
Hiring Laws
New Hire Reporting
Employment Agreements
Independent Contractors
Temporary Workers
Firing Laws
Discrimination Laws
Sexual Harassment
Wage and Hour Laws
Pension and Benefit Laws
Family and Medical Leave Law
Child Labor Laws

Immigration Laws
Hiring Off the Books
Federal Contracts
Miscellaneous Laws

Chapter 12: Advertising and Promotion Laws.... 123
Advertising Laws and Rules
Internet Sales Laws
Home Solicitation Laws
Telephone Solicitation Laws
Pricing, Weights, and Labeling
Email Advertising

Chapter 13: Payment and Collection 135
Cash
Checks
Credit Cards
Financing Laws
Usury
Collections

Chapter 14: Business Relations Laws............ 141
The Uniform Commercial Code
Commercial Discrimination
Restraining Trade
Intellectual Property Protection

Chapter 15: Endless Laws..................... 147
Federal Laws
Massachusetts Laws

Chapter 16: Your Business and the Internet 159
Domain Names
Web Pages

Legal Issues
Hiring a Website Designer
Financial Transactions
FTC Rules
Fraud

Chapter 17: Bookkeeping and Accounting 175
Initial Bookkeeping
Accountants
Computer Programs
Tax Tips

Chapter 18: Paying Federal Taxes............... 179
Federal Income Tax
Federal Withholding, Social Security, and Medicare Taxes
Federal Excise Taxes
Federal Unemployment Compensation Taxes

Chapter 19: Paying Massachusetts Taxes 185
Sales and Use Tax
Corporate Excise (Income) Tax
Unemployment Compensation Taxes

Chapter 20: Out-of-State Taxes 189
Business Taxes
Internet Taxes
Canadian Taxes

Chapter 21: The End...and the Beginning........ 191

Glossary 193

Appendix A: Sample, Filled-In Forms............ 201

**Appendix B: Tax Timetable and
Ready-to-Use Forms** **225**

Index **267**

Using Self-Help Law Books

Before using a self-help law book, you should realize the advantages and disadvantages of doing your own legal work and understand the challenges and diligence that this requires.

The Growing Trend

Rest assured that you will not be the first or only person handling your own legal matter. For example, in some states, more than 75% of the people in divorces and other cases represent themselves. Because of the high cost of legal services, this is a major trend, and many courts are struggling to make it easier for people to represent themselves. However, some courts are not happy with people who do not use attorneys and refuse to help them in any way. For some, the attitude is, "Go to the law library and figure it out for yourself."

We write and publish self-help law books to give people an alternative to the often complicated and confusing legal books found in most law libraries. We have made the explanations of the law as simple and easy to understand as possible. Of course, unlike an attorney advising an individual client, we cannot cover every conceivable possibility.

Cost/Value Analysis

Whenever you shop for a product or service, you are faced with various levels of quality and price. In deciding what product or service to buy, you make a cost/value analysis on the basis of your willingness to pay and the quality you desire.

When buying a car, you decide whether you want transportation, comfort, status, or sex appeal. Accordingly, you decide among choices such as a Neon, a Lincoln, a Rolls Royce, or a Porsche. Before making a decision, you usually weigh the merits of each option against the cost.

When you get a headache, you can take a pain reliever (such as aspirin) or visit a medical specialist for a neurological examination. Given this choice, most people, of course, take a pain reliever, since it costs only pennies, whereas a medical examination costs hundreds of dollars and takes a lot of time. This is usually a logical choice because it is rare to need anything more than a pain reliever for a headache. But in some cases, a headache may indicate a brain tumor, and failing to see a specialist right away can result in complications. Should everyone with a headache go to a specialist? Of course not, but people treating their own illnesses must realize that they are betting, on the basis of their cost/value analysis of the situation, that they are taking the most logical option.

The same cost/value analysis must be made when deciding to do one's own legal work. Many legal situations are very straightforward, requiring a simple form and no complicated analysis. Anyone with a little intelligence and a book of instructions can handle the matter without outside help.

But there is always the chance that complications are involved that only an attorney would notice. To simplify the law into a book like this, several legal cases often must be condensed into a single sentence or paragraph. Otherwise, the book would be several hundred pages long and too complicated for most people. However, this simplification necessarily leaves out many details and nuances that would apply to special or unusual situations. Also, there are many ways to interpret most legal questions. Your case may come before a judge who disagrees with the analysis of our authors.

Therefore, in deciding to use a self-help law book and to do your own legal work, you must realize that you are making a cost/value analysis. You have decided that the money you will save in doing it yourself outweighs the chance that your case will not turn out to your satisfaction. Most people handling their own simple legal matters never have a problem, but occasionally people find that it ended up costing them more to have an attorney straighten out the situation than it would have if they had hired an attorney in the beginning. Keep this in mind while handling your case, and be sure to consult an attorney if you feel you might need further guidance.

Local Rules   The next thing to remember is that a book that covers the law for the entire nation, or even for an entire state, cannot possibly include every procedural difference of every jurisdiction. Whenever possible, we provide the exact form needed; however, in some areas, each county, or even each judge, may require unique forms and procedures. In our state books, our forms usually cover the majority of counties in the state or provide examples of the type of form that will be required. In our national books, our forms are sometimes even more general in nature but are designed to give a good idea of the type of form that will be needed in most locations. Nonetheless, keep in mind that your state, county, or judge may have a requirement, or use a form, that is not included in this book.

You should not necessarily expect to be able to get all the information and resources you need solely from within the pages of this book. This book will serve as your guide, giving you specific information whenever possible and helping you to find out what else you will need to know. This is just like if you decided to build your own backyard deck. You might purchase a book on how to build decks. However, such a book would not include the building codes and permit requirements of every city, town, county, and township in the nation; nor would it include the lumber, nails, saws, hammers, and other materials and tools you would need to actually build the deck. You would use the book as your guide, and then do some work and research involving such matters as whether you need a permit of some kind, what type and grade of wood is available in your area, whether to use hand tools or power tools, and how to use those tools.

Before using the forms in a book like this, you should check with your court clerk to see if there are any local rules of which you should be aware or local forms you will need to use. Often, such forms will require the same information as the forms in the book but are merely laid out differently or use slightly different language. They will sometimes require additional information.

Changes in the Law   Besides being subject to local rules and practices, the law is subject to change at any time. The courts and the legislatures of all fifty states are constantly revising the laws. It is possible that while you are reading this book, some aspect of the law is being changed.

In most cases, the change will be of minimal significance. A form will be redesigned, additional information will be required, or a waiting period will be extended. As a result, you might need to revise a form, file an extra form, or wait out a longer time period. These types of changes will not usually affect the outcome of your case. On the other hand, sometimes a major part of the law is changed, the entire law in a particular area is rewritten, or a case that was the basis of a central legal point is overruled. In such instances, your entire ability to pursue your case may be impaired.

Introduction

Each year, thousands of new corporations and limited liability companies are registered in Massachusetts and thousands more partnerships and proprietorships open for business. Entrepreneurship is alive and well in Massachusetts. From restaurants to shopping services to indoor golf courses, the new businesses just keep growing.

The best way to take part in this boom is to run your own business. Be your own boss and be as successful as you dare to be. But if you do not follow the laws of the state, your progress can be slowed or stopped by government fines, civil judgments, or even criminal penalties.

This book is intended to give you the framework for legally opening a business in Massachusetts. It also includes information on where to find special rules for each type of business. If you have problems that are not covered by this book, you should consult an attorney who can be available for your ongoing needs.

In order to cover all the aspects of any business you are thinking of starting, you should read through this entire book, rather than skipping to the parts that look most interesting. There are many laws that may not sound like they apply to you, but that do have provisions that will affect your business.

The forms included in this book were the most recent available at the time of publication. It is possible that some may be revised by the time you read this book. Always check with the Secretary of State or other appropriate authority to be sure you are using the latest forms.

Good luck with your new business!

Deciding to Start a Business

If you are reading this book, you have probably made the serious decision to take the plunge and start your own business. Hundreds of thousands of people make the same decision each year and many of them become very successful. Some merely eke out a living, others become billionaires, but a lot of them also fail. Knowledge can only help your chances of success. You need to know why some succeed while others fail. Some of what follows may seem obvious, but to someone wrapped up in a new business idea, some of this information is occasionally overlooked.

KNOW YOUR STRENGTHS

The last thing a budding entrepreneur wants to hear is that he or she is not cut out for running his or her own business. Those *do you have what it takes* quizzes are ignored with the fear that the answer might be one the entrepreneur does not want to hear. But even if you lack some skills, you can be successful if you know where to get them.

You should consider all the skills and knowledge necessary to run a successful business and decide if you have what it takes. If you do not, it does not necessarily mean you are doomed to be an employee all your life. Perhaps you just need a partner who has the skills you lack. Perhaps you can hire someone with the skills you need or can structure your business to avoid areas where you are weak. If those options do not work, maybe you can learn the skills.

For example, if you are not good at dealing with employees (either you are too passive and get taken advantage of or you are too tough and scare them off), you can:

✪ handle product development yourself and have a partner or manager deal with employees;

✪ take seminars in employee management; or,

✪ structure your business so that you do not need employees. Either use independent contractors or set yourself up as an independent contractor.

Here are some of the factors to consider when planning your business.

✪ *If it takes months or years before your business turns a profit, do you have the resources to stay afloat?* Businesses have gone under or been sold just before they were about to succeed. Staying power is an important ingredient to success.

✪ *Are you willing to put in a lot of overtime to make your business a success?* Owners of businesses do not set their own hours— the business sets the hours for the owner. Many business owners work long hours, seven days a week, but they enjoy running their businesses more than family picnics or fishing.

✪ *Are you willing to do the dirtiest or most unpleasant work of the business?* Emergencies come up and employees are not always dependable. You might need to mop up a flooded room, spend a weekend stuffing 10,000 envelopes, or work Christmas if someone calls in sick.

✪ *Do you know enough about the product or service? Are you aware of the trends in the industry and what changes new technology might bring?* Think of the people who started typesetting or printing businesses just before type was replaced by laser printers.

✪ *Do you know enough about accounting and inventory to manage the business?* Some people naturally know how to save money and do things profitably. Others are in the habit of buying the best and the most expensive of everything. The latter can be fatal to a struggling new business.

✪ *Are you good at managing employees?* While you can start a business on your own, it is usually difficult to *grow* the business without the help of additional employees. Hiring compatible and competent help is essential to your success.

✪ *Do you know how to sell your product or service?* You can have the best product on the market but find that people are not beating a path to your door. If you are a wholesaler, shelf space in major stores is hard to get, especially for a new company without a record, a large line of products, or a large advertising budget.

✪ *Do you know enough about getting publicity?* The media receive thousands of press releases and announcements each day and most are thrown away. Do not count on free publicity to put your name in front of the public.

KNOW YOUR BUSINESS

You do not only need to know the concept of a business; you also need the experience of working in a business. Maybe you always dreamed of running a bed and breakfast or having your own pizza place, and now that you are laid off you think it is time to use your savings to fulfill your dream. Have you ever worked in such a business? If not, you may have no idea of the day-to-day headaches and problems of the business. For example, do you really know how much to allow for theft, spoilage, and unhappy customers?

You might feel silly taking an entry level job at a pizza place when you would rather start your own, but it might be the most valuable preparation you could have. A few weeks of seeing how a business operates could mean the difference between success and failure.

Working in a business as an employee is one of the best ways to be a success at running such a business. New people with new ideas who work in old stodgy industries have been known to revolutionize them with obvious improvements that no one ever dared to try.

SOURCES FOR FURTHER GUIDANCE

There are many things to consider as you prepare to start your own business. Most likely, you will have numerous questions that need to be answered before opening your doors for the first time. Luckily, there are many resources available for help. The sources discussed in this section offer free or low-cost guidance for new businesses.

Small Business Administration. Provides information on starting, financing, and expanding a business. Call 617-565-5590 or visit their website at **www.sba.gov/index.html**.

National Association for the Self-Employed. A 300,000-member group of small-business owners tracking legislative activities, stimulating and encouraging grassroots businesses, and providing members with educational opportunities and health benefits. Call 800-232-6273 or visit their website at **www.nase.org**.

Business Resource Center. Provides information for small businesses on getting started, marketing, management, financing, etc. Visit their website at **www.morebusiness.com**.

SCORE   *Service Corps of Retired Executives*. Retired business executives volunteer their time to share their management and technical expertise with present and prospective owners and managers of small businesses.

Beverly
Danvers Savings Bank
181 Eliot Street
100 Cummings Center, Suite 101K
Beverly, MA 01915
978-927-2282

Boston
10 Causeway Street, Room 265
Boston, MA 02222
617-565-5591

Brockton
60 School Street
Brockton, MA 02301
508-587-2673

Cape Cod
270 Communications Way
Independence Park, Suite 5-B
Hyannis, MA 02601
508-775-4884

Springfield
Scibelli Enterprise Center
One Federal Square
Springfield, MA 01105
413-785-0314

Worcester
Worcester Regional Chamber of Commerce
339 Main Street
Worcester, MA 01608
508-753-2929

Visit their website at **www.score.org**.

Massachusetts Development Centers

Executive Office of Housing and Economic Development. The Executive Office of Housing and Economic Development (EOHED) is a state agency responsible for job creation and economic development in Massachusetts. Call 617-727-8380, or visit them on the Web at **www.mass.gov**. Click on the "For Government" tab and go to the "Exec. Departments" link under "Branches & Departments." You should see a link for the Housing and Economic Development office under "Governor & Executive Departments." If you click on it, it will take you to a listing of the departments in the EOHED, where you can find links to the Department of Business and Technology and the

Office of Business Development. The *Massachusetts Department of Business and Technology* provides a variety of information for new businesses. The *Massachusetts Office of Business Development* is a division of the Department of Business and Technology. This office provides financial, technical, informational, and various other types of assistance to businesses in Massachusetts. Call 617-973-8600 for more information. You can also call the regional offices in the following list.

Greater Boston Region:	617-788-3637
Central Region (Worcester):	508-792-7506
Northeast Region (Lowell):	978-970-1193
Southeast Region (Fall River):	508-730-1438
Western Region (Westfield):	413-784-1580

SOMWBA   *The State Office of Minority and Women's Business Assistance.* SOMWBA is also a division of the Massachusetts Department of Business and Technology. This agency promotes the development of certified minority business enterprises, women-owned business enterprises, and minority nonprofit and women's nonprofit organizations. Call 617-973-8692 or visit their website at **www.somwba.state.ma.us**.

Corporation Development   *The Commonwealth Corporation.* The Commonwealth Corporation is a government-sponsored entity that provides services to business owners and employees to promote economic growth in Massachusetts. Call 617-727-8158 or visit their website at **www.commcorp.org**.

Small Business Developement Centers   *Massachusetts Technology Development Corporation.* The Technology Development Corporation provides funding for the start-up and expansion of early stage technology companies operating in Massachusetts. Call 617-723-4920 or visit their website at **www.mtdc.com**.

Massachusetts Small Business Development Centers. Small Business Development Centers stem from a program sponsored by a consortium of colleges and universities, providing management, technical assistance counseling, and educational programs to small businesses.

State Office: 413-545-6301

Counseling Centers:

Clark University SBDC:	508-793-7615
Mass. Export Center:	617-973-8664
Procurement Technical Assistance Center:	413-545-6303
Salem State College SBDC:	978-542-6343
Southeastern Mass. Regional SBDC:	508-673-9783
UMass Boston SBDC & Minority Business Center:	617-287-7750
Western Mass. Regional Office:	413-737-6712

Or, visit their website at **http://msbdc.som.umass.edu**.

Massachusetts Alliance for Economic Development. The Massachusetts Alliance for Economic Development is a private, nonprofit corporation dedicated to fostering economic growth in Massachusetts. It provides free, customized information relating to facility relocation and expansion. Call 781-489-6262 or visit their website at **www.massecon.com**.

Boston Entrepreneurs' Network. The Boston Entrepreneurs' Network provides resources for starting and building businesses. Visit their website at **www.boston-enet.org**.

Worcester Regional Chamber of Commerce. The Worcester Regional Chamber of Commerce is the largest Chamber of Commerce in New England. It provides many networking opportunities and more. Call 508-753-2924 or visit their website at **www.worcesterchamber.org**.

Cambridge Business Development Center. The Business Development Center in Cambridge provides resources and support for emerging businesses, including counseling, referrals, and sponsored events. Call 617-349-4690 or visit their website at **www.cbdc.org**.

Foundation for Continuing Education. The Foundation for Continuing Education is a nonprofit educational resource that presents seminars and publishes books in the areas of finance, estate and business planning, taxes, business development, and computer programming. Call 978-468-6528 or visit their website at **www.fce.org**.

The Enterprise Center at Salem State College. The Enterprise Center is a mixed-use business park with space available to established and start-up companies. On-site support services, a business incubator program, and an entrepreneurs' network are available to help new and emerging businesses on the North Shore. Call 978-542-7528 or visit their website at **www.enterprisectr.org**.

chapter 2

Choosing the Form of Your Business

The six most common forms of business entities in Massachusetts are proprietorship, partnership, corporation, limited partnership, limited liability company, and limited liability partnership. Some of the characteristics, advantages, and disadvantages of each are described in this chapter.

PROPRIETORSHIP

A *proprietorship* is one person doing business in his or her own name or under a *fictitious name*.

Advantages Simplicity is a proprietorship's greatest advantage. There is also no organizational expense and no extra tax forms or reports.

Disadvantages The proprietor is personally liable for all debts and obligations. There is also no continuation of the business after death. All profits are directly taxable, which is certainly a disadvantage for the proprietor, and business affairs are easily mixed with personal affairs.

GENERAL PARTNERSHIP

A *general partnership* involves two or more people carrying on a business together and sharing the profits and losses.

Advantages

Partners can combine expertise and assets. A general partnership allows liability to be spread among more persons. Also, the business can be continued after the death of a partner if bought out by a surviving partner.

Disadvantages

Each partner is liable for acts of other partners within the scope of the business. This means that if your partner harms a customer or signs a million-dollar credit line in the partnership's name, you can be personally liable. All profits are taxable, even if left in the business. Control is shared by all parties and the death of a partner may result in liquidation. In a general partnership, it is often hard to get rid of a bad partner.

CORPORATION

A *corporation* is an artificial *legal person* that carries on business through its officers and directors for its shareholders. (In Massachusetts, one person may form a corporation and be the sole shareholder, director, and officer.) The corporation carries on business in its own name and shareholders are usually not liable for its acts. Since July 1, 2004, laws covering most business corporations have been contained in Massachusetts General Laws (Mass. Gen. Laws), Chapter (Ch.) 156D. This act superseded Chapter 156B.

In a corporation, the *shareholders* elect the directors. The directors then elect the officers. In Massachusetts, the law until June 30, 2004, required that if the corporation had three or fewer shareholders, it had to have at least the same number of directors. Since July 1, 2004, a corporation may avoid this rule (*e.g.*, have any number of directors regardless of the number of shareholders) by providing otherwise in its articles of organization. The officers have authority to run the day-to-day operations, but they need directors' approval to do anything out of the ordinary, such as sign a lease for business space, hire an executive employee, or start a new line of business. For even more major decisions, such as a sale of all or substantially all the assets of the corporation, merger, reorganization, consolidation, or amendment to the articles of organization, a shareholders' vote is required.

An *amendment* to the articles of organization is required in order to increase the number of authorized shares of stock, add another class or series of stock (unless a bank of undesignated shares has been previously authorized in the articles), change the corporation's name, and to take various other actions. In Massachusetts, a majority shareholder vote is required to authorize certain amendments to the articles of organization, including a change of the corporation's name or a stock split. For more major matters, such as a merger, consolidation, or sale of all or substantially all the assets, a two-thirds vote is required, unless the company's articles of organization provide for a lesser vote.

Types *S corporation.* An *S corporation* is a corporation that has filed IRS Form 2553, choosing to have all profits taxed to, and other tax attributes flow through to, the shareholders rather than to the corporation. An S corporation files a tax return but pays no federal tax. The profits (or losses) shown on the S corporation tax return are reported on the owners' tax returns. In Massachusetts, even an S corporation must pay the minimum state excise tax of $456 per year.

Generally, to elect S corporation status, the following conditions must be satisfied:

○ the corporation must be a U.S. corporation;

○ there must be no more than one hundred shareholders;

○ shareholders may only be individuals, estates, specified types of trusts, or certain exempt organizations; and,

○ only one class of stock is allowed, although the voting rights can differ.

C corporation. A *C corporation* is any business corporation that has not elected to be taxed as an S corporation. A C corporation pays both state and federal income tax on its profits. The effect of having business profits taxed at the corporate level, unlike the S corporation, is that the profits are taxed twice—once at the corporate level (as income to the corporation) and a second time at the shareholder level (as dividend income to the shareholder).

Professional corporation. A *professional corporation* is a corporation formed by a professional, such as a doctor or an accountant. Massachusetts has special rules for professional corporations that differ slightly from those of other corporations. These rules are included in Chapter 156A of the Massachusetts General Laws. A professional corporation may be an S corporation.

Massachusetts laws require a majority of the directors and all the officers other than treasurer, secretary, assistant treasurer, and assistant secretary of a professional corporation to be licensed practitioners of the profession that the corporation has been organized to practice. When filing the organizational documents, the incorporators of a professional corporation have to obtain proof from the appropriate licensing board that the necessary persons are duly licensed.

In addition, Massachusetts law prohibits the issuance or transfer of shares to a person who is not professionally licensed. The various licensing boards also often have authority, by statute, to promulgate additional requirements with which professional corporations must comply.

Nonprofit corporation. A *nonprofit corporation* is usually used for organizations such as churches and condominium associations. However, with careful planning, some types of businesses can be set up as nonprofit corporations and save a fortune in taxes. While a nonprofit corporation cannot pay dividends, it can pay its officers and employees fair salaries. Some of the major American nonprofit organizations pay their officers well over $100,000 a year. Massachusetts' special rules for nonprofit corporations are included in Chapter 180 of the Massachusetts General Laws.

Advantages   If a corporation is properly organized and maintained, shareholders have no liability for corporate debts and lawsuits. Also, officers and directors usually have no personal liability for their corporate acts. The existence of a corporation may be perpetual; that is, it will survive changes in owners. There are tax advantages allowed only to corporations. There is prestige in owning a corporation.

Capital may be raised by issuing stock and it is fairly easy to transfer ownership upon death. A small corporation can be set up as an S corporation to avoid corporate taxes but still retain corporate advantages, such as limited liability. Some types of businesses can be set up as nonprofit corporations, which provide significant tax savings.

Disadvantages

There are start-up costs for forming a corporation. Plus, there are certain formalities that must be followed, such as annual meetings, separate bank accounts, and special tax forms. Unless a corporation registers as an S corporation, it must pay federal income tax separate from the tax paid by the owners, and may pay more than the minimum state excise tax.

LIMITED PARTNERSHIP

A *limited partnership* has characteristics similar to both a corporation and a partnership. There are *general partners* who have the control and personal liability, and there are *limited partners* who only put up money and whose liability is limited to what they paid for their share of the partnership (like corporate stock).

Advantages

Capital can be contributed by limited partners who have no control of the business or liability for its debts.

Disadvantages

A great disadvantage is high start-up costs. Also, an extensive partnership agreement is required because general partners are personally liable for partnership debts and for the acts of each other. (One solution to this problem is to use a corporation as the general partner.)

LIMITED LIABILITY COMPANY

Massachusetts was one of the last states to allow the formation of a limited liability company. Previously, Massachusetts required LLCs to have at least two members. Fortunately, this law has been changed so that now one-member LLCs are allowed. As an alternative to the corporate form, the LLC is steadily gaining in popularity. This entity is like a limited partnership without general partners. It has characteristics of both a corporation and a partnership. None of the members have liability and all can have some control. It does not have to be taxed for federal purposes at the company level but can choose to be taxed like a partnership (unless it has only one member, in which case it will be taxed like a sole proprietorship).

Advantages   The limited liability company offers the tax benefits of a partnership (if the entity chooses to be taxed as a partnership rather than a corporation) with the protection from liability of a corporation. It offers more tax benefits and flexibility than an S corporation because it may pass through more depreciation and deductions. Allocations of income, gain, loss, deduction, and credit can be made in proportions that are different than the equity owners' respective ownership interests, subject to various limitations.

It may have different classes of ownership, an unlimited number of members, and aliens as members. If it owns appreciated property, it has more favorable tax treatment upon dissolution than an S corporation. The limited liability company is also extremely flexible in structure and operational aspects, since those are not dictated strictly by statute as they are for corporations.

Disadvantages   There are higher start-up costs than for a corporation. Due to the flexibility in structural and operational aspects, the governing documents are more complex and expensive to have properly prepared than those of a corporation. The LLC may also be subject to personal property tax on inventory in Massachusetts to which a corporation would not be subject.

LIMITED LIABILITY PARTNERSHIP

The limited liability partnership is like a general partnership, but without personal liability. It was devised to allow partnerships of lawyers and other professionals to limit their personal liability without losing their partnership structure.

NOTE: *The law does not allow professionals to limit their liability for negligence in their own professional functions, i.e., malpractice.*

This is important because converting to an LLC could have tax consequences, and some states do not allow professionals to operate as LLCs. Both general and limited partnerships can register as LLPs.

Advantages The LLP offers the flexibility and tax benefits of a partnership with the protection from liability of a corporation.

Disadvantages Start-up and annual fees are higher for limited liability partnerships than for a corporation.

MASSACHUSETTS S CORPORATIONS VERSUS MASSACHUSETTS LLCS

Often the start-up will narrow down its choices of entity to two—the S corporation and the LLC. Both entities will protect the principals from any personal liability for the business's debts and obligations, assuming formalities are followed and no circumstances lend themselves to a creditor's being able to *pierce the corporate veil*. Both entities also have their income taxed to the principals on a pass-through basis, such that there is no tax at the entity level, but only at the individual owner level. However, the S corporation must pay an annual minimum excise tax of $456 to the Commonwealth of Massachusetts. If an S corporation's annual receipts exceed $6 million, the entity could become liable for substantial state income taxes. The LLC is not liable for any state excise tax.

Different circumstances may point to a choice of one type of entity or another. There are always pros and cons to both choices. But being aware of the differences and similarities between these two types of entities will help you to make the right choice.

Filing Fees The cost of the annual filing fee for the LLC makes up for the lack of excise tax liability. The fee for filing an LLC's annual report with the Secretary of State is $500, while the S corporation's annual filing fee is $125. The initial filing fees for forming the entities are $500 for an LLC and $275 (minimum, depending on the amount of stock authorized) for the S corporation. Thus, while the initial fees differ by $225, the annual fees for upkeep for the two types of entities are substantially similar.

Restrictions On Transfer   Both the LLC and the S corporation lend themselves easily to restrictions on transfer to protect the principals from having outsiders as co-owners. The LLC's operating agreement can include these restrictions on transfer and buy-sell provisions. The shares in an S corporation can be made subject to such provisions by their inclusion in the articles of organization or by contract.

Some practitioners and businesspeople assume that *newer is better*. They automatically choose the LLC over the S corporation because the LLC is new, more modern, and therefore, must be better. As when you choose a computer or a word-processing program, you should evaluate how you plan to use it, what you plan to do with it in the future, and other various implications of the choice in order to select the model that is right for you.

Statutes   The structure and function of the S corporation are governed by statute. With the recent change in the corporations law in Massachusetts, the private corporation now can be governed with almost as much flexibility as an LLC. The new law allows the corporation to dispense with the Board of Directors entirely, make distributions disproportionate to stock ownership, delegate authority in a broader manner, and change other governing provisions, as long as the change is not contrary to public policy. However, the LLC still carries many more choices than the S corporation with respect to setup, operation, and termination.

Although flexibility can be a bonus, it carries with it a certain level of complexity that some people would rather avoid. The flexibility that comes with an LLC necessarily involves decision-making, which some may find daunting.

In making this decision, you should also consider whether your business is likely to ever go public. If so, an LLC will not work. The business could, however, convert from an LLC to a corporation prior to going public, without too much trouble or tax consequence.

Owners/ Members   Another major difference between the LLC and the S corporation relates to the number and type of owners or members. In Massachusetts, there are no restrictions on how many members an LLC may have or who they may be (*e.g.*, individuals, corporations, or other entities). The S corporation may have as few as one shareholder but no more than one hundred (husband and wife are treated as one), and they must meet certain criteria. They must be individuals, estates, certain types of trusts, or certain exempt organizations, and they may not be nonresident aliens. The S corporation can only have one class of stock (although differences solely in voting rights are allowed). The LLC can have many different types of owners and equity interests in one entity.

Taxes   Although the tax treatment of the two types of entities is generally similar (*i.e.*, tax attributes flow through to the equity owner level and there is no entity level tax), there are some differences that should be considered.

One tax aspect to consider is that the income of an LLC that flows through to persons involved with the business will generally be subject to self-employment tax. With an S corporation, only salaries are subject to self-employment tax. If other income is paid out as S corporation distributions, it will not be subject to self-employment tax.

NOTE: *In this regard, the IRS has broad authority to characterize income as it sees fit.*

A second tax difference between the two entities is that in an LLC, distributions of appreciated property will generally be tax-free, and the members will have a carry over basis in the distributed assets. This is not so with an S corporation. Distributed appreciated assets will cause shareholders in an S corporation to have taxable income and take a basis of current fair market value in the assets. This is the major reason that conversion from an S corporation to an LLC creates tax issues, while conversion from an LLC to an S corporation generally does not.

A third, and very important, tax difference is that in an LLC, owners generally can have different allocations of tax benefits, like depreciation and losses, without regard to their *pro rata* ownership interests. The S corporation cannot make special allocations of these tax items.

There can be a major tax problem for Massachusetts LLCs that carry inventory. The personal property tax statutes specifically exempt personal property of domestic business corporations, but not of LLCs. This means that an LLC with substantial personal property (*e.g.,* inventory such as automobiles) will be liable for property tax that the business would not have been liable for had it been formed as a corporation. This legislative omission could be a costly trap for some businesses.

The LLC is generally preferable to the S corporation when the entity will own real estate subject to substantial debt because the LLC provides the benefit of member-level tax basis adjustments for LLC liabilities and the allowance of an adjustment in the tax basis of the entity's assets upon the sale of a member's interest. The S corporation shareholder cannot include any part of the corporation's debt in the tax basis of his or her stock, unless he or she loaned the money to the corporation. Because of these differences, LLC members are able to deduct more of the entity's tax losses as they occur than S corporation shareholders.

START-UP PROCEDURES

Except for a sole proprietorship, you must prepare some paperwork to start your business, and for some types, you must file the paperwork and pay a registration fee. For those entities that are required to make filings with the Secretary of State, the Corporations Division's website has a lot of information and forms. It is located at **www.sec.state.ma.us/cor/coridx.htm**.

Proprietorship

In a proprietorship, all accounts, property, and licenses are taken in the name of the owner. (See Chapter 3 for using a fictitious name.)

Partnership

To form a partnership, a written agreement should be prepared to spell out rights and obligations of the parties. (See Chapter 3 for using a fictitious name.) Most accounts, property, and licenses can be in either the partnership name or that of the partners.

Corporation

To form a corporation, **ARTICLES OF ORGANIZATION** (form 5, p.237) must be filed with the Secretary of State in Boston, along with a minimum filing fee of $275. An organizational meeting is then held at which officers are elected, stock issued, and other formalities observed. If these formalities are not followed, you risk the possibility of a creditor being able to *pierce the corporate veil*, or have the corporate entity set aside in order to render shareholders personally liable for the company's obligations. Contracts, licenses, accounts, and the like are in the name of the corporation.

Limited Partnership

A *Certificate of Limited Partnership* must be drawn up and registered with the Secretary of State in Boston, and generally, a lengthy disclosure document must be given to all prospective limited partners. Because of the complexity of securities laws and the criminal penalties for violation, it is advantageous to have an attorney organize a limited partnership.

Limited Liability Company

One or more persons may form a *limited liability company* by filing a *Certificate of Formation* with the Secretary of State in Boston. The filing fee is $500. Contracts, licenses, and accounts are in the name of the company.

Limited Liability Partnership

Two or more persons may form a limited liability partnership by filing a registration form with the Secretary of State in Boston. The filing fee is $500. Licenses and accounts are in the name of the company.

Required Contacts

TYPES OF BUSINESS	AGENCY	DIVISION	TELEPHONE	REQUIREMENTS	FREQUENCY
Business Corporation	Secretary of Commonwealth	Corporations	617-727-9640	• file Articles of Organization • file Articles of Amendment • file Annual Report • file Articles of Dissolution	Once When Necessary Annually Upon termination
Professional Corporation	Secretary of Commonwealth	Corporations	617-727-9640	• same as for business corporation, plus; - a certificate of the appropriate regulating board(s) that each of the incorporators, the president, and any vice presidents, a majority of the directors and each shareholder is duly licensed, must accompany Articles of Organization	Once
Nonprofit Corporation	Secretary of Commonwealth	Corporations	617-727-9640	• same as for business corporations except: - file Annual Report - dissolved through court action	Annually on November 1
Foreign Corporation	Secretary of Commonwealth	Corporations	617-727-9640	• file Certificate of Registration • file amended certificate • file Annual Report • file Certificate of Withdrawal	Once When necessary Annually Upon cessation of business in the Commonwealth
Limited Partnership	Secretary of the Commonwealth	Corporations	617-727-2859	• file Certificate of Limited Partnership • file amended certificate • file Certificate of Cancellation	Once When necessary Upon dissolution
Foreign Limited Partnership	Secretary of the Commonwealth	Corporations	617-727-2859	• file Certificate of Registration • file amended certificate • file Certificate of Withdrawal	Once When necessary Upon cessation of business in the Commonwealth Upon dissolution
Business Trust	Secretary of the Commonwealth	Corporations	617-727-2859	• file Declaration of trust • file amended declaration • file Annual Report	Once When Necessary Annually
	Secretary of the Commonwealth	Securities Division	617-727-3548 800-269-5428	• broker/dealer registration • investment advisor registration • corporate finance section	When necessary When necessary When necessary

TYPE OF BUSINESS	AGENCY	DIVISION	TELEPHONE	REQUIREMENTS	FREQUENCY
Limited Liability Companies	Secretary of the Commonwealth	Corporations	617-727-2859	Domestic: • file Certificate of Formation • file Certificate of Amendment • file Annual Report • file Certificate of Cancellation Foreign: • file Registration • file Amendment • file Annual Report • file Certificate of Withdrawal	Once When necessary Annually Upon dissolution Once When necessary Annually Upon dissolution
Limited Liability Partnerships	Secretary of the Commonwealth	Corporations	617-727-2859	Domestic and Foreign: • file Certificate of Registration • file Amendment Registration • file Annual Report • file Certificate of Withdrawal	Once When necessary Annually Upon withdrawal of registration or dissolution

BUSINESS COMPARISON CHART

	Sole Proprietorship	General Partnership	Limited Partnership	Limited Liability Co.	Limited Liability Partnership	Corporation C or S	Nonprofit Corporation
Liability Protection	No	No	For limited partners	For all members	For all members	For all shareholders	For all members
Taxes	Pass through	Pass through	Pass through	Pass through	Pass through	S corps. pass through; C corps. pay tax	None
Minimum # of Members	1	2	2	1	2	1	1
Start-up Fee	None	None	$200	$500	$500	Min $275	$35
Annual Fee	None	None	N/A	$500	$500	$125	$15
Diff. Classes of Ownership	No	No	Yes	Yes	Yes	S corps. No C corps. Yes	No ownership Diff. classes of membership
Survives after Death	No	No	Yes	Yes	No	Yes	Yes
Best for	1 person low-risk business or no assets	Low-risk business	Low-risk business with silent partners	All types of businesses	Law Firms	All types of businesses	Educational

BUSINESS START-UP CHECKLIST

❏ Make your plan
- ❏ Obtain and read all relevant publications on your type of business
- ❏ Obtain and read all laws and regulations affecting your business
- ❏ Calculate whether your plan will produce a profit
- ❏ Plan your sources of capital
- ❏ Plan your sources of goods or services
- ❏ Plan your marketing efforts

❏ Choose your business name
- ❏ Check other business names and trademarks
- ❏ Register your name, trademark, etc.

❏ Choose the business form
- ❏ Prepare and file organizational papers
- ❏ Prepare and file a fictitious name if necessary

❏ Choose the location
- ❏ Check competitors
- ❏ Check zoning

❏ Obtain necessary licenses
- ❏ City?
- ❏ County?
- ❏ State?
- ❏ Federal?

❏ Choose a bank
- ❏ Checking
- ❏ Credit card processing
- ❏ Loans

❏ Obtain necessary insurance
- ❏ Workers' Comp
- ❏ Unemployment
- ❏ Health
- ❏ Life/disability
- ❏ Automobile
- ❏ Liability
- ❏ Hazard

❏ File necessary federal tax registrations

❏ File necessary state tax registrations

❏ Set up a bookkeeping system

❏ Plan your hiring
- ❏ Obtain required posters
- ❏ Obtain or prepare employment application
- ❏ Obtain new hire tax forms
- ❏ Prepare employment policies
- ❏ Determine compliance with health and safety laws

❏ Plan your opening
- ❏ Obtain all necessary equipment and supplies
- ❏ Obtain all necessary inventory
- ❏ Do all necessary marketing and publicity
- ❏ Obtain all necessary forms and agreements
- ❏ Prepare your company policies on refunds, exchanges, returns

Your Business Name

Before deciding on a name for your business, you should be sure that it is not already being used by someone else. Many business owners spend thousands of dollars on publicity and printing, only to throw it all away because another company owned the name. A company that owns a name can take you to court and force you to stop using that name. It can also sue you for damages if it thinks your use of the name caused it a financial loss.

If you will be running a small local shop with no plans for expansion, you should at least check out whether the name has been trademarked. If someone else is using the same name anywhere in the country and has registered it as a federal trademark, he or she can sue you. If you plan to expand or to deal nationally, you should do a more thorough search of the name.

NAME SEARCHES

To search for a name you are considering using, the first places to look are the local phone books and city or town clerk's office (for a fictitious name filing). Next, you should check with the Secretary of State's office in Boston to see if someone has registered a corporate or an

LLC name that is the same as, or confusingly similar to, the one you have chosen. The Secretary of State's office can be reached at 617-727-2850 or 617-727-9640.

To do a national search, you should check trade directories and phone books of major cities. These can be found at many libraries, but they usually can only be used at the library and not checked out. The *Trade Names Directory* is a two-volume set of names compiled from many sources and published by Gale Research Company. If you have a computer with Internet access, you can use it to search the Yellow Pages at **www.yellowpages.com**.

To be sure that your use of the name does not violate someone else's trademark rights, you should have a trademark search done in the United States Patent and Trademark Office (USPTO). In the past, this required a visit to their offices or the ordering of a search for hundreds of dollars. Now you can search the trademark records online at **www.uspto.gov**. Keep in mind that this database is not kept altogether current.

If you do not have access to the Internet, you might be able to do it on a computer at a public library or have one of their employees order an online search for a small fee. If this is not available to you, you can have the search done through a firm, such as Thomson CompuMark at **www.thomson-thomson.com** or 800-692-8833.

No matter how thorough your search, there is no guarantee that there is not a local user somewhere with rights to the mark. If, for example, you register a name for a new chain of restaurants and later find out that someone in Tucumcari, New Mexico, has been using the name longer than you, that person will still have the right to use the name, but probably just in that local area. If you do not want that restaurant to cause confusion with your chain, you can offer to buy it. Similarly, if you are operating a small business under a unique name and a law firm in New York writes and offers to buy the right to your name, you can assume that some large corporation wants to start a major expansion under that name.

The best way to make sure a name you are using is not already owned by someone else is to make up a name. Names such as Xerox, Kodak, and Exxon were made up and did not have any meaning prior to their use. Remember that there are millions of businesses, so even something you make up may already be in use. Do a search to be sure.

FICTITIOUS NAMES

In Massachusetts, as in most states, unless you do business in your own legal name, you must register the business name (called a *fictitious name*) you are using. The name must be registered with the clerk of each city and town where you have an office.

A fictitious name registration is good for four years and can be renewed for additional four-year periods. Failure to make the required filings can result in fines of $300 per month.

If your name is Jennifer Anne and you are operating a fan store, you may operate your business as *Jennifer Anne, Portable Fans* without registering the name. But variations on your name, such as *Jenny Anne, the Fan Fan*, should be registered.

You cannot use the words *corporation, incorporated, corp.,* or *inc.,* unless you are a corporation. However, a corporation does not have to register the name it is using unless it is different from its registered corporate name. A partnership does not have to register the name it is using as long as it contains the surname of any partner.

Legally, when you use a fictitious name, you are *doing business as* (DBA) whatever name you are using. For example, *Jennifer Anne DBA Jenny Anne, The Fan Fan*.

As discussed in the previous section, you should do some research to see if the name you intend to use is already being used by anyone else. Even persons who have not registered a name can acquire legal rights to the name through use.

Most cities and towns have their own fictitious name form. You should call the city or town clerk and ask them to send it to you. If they do not have one, you can use the **CERTIFICATE STATING REAL NAME OF PERSON TRANSACTING BUSINESS** (form 3, p.231).

CORPORATE NAMES

A corporation does not have to register a fictitious name unless it uses a name that is different from its true legal name. In the judgment of the Secretary of State, the name of a corporation must include a word or words indicating that it is a corporation. Regulations indicate that one of the following words (or its abbreviation) will suffice:

Incorporated	Inc.
Corporation	Corp.
Limited	Ltd.
Company	Co.

If the name of the corporation does not contain one of the approved words, it will probably be rejected by the Secretary of State. It will also be rejected if the name is already taken or is similar to the name of another corporation, or if it uses a forbidden word such as *Bank* or *Trust*. To check on a name, you may call the Secretary of State at 617-727-2850.

If a name you choose is taken by another company, you may be able to change it slightly and have it accepted. For example, if there is already a Fisher Cut Bait, Inc., in a different county, you may be allowed to use Fisher Cut Bait, Inc., of Dukes County. But even if this is approved by the Secretary of State, you may get sued by the other company if your business is close to theirs or there is a likelihood of confusion.

Also, do not have anything printed with your business name on it until you have final approval. If you register online, you will get an email approval that the articles are filed. If you file by mail, you should wait until you receive the copy back with the filing date on it.

Once you have chosen a corporate name and know it is available, you should immediately form your corporation. A name can be *reserved* for a month for $15, but it is easier just to form the corporation than to waste time on the name reservation.

If a corporation wants to do business under a name other than its corporate name, it can register a fictitious name such as *Luke the Duke of Earl, Inc., DBA Luke the Duke*. However, if the name used leads people to believe that the business is not a corporation, there may be some risk of losing the right to limited liability that the corporate entity provides. If such a name is used, it should always be accompanied by the corporate name.

PROFESSIONAL CORPORATIONS

Professional corporations are corporations formed by professionals, such as attorneys, doctors, dentists, and architects. In Massachusetts, a professional corporation can use any of the usual corporate designations—Inc., Corp., and so on—or the words *Professional Corporation* or the abbreviation *P.C.*

THE WORD *LIMITED*

The words *Limited* or *Ltd.* at the end of a name can be used for a corporation, although some people find this confusing because they associate the word with a limited partnership. The phrase *Limited Liability Company*, or its abbreviation, *L.L.C.*, should only be used if you are doing business in the form of a limited liability company.

DOMAIN NAMES

A discussion of domain names is contained in Chapter 16 of this book.

TRADEMARKS

As your business builds goodwill, its name will become more valuable and you will want to protect it from others who may wish to copy it. To protect a name used to describe your goods or services, you can register it as a trademark (for goods) or a service mark (for services) with either the Secretary of State of Massachusetts or with the United States Patent and Trademark Office.

You cannot register a trademark for the name of your business unless that name is also the name of goods or services you are selling. In many cases, you use your company name on your goods as your trademark. In effect, it protects your company name. Another way to protect your company name is to incorporate. A unique corporate name can only be registered by one company in Massachusetts.

State Registration

State registration would be useful if you only expect to use your trademark within Massachusetts. Federal registration would protect your mark anywhere in the country. Use of a mark without registration does give you some legal rights to the mark, but registration of the mark gives you much better protection. The registration of a mark constitutes proof that you are the exclusive owner of the mark for the types of goods or services for which it is registered. The only exception is persons who have already been using the mark. People who have been using the mark prior to your registration may have superior rights even though they have not registered the mark.

The procedure for state registration is simple and the cost is $50. First, you should write to the Secretary of State, or call 617-727-2859 to ask them to search your name and tell you if it is available. For questions about filing the application, call the same number. The Secretary of State can be reached by mail at:

Secretary of State
Trademark Division
1 Ashburton Place, Room 1611
Boston, MA 02108

Before a mark can be registered, it must be used in Massachusetts. For goods, this means it must be used on the goods themselves or on containers, tags, labels, or displays of the goods. For services, it must be used in the sale or advertising of the services. The use must be in an actual transaction with a customer. A sample mailed to a friend is not considered acceptable use.

The $50 fee will register the mark in only one *class of goods*. If the mark is used on more than one class of goods, a separate registration must be filed. Three *specimens* of use of the mark must also be filed.

The registration is good for ten years. It must be renewed six months prior to its expiration. The renewal fee is $50 for each class of goods.

An **APPLICATION FOR REGISTRATION OF A TRADEMARK** (form 4, p.233) is included in the back of this book. At the end of this chapter is the *Massachusetts Classification of Goods and Services* (similar, but not identical to, the federal classifications), which you will need to fill out your application.

Federal Registration   The procedure for federal registration is a little more complicated. There are two types of applications depending upon whether you have already made actual use of the mark or whether you merely have an intention to use the mark in the future. For a trademark that has been in use, you must file an application form along with specimens showing actual use and a drawing of the mark that complies with all the rules of the United States Patent and Trademark Office. For an *intent to use* application, you must file two separate forms: one when you make the initial application, and the other after you have made *actual use* of the mark as well as the specimens and drawing. Before a mark can be entitled to federal registration, the use of the mark must be in *interstate commerce* or in commerce with another country. The fee for registration is either $275 or $325 if you file online, depending on whether you use a pre-approved description of goods or services; the fee is $375 if you file on paper. If you file an *intent to use* application, there is a second fee of $100 for the filing after actual use.

For more information on federal registration and to complete an online application, visit **www.uspto.gov**.

MASSACHUSETTS CLASSIFICATION OF GOODS

Class 1: Chemicals

Chemicals used in industry, science, photography, as well as in agriculture, horticulture, forestry; unprocessed resins, unprocessed plastics; manures; fire extinguishing compositions; tempering and soldering preparations; chemical substances for preserving foodstuffs; tanning substances; adhesives used in industry.

Class 2: Paints

Paints, varnishes, lacquers; preservatives against rust and against deterioration of wood; colorants, mordants; raw natural resins; metals in foil and powder form for painters, decorators, printers, and artists.

Class 3: Cosmetics and Cleaning Preparations

Bleaching preparations and other substances for laundry use; cleaning, polishing, scouring, and abrasive preparations; soaps; perfumery, essential oils, cosmetics, hair lotions; dentifrices.

Class 4: Lubricants and Fuels

Industrial oils and greases; lubricants; dust absorbing compositions; wetting and binding compositions; fuels (including motor spirit) and illuminants; candles and wicks for lighting.

Class 5: Pharmaceuticals

Pharmaceutical and veterinary preparations; sanitary preparations for medical purposes; dietetic substances adapted for medical use; food for babies; plasters; materials for dressings; materials for stopping teeth, dental wax; disinfectants; preparations for destroying vermin; fungicides, herbicides.

Class 6: Metal Goods

Common metals and their alloys; metal building materials; transportable buildings of metal; materials of metal for railway tracks; nonelectric cables and wires of common metal; ironmongery, small items of metal hardware; pipes and tubes of metal; safes; goods of common metal not included in other classes; ores.

Class 7: Machinery
Machines and machine tools; motors and engines (except for land vehicles); machine coupling and transmission components (except for land vehicles); agricultural implements other than hand-operated; incubators for eggs.

Class 8: Hand Tools
Hand tools and implements (hand-operated); cutlery; side arms; razors.

Class 9: Electrical and Scientific Apparatus
Scientific, nautical, surveying, photographic, cinematographic, optical, weighing, measuring, signaling, checking (supervision), life-saving and teaching apparatus and instruments; apparatus and instruments for conducting, switching, transforming, accumulating, regulating, or controlling electricity; apparatus for recording, transmission, or reproduction of sound or images; magnetic data carriers, recording discs; automatic vending machines and mechanisms for coin-operated apparatus; cash registers, calculating machines, data-processing equipment and computers; fire extinguishing apparatus.

Class 10: Medical Apparatus
Surgical, medical, dental, and veterinary apparatus and instruments; artificial limbs, eyes, and teeth; orthopedic articles; suture materials.

Class 11: Environmental Control Apparatus
Apparatus for lighting, heating, steam generating, cooking, refrigerating, drying, ventilating, water supply, and sanitary purposes.

Class 12: Vehicles
Vehicles; apparatus for locomotion by land, air, or water.

Class 13: Firearms
Firearms, ammunition, and projectiles; explosives; fireworks.

Class 14: Jewelry
Precious metals and their alloys and goods in precious metals or coated therewith, not included in other classes; jewelry, precious stones, horological, and other chronometric instruments.

Class 15: Musical Instruments
Musical instruments.

Class 16: Paper Goods and Printed Matter
Paper, cardboard, and goods made from these materials, not included in other classes; printed matter; bookbinding material, photographs; stationery, adhesives for stationery or household purposes; artists' materials; paint brushes; typewriters and office requisites (except furniture); instructional and teaching material (except apparatus); plastic materials for packaging (not included in other classes); printers' type; printing blocks.

Class 17: Rubber Goods
Rubber, gutta-percha, gum, asbestos, mica, and goods made from these materials and not included in other classes; plastics in extruded form for use in manufacture, packing, stopping, and insulating materials; flexible pipes, not of metal.

Class 18: Leather Goods
Leather and imitations of leather, and goods made from these materials and not included in other classes; animal skins, hides; trunks and traveling bags; umbrellas, parasols, and walking sticks; whips, harnesses, and saddlery.

Class 19: Nonmetallic building materials
Building materials (nonmetallic); nonmetallic rigid pipes for building; asphalt, pitch, and bitumen; nonmetallic transportable buildings; monuments, not of metal.

Class 20: Furniture and Articles Not Otherwise Classified
Furniture, mirrors, picture frames, goods (not included in other classes) of wood, cork, reed, cane, wicker, horn, bone, ivory, whalebone, shell, amber, mother-of-pearl, meerschaum, and substitutes for all these materials, or of plastics.

Class 21: Housewares and Glasses
Household or kitchen utensils and containers (not of precious metal or coated therewith); combs and sponges; brushes (except paint brushes); brush-making materials; articles for cleaning purposes; steel wool; unworked or semi-worked glass (except glass used in

building); glassware, porcelain, and earthenware, not included in other classes.

Class 22: Cordage and Fibers

Ropes, string, nets, tents, awnings, tarpaulins, sails, sacks, and bags (not included in other classes); padding and stuffing materials (except of rubber or plastics); raw fibrous textile materials.

Class 23: Yarns and Threads

Yarns and threads for textile use.

Class 24: Fabrics

Textiles and textile goods, not included in other classes; bed and table covers.

Class 25: Clothing

Clothing, footwear, and headgear.

Class 26: Fancy Goods

Lace and embroidery, ribbons and braid; buttons, hooks and eyes, pins and needles; artificial flowers.

Class 27: Floor Coverings

Carpets, rugs, mats, and matting; linoleum and other materials for covering floors; wall hangings (non-textile).

Class 28: Toys and Sporting Goods

Games and playthings; gymnastic and sporting articles not included in other classes; decorations for Christmas trees.

Class 29: Meats and Processed Foods

Meat, fish, poultry, and game; meat extracts; preserved, dried, and cooked fruits and vegetables; jellies, jams, compotes; eggs, milk, and milk products; edible oils and fats.

Class 30: Staple Foods

Coffee, tea, cocoa, sugar, rice, tapioca, sago, artificial coffee; flour, and preparations made from cereals, bread, pastry and confectionery, ices;

honey, treacle; yeast, baking-powder; salt, mustard; vinegar, sauces (condiments); spices; ice.

Class 31: Natural Agricultural Products
Agricultural, horticultural, and forestry products and grains not included in other classes; living animals; fresh fruits and vegetables; seeds; natural plants and flowers; foodstuffs for animals, malt.

Class 32: Light Beverages
Beers; mineral and aerated waters and other nonalcoholic drinks; fruit drinks and fruit juices; syrups and other preparations for making beverages.

Class 33: Wines and Spirits
Alcoholic beverages (except beers).

Class 34: Smokers' Articles
Tobacco; smokers' articles; matches.

MASSACHUSETTS CLASSIFICATION OF SERVICES

Class 35: Advertising and Business Management
Advertising; business management; business administration; office functions.

Class 36: Insurance and Financial
Insurance; financial affairs; monetary affairs; real estate affairs.

Class 37: Building Construction and Repair
Building construction; repair; installation services.

Class 38: Telecommunications
Telecommunications.

Class 39: Transportation and Storage
Transportation and storage of goods; travel arrangement.

Class 40: Treatment of Materials
Treatment of Materials.

Class 41: Education and Entertainment
Education; providing of training; entertainment; sporting and cultural activities.

Class 42: Computer, Scientific, and Legal
Computer, scientific and technological services and research, and design relating thereto; industrial analyses and research services; design and development of computer hardware and software; legal services.

Class 43: Hotels and Restaurants
Services for providing food and drink; temporary accommodations.

Class 44: Medical, Beauty, and Agriculture
Medical services; veterinary services; hygienic and beauty care for human beings or animals; agriculture, horticulture, and forestry services.

Class 45: Personal
Personal and social services rendered by others to meet the needs of individuals; security services for the protection of property and individuals.

Preparing a Business Plan

Not everyone needs a business plan to start a business, but if you have one it might help you avoid mistakes and make better decisions. For example, if you think it would be a great idea to start a candle shop in a little seaside resort, you might find out after preparing a business plan that considering the number of people who might stop by, you could never sell enough candles to pay the rent.

A business plan lets you look at the costs, expenses, and potential sales, and see whether or not your plan can be profitable. It also allows you to find alternatives that might be more profitable. In the candle shop example, you might find that if you chose a more populous location or if you sold something else in addition to the candles, you would be more likely to make a profit.

ADVANTAGES AND DISADVANTAGES OF A BUSINESS PLAN

Other than helping you figure out if your business will be profitable, a business plan would also be useful if you hope to borrow money or have investors buy into your business. Lenders and equity investors always require a business plan before they will provide money to a business.

If your idea is truly unusual, a business plan may discourage you from starting your business. A business idea might look like a failure on paper, but if in your gut you know it would work, it might be worth trying without a business plan.

Example:

When Chester Carlson invented the first photocopy machine, he went to IBM. They spent $50,000 to analyze the idea and concluded that nobody needed a photocopy machine because people already had carbon paper—which was cheaper. However, he believed in his machine and started Xerox Corporation, which became one of the biggest and hottest companies of its time.

However, even with a great concept, you need to at least do some basic calculations to see if the business can make a profit.

❂   If you want to start a retail shop, figure out how many people are close enough to become customers and how many other stores will be competing for those customers. Visit some of those other shops and see how busy they are. Without giving away your plans to compete, ask some general questions like "how's business?" and maybe they will share their frustrations or successes.

❂   Whether you sell a good or a service, do the math to find out how much profit is in it. For example, if you plan to start a house painting company, find out what you will have to pay to hire painters, what it will cost you for all the insurance, what bonding and licensing you will need, and what the advertising will cost you. Figure out how many jobs you can do per month and what other painters are charging. In some industries, in different areas of the state there may be a large margin of profit, while in other areas there may be almost no profit.

✪ Find out if there is a demand for your product or service. Suppose you have designed a beautiful new kind of candle and your friends all say you should open a shop because "everyone will want them." Before making a hundred of them and renting a store, bring a few to craft shows or flea markets and see what happens.

✪ Figure out what the income and expenses would be for a typical month of your new business. List monthly expenses, such as rent, salaries, utilities, insurance, taxes, supplies, advertising, services, and other overhead. Then, figure out how much profit you will average from each sale. Next, figure out how many sales you will need to cover your overhead and divide by the number of business days in the month. Can you reasonably expect that many sales? How will you get those sales?

Most types of businesses have trade associations, which often have figures on how profitable its members are. Some even have start-up kits for people wanting to start businesses. One good source of information on such organizations is the *Encyclopedia of Associations* published by Gale Research Inc., available in many library reference sections. Suppliers of products to the trade often give assistance to small companies getting started, to win their loyalty. Contact the largest suppliers of the products your business will be using and see if they can be of help.

OUTLINE FOR YOUR BUSINESS PLAN

While you may believe that you do not need a business plan, conventional wisdom says you do and it only makes good business sense to have one. A typical business plan has sections that cover topics such as the following:

✪ executive summary;

✪ product or service;

✪ market;

- ✪ competition;

- ✪ marketing plan;

- ✪ production plan;

- ✪ organizational plan;

- ✪ financial projections;

- ✪ management team; and,

- ✪ risks.

The following is an explanation of each.

Executive Summary The executive summary is an overview of what the business will be and why it is expected to be successful. If the business plan will be used to lure investors, this section is the most important, since many might not read any further if they are not impressed with the summary.

Product or Service This is a detailed description of what you will be selling. You should describe what is different about it and why people would need it or want it.

Market The market section should analyze who the potential buyers of your product or service are. Describe both the physical location of the customers and their demographics. For example, a bodybuilding gym would probably mostly appeal to males in the 18 to 40 age bracket in a ten- to twenty-mile radius, depending on the location.

If you will sell things from a retail shop, you might also want to sell from mail order catalogs or over the Internet if your local customer base would not be large enough to support the business. Describe what you will be doing for those ventures.

If you are manufacturing things, you should find out who the wholesalers and distributors are, and their terms. This information should also be included in this section.

Competition   Before opening your business, you should know who and where your competitors are. If you are opening an antique shop, you might want to be near other antique shops so more customers come by your place, since antiques are unique and do not really compete with other antiques. However, if you open a florist shop, you probably do not want to be near other florist shops since most florists sell similar products and a new shop would just dilute the customer base.

If you have a truly unique way of selling something, you might want to go near other similar businesses to grab their existing customer base and expand your market share. However, if they could easily copy your idea, you might not take away the business for long and end up diluting the market for each business. (see Chapter 6.)

Marketing Plan   Many a business has closed just a few months after opening because not enough customers showed up. How do you expect customers to find out about your business? Even if you get a nice write-up in the local paper, not everyone reads the paper, many people do not read every page, and lots of people forget what they read.

Your marketing plan describes how you will advertise your business. List how much the advertising will cost, and describe how you expect people to respond to the advertising.

Production Plan   The production plan needs to address and answer questions such as the following.

- If you are manufacturing a product, do you know how you will be able to produce a large quantity of it?

- Do you know all the costs and the possible production problems that could come up?

- If Wal-Mart orders 100,000 of a product, could you get the order made in a reasonable amount of time?

The production plan needs to anticipate the normal schedule you intend to use, as well as how to handle any changes, positive or negative, to that schedule.

If you are selling a service and will need employees to perform those services, your production plan should explain how you will recruit and train those employees.

Organizational Plan

If your business will be more than a mom and pop operation, what will the organizational plan be? How many employees will you need and who will supervise whom? How much of the work will be done by employees and how much will be hired out to other businesses and independent contractors? Will you have a sales force? Will you need manufacturing employees? Will your accounting, website maintenance, and office cleaning and maintenance be contracted out or done by employees?

Financial Projections

Tying all the previously discussed topics together is what your financial plan will discuss. You should know how much rent, utilities, insurance, taxes, marketing, and product costs or wages for labor will cost you for the first year. Besides listing known, expected expenses, you should calculate your financial well-being under a number of different possible scenarios. Some of the questions to think about and answer will be: *How long will you be in business if you have very few customers the first few months?* and *If Wal-Mart orders 100,000 of your products, could you afford to manufacture them, knowing you will not be paid for months?*

Management Team

If you will be seeking outside funding, you will need to list the experience and skills of the management of the business. Investors want to know that the people have experience and know what they are doing.

Risks

A good business plan weighs all the risks of the new enterprise. Is new technology in the works that will make the business obsolete? Would a rise in the price of a particular needed supply eliminate all your profits? What are the chances of a new competitor entering the market if you show some success, and what are you going to do about it? Part of your analysis should be to look at all the possible things that could happen in the field you choose and to gauge the likelihood of success.

Gathering Information

Some of the sections of your business plan require a lot of research. People sometimes take years to prepare them. Today, the Internet puts a nearly infinite amount of information at your fingertips, but you might also want to do some personal research.

Sometimes the best way to get the feel for a business is to get a job in a similar business. At a minimum, you should visit similar businesses and perhaps sit outside of one, and see how many customers they have and how much business they do. There are start-up guides for many types of businesses, which can be found at Amazon.com, your local bookstores, and the library. Your local chamber of commerce, business development office, or SCORE office might also have materials to help your research.

SAMPLE BUSINESS PLAN

The following plan is one for a simple one-person business that will use its owner's assets to start. Of course, a larger business, or one that needs financing, will need a much longer and more detailed plan.

A website with sixty sample business plans and information on business plan software is **www.bplans.com.**

Executive Summary

This is the plan for a new business, Reardon Computer Repair, LLC, by Henry Reardon, to be started locally and then expanded throughout the state and perhaps farther if results indicate it is feasible.

The mission of Reardon Computer Repair (RCR) is to offer fast, affordable repairs to office and home computers. The objective is to become profitable within the first three months and to grow at a quick but manageable pace.

In order to offer customers the quickest service, RCR will rely on youthful computer whizzes who are students and have the time and expertise to provide the service. They will also have the flexibility to arrive quickly and the motivation to show off their expertise.

To reach customers, we will use limited advertising, but primarily the Internet and word of mouth from happy customers.

With nearly every business and family having several computers and the lack of fast service currently available, it is expected this business could be successful quickly and could grow rapidly.

Product or Service

The company will offer computer repair services both at its shop and at customers' offices and homes. It will sell computer parts as necessary to complete the repairs and it will also carry upgrades, accessories, and peripherals, which will most likely be of value to customers needing repairs.

Market

The market would be nearly every business and family at every address in the city, state, and country, since today nearly everyone has a computer. Figures show nearly 250 million computers in use in America, and that number is expected to grow to over 300 million in five years.

The market for the initial shop would be a fifteen-mile radius, which is a reasonable driving distance for our employees. The population in that area is 300,000 people, which would mean 240,000 potential customers, based on the current level of 800 computers per 1,000 people.

The market would not include new computers, which typically come with a one-year guarantee. It would also not include people who bought extended guarantees.

The growth trend for the industry is 8–10% for the next decade.

Competition

The competition would be the authorized repair shops working with the computer manufacturers. While these have the advantage of being authorized, research and experience have shown that they are slow and do not meet customers' need for an immediate repair.

There is one computer repair shop within a ten-mile radius of the proposed shop and two more within a twenty-five-mile radius. Average wait time for a dropped off repair is one week. The two closest repair services offer no on-site repair. Shipping a computer to a dealer for repair takes one to two weeks. Most customers need their computers fixed within a day or two.

One potential source for competition would be from employees or former employees who are asked to work for customers on the side at a reduced rate. To discourage this, the company will have a contract with employees with a non-compete agreement that specifies that they will pay the company three times what they earn. Also, agreements with customers will include a clause that they have the option to hire away one of our employees for a one-time $2,000 fee.

Marketing Plan

The business will be marketed through networking, Internet marketing, advertising, and creative marketing.

Networking will be through the owner's contacts and local computer clubs and software stores. Some local retailers do not offer service and they have already indicated that they would promote a local business that could offer fast repairs.

A website would be linked to local businesses and community groups, and to major computer repair referral sites.

Advertising would include the Yellow Pages and local computer club newsletters. Studies have shown that newspaper and television advertising would be too expensive and not cost-effective for this type of business.

Creative advertising would include vinyl lettering on the back window of the owner's vehicle.

Production Plan

The company will be selling the services of computer technicians and computer parts. The owner will supply most of the services in the beginning and then add student technicians as needed.

The parts will all be purchased ready-made from the manufacturers, except for cables, which can be made on an as-needed basis much cheaper than ready-made ones.

Employees

The employees will be students who are extremely knowledgeable about computers. Some would call them computer geeks—in a nice way. They have extensive knowledge of the workings of computers, have lots of free time, need money, and would love to show off how knowledgeable they are.

As students, they already have health insurance and do not need full-time work. They would be available as needed. The company would pay them $12 an hour plus mileage, which is more than any other jobs available to students, but is not cost prohibitive, considering the charge to customers of $50 per hour.

Financial Projections

The minimum charge for a service call will be $75 on-site and $50 in-shop, which will include one hour of service. The parts markup will be the industry standard of 20%. The average customer bill will be estimated to be $100 including labor and markup.

The labor cost is estimated to be $30 per call including time, taxes, insurance, and mileage. The owner will be estimated to handle 75% of the work the first six months and 50% the second six months.

Rent, utilities, insurance, taxes, and other fixed costs are estimated to be $3,000 per month.

Advertising and promotion expenses are expected to be $3,000 per month.

Estimated number of customers will be:

First three months   10 per week

Second three months   20 per week

Third three months   35 per week

Fourth three months   50 per week

Estimated monthly revenue:

First three months $4,000

Second three months $8,000

Third three months $14,000

Fourth three month $20,000

Monthly income and expense projection:

First three months:

Income $4,000

Labor $300

Fixed costs $3,000

Advertising $3,000

Net $2,300 loss per month

Second 3 months:

Income $8,000

Labor $600

Fixed costs $3,000

Advertising $3,000

Net $1,400 profit per month

Third 3 months:

Income $14,000

Labor $2,100

Fixed costs $3,000

Advertising	$3,000
Net	$5,900 profit per month

Fourth 3 months:

Income	$20,000
Labor	$3,000
Fixed costs	$3,000
Advertising	$3,000
Net	$11,000 profit per month

Organization Plan

The business will start with the owner, Henry Reardon, and three students who are experts at computer repair and available as part-time workers on an as-needed basis.

The owner will manage the business and do as many repairs as are possible with the time remaining in the week.

One of the students, Peter Galt, will work after school in the shop, and the others, Dom Roark and Howard Taggert, are willing to work on an on-call basis, either at the shop or at customers' homes.

As business grows, the company will recruit more student employees through the school job placement offices and at computer clubs.

Management Team

The owner, Henry Reardon, will be the sole manager of the company. He will use the accounting services of his accountant, Dave Burton. The owner anticipates being able to supervise up to ten employees. When there are more than ten, the company will need a manager to take over scheduling and some of the other management functions.

Risks

Because the business does not require a lot of capital, there will be a low financial risk in the beginning. The biggest reason for failure would be an inability to get the word out that the company exists and can fill a need when it arises. For this reason, the most important task in the beginning will be marketing and promotion.

As the company grows, the risk will be that computers will need fewer repairs, become harder to repair, and become so cheap they are disposable. To guard against this possibility, the company will add computer consulting services as it grows so that it will always have something to offer computer owners.

Financing Your
Business

The way to finance your business is determined by how fast you want your business to grow and how much risk of failure you are able to handle. Letting the business grow with its own income is the slowest but safest way to grow. Taking out a personal loan against your house to expand quickly is one of the fastest but riskiest ways to grow.

GROWING WITH PROFITS

Many successful businesses have started out with little money and used the profits to grow bigger and bigger. If you have another source of income to live on (such as a job or a spouse), you can plow all the income of your fledgling business into growth.

Some businesses start as hobbies or part-time ventures on the weekend while the entrepreneur holds down a full-time job. Many types of goods or service businesses can start this way. Even some multimillion dollar corporations, such as Apple Computer, started out this way.

This allows you to test your idea with little risk. If you find you are not good at running that type of business or the time or location was not right for your idea, all you have lost is the time you spent and your start-up capital.

However, a business can only grow so big from its own income. In many cases, as a business grows, it gets to a point where the orders are so big that money must be borrowed to produce the product to fill them. With this kind of order, there is the risk that if the customer cannot pay or goes bankrupt, the business will also fail. At such a point, a business owner should investigate the credit-worthiness of the customer and weigh the risks. Some businesses have grown rapidly, some have gone under, and others have decided not to take the risk and stayed small. You can worry about that down the road.

USING YOUR SAVINGS

If you have savings you can tap to get your business started, that is the best source. You will not have to pay high interest rates, and you will not have to worry about paying anyone back.

Home Equity   If you have owned your home for several years, it is possible that the equity has grown substantially and you can get a second mortgage to finance your business. If you have been in the home for many years and have a good record of paying your bills, some lenders will make second mortgages that exceed the equity. Just remember, if your business fails, you may lose your house.

Retirement Accounts   Be careful about borrowing from your retirement savings. There are tax penalties for borrowing from or against certain types of retirement accounts. Also, your future financial security may be lost if your business does not succeed.

Having Too Much Money   It probably seems impossible to have too much money to start a business with, but many businesses have failed for that reason. With plenty of start-up capital available, a business owner does not need to watch expenses and can become wasteful. Employees get used to lavish spending. Once the money runs out and the business must run on its own earnings, it fails.

Starting with the bare minimum forces a business to watch its expenses and be frugal. It necessitates finding the least expensive solutions to problems that crop up and creative ways to be productive.

BORROWING MONEY

It is extremely tempting to look to others to get the money to start a business. The risk of failure may be less worrisome and the pressure may be lower. However, there is a problem with borrowing. You may not have the same incentive to succeed if you are using someone else's money as you would if everything you own is on the line.

Actually, you should be even more concerned when using the money of others. Your reputation is at risk, and if you do not succeed, you probably will still have to pay back the loan.

Family   Depending on how much money your family can spare and the status of your relationship, borrowing from family members may be the most comfortable or most uncomfortable source of funds for you. If you have been assured a large inheritance and your parents have more funds than they need to live on, you may be able to borrow against your inheritance without worry. It will be your money anyway and you need it much more now than you will ten or more years from now. If you lose it all, it is your own loss anyway.

However, if you are borrowing your widowed mother's only source of income or asking her to cash in a CD she lives on to finance your get-rich-quick scheme, you should have second thoughts about it. Stop and consider all the real reasons your business might not take off and what your mother would do without the income.

Friends   Borrowing from friends is like borrowing from family members. If you know they have the funds available and could survive a loss, you may want to risk it. However, if they would be loaning you their only resources, do not chance it.

Financial problems can be the worst thing for a relationship, whether it is a casual friendship or a long-term romantic involvement. Before you borrow from a friend, try to imagine what would happen if you could not pay it back and how you would feel if it caused the end of your relationship.

The ideal situation is if your friend were a co-venturer in your business, and the burden would not be totally on you to see how the funds were spent. Still, realize that such a venture will put extra strain on the relationship.

Banks   In a way, a bank can be a more comfortable party from which to borrow because you do not have a personal relationship with the bank as you do with a friend or family member. If you fail, they will write your loan off rather than disown you. However, a bank can also be the least comfortable party to borrow from because it will demand realistic projections and be on top of you to perform. If you do not meet the bank's expectations, it may call your loan just when you need it most.

The best thing about a bank loan is that it will require you to do your homework. You must have plans that make sense to a banker. If the bank approves your loan, you know that your plans are at least reasonable.

Bank loans are not cheap or easy. You will be paying a good interest rate, and you will have to put up collateral. If your business does not have equipment or receivables, the bank may require you to put up your house and other personal property to guarantee the loan.

Banks are a little easier to deal with when you get a *Small Business Administration* (SBA) loan. That is because the SBA guarantees that it will pay the bank if you default on the loan. SBA loans are obtained through local bank branches.

Credit Cards   Borrowing against a credit card is one of the fastest growing ways of financing a business, but it can be one of the most expensive ways, as the rates can go higher than 20%. However, there are many cards that offer lower rates and some people are able to get numerous cards. Some successful businesses have used the partners' credit cards to get off the ground or to weather through a cash crunch, but if the business does not begin to generate the cash to make the payments, you could soon end up in bankruptcy. A good strategy is to only use credit cards for a long-term asset, like a computer, or for something that will quickly generate cash, like buying inventory to fill an order. Do not use credit cards to pay expenses that are not generating revenue.

GETTING A RICH PARTNER

One of the best business combinations is a young entrepreneur with ideas and ambition and a retired investor with business experience and money. Together, they can supply everything the business needs.

How to find such a partner? Be creative. You should have investigated the business you are starting and know others who have been in such businesses. Have any of them had partners retire over the last few years? Are any of them planning to phase out of the business?

SELLING SHARES OF YOUR BUSINESS

Silent investors are the best source of capital for your business. You retain full control of the business and if it happens to fail you have no obligation to them. Unfortunately, few silent investors are interested in a new business. It is only after you have proven your concept to be successful and built up a rather large enterprise that you will be able to attract such investors.

The most common way to obtain money from investors is to issue other types of stock or ownership interests to them. The best types of business entities for this are the corporation and the limited liability company. There is almost unlimited flexibility in the number and kinds of ownership interests you can issue.

If you do sell ownership interests in your business to outsiders, and even if you have co-owners who are involved in the business with you, you should make sure to have arrangements in place that govern what happens to those ownership interests if the owner dies, tries to voluntarily sell his or her interest, becomes disabled, or otherwise leaves the business. Disaster can strike when ownership interests pass to heirs or other transferees who you never contemplated having as business partners.

Buy-Sell Agreements

You can also protect yourself by providing yourself and your heirs with a way to cash out in the event that you die or become disabled. These arrangements are usually contained in a *buy-sell agreement*, in a corporation's *shareholders' agreement*, and in the *operating agreement* of a limited liability company. These agreements are complex and involve differing tax consequences. Consult an attorney to get the proper arrangements in place.

Securities Laws   There is one major problem with selling stock in your business, and that is all the federal and state regulations with which you must comply. Both the state and federal governments have long and complicated laws dealing with the sales of *securities*. There are also hundreds of court cases attempting to explain what these laws mean. A thorough explanation of this area of law is beyond the scope of this book.

Basically, securities have been held to exist in any case in which a person provides money to someone with the expectation of getting a profit through the efforts of that person. This can apply to any situation in which someone buys stock or other ownership interest in, or makes a loan to, your business. What the laws require is disclosure of the risks involved and other material information that a person would use to decide whether to make the investment or not. In some cases, *registration* of the securities with the government is required. There are some *exemptions* to registration, such as for small amounts of money being raised and for limited numbers of investors.

Penalties for violation of securities laws are severe and include triple damages and prison terms. Consult a specialist in securities laws before issuing any security. You can often get an introductory consultation at a reasonable rate to learn your options.

USING THE INTERNET TO FIND CAPITAL

In 1995, the owners of Wit Beer made headlines in all the business magazines by successfully raising $1.6 million for their business on the Internet. It seemed so easy—every business wanted to try. What was not made clear in most of the stories was that the owner was a corporate securities lawyer and that he did all the necessary legal work to prepare a prospectus and properly register the stock, something that would have cost anyone else over $100,000 in legal fees. Also, most of the interest in the stock came from the articles, not from the Internet promotion. Today, a similar effort would probably not be nearly as successful.

Before attempting to market your company's shares on the Internet, be sure to get an opinion from a securities lawyer or do some serious research into securities laws.

The Internet does have some sources of capital listed. The following sites may be helpful.

America's Business Funding Directory
www.businessfinance.com

Active Capital
http://activecapital.org

Small Business Administration
www.sba.gov

FinanceHub
www.financehub.com

NVST
www.nvst.com

***Inc.* Magazine**
http://mothra.inc.com/resources/finance

The Capital Network
www.thecapitalnetwork.org

Locating Your Business

The right location for your business will be determined by what type of business it is and how fast you expect it to grow. For some types of businesses, the location will not be important to your success or failure. In others, it will be crucial.

WORKING OUT OF YOUR HOME

Many small businesses get started out of the home. Chapter 7 discusses the *legalities* of home businesses. This section discusses the *practicalities*.

Starting a business out of your home can save you the rent, electricity, insurance, and other costs of setting up at another location. For some people this is ideal, and they can combine their home and work duties easily and efficiently. For others, it is a disaster. A spouse, children, neighbors, television, and household chores can be so distracting that no other work gets done.

Phone Lines   You also should consider whether the type of business you are starting is compatible with a home office. For example, if your business mostly consists of making phone calls or calling clients, the home may be an ideal place to run it. The home may not be a good location if your clients need to visit you or you will need daily pickups and deliveries by truck. This is discussed in more detail in the next chapter.

Since residential rates are usually lower than business lines, many people use their residential telephone line to conduct business or add a second residential line. However, if you wish to be listed in the Yellow Pages, you will need to have a business line in your home. If you are running two or more types of businesses, you can probably add their names as additional listings on the original number and avoid paying for another business line.

CHOOSING A RETAIL SITE

For most types of retail stores, the location is of prime importance. Such things to consider are how close it is to your potential customers, how visible it is to the public, and how easily accessible it is to both automobiles and pedestrians. The attractiveness and safety should also be considered.

Location would be less important for a business that was the only one of its kind in the area. For example, if there was only one moped parts dealer or Armenian restaurant in a metropolitan area, people would have to come to wherever you are if they wanted your products or services. However, even with such businesses, keep in mind that there is competition. People who want moped parts can order them by mail and restaurant customers can choose another type of cuisine.

You should look up all the businesses like the one you plan online or in the phone book and mark them on a map. For some businesses, like a cleaners, you would want to be far from the others. But for other businesses, like antique stores, you would want to be near the others. (Antique stores usually do not carry the same things, they do not compete, and people like to go to an *antique district* and visit all the shops.)

CHOOSING OFFICE, MANUFACTURING, OR WAREHOUSE SPACE

If your business will be the type in which customers will not come to you, such as a manufacturing operation or warehouse facility, locating it near customers is not as much of a concern. You can probably save money by locating away from the high-traffic, central business districts. However, you should consider the convenience for employees and not locate in an area that would be unattractive to them or too far from where they would likely live.

For manufacturing or warehouse operations, you should consider your proximity to a post office, trucking company, or rail line. Where several sites are available, you might consider which one has the earliest or most convenient pick-up schedule for the carriers you plan to use.

LEASING A SPACE

A lease of space can be one of the biggest expenses for a small business, so you should do a lot of homework before signing one. There are a lot of terms in a commercial lease that can make or break your business. The following are the most critical.

Zoning

Before signing a lease, you should be sure that everything that your business will need to do is allowed by the zoning of the property.

Restrictions

In some shopping centers, existing tenants have guarantees that other tenants will not compete with them. For example, if you plan to open a restaurant and bakery, you may be forbidden to sell carry-out baked goods if the supermarket has a bakery and a noncompete clause.

Signs

Business signs are regulated by zoning laws, sign laws, and property restrictions. If you rent a hidden location with no possibility for adequate signage, your business will have a lot smaller chance of success than with a more visible site or much larger sign.

ADA Compliance

The *Americans with Disabilities Act* (ADA) requires that reasonable accommodations be made to make businesses accessible to the handicapped. When a business is remodeled, many more changes are required than if no remodeling is done. When renting space, you should be sure that it complies with the law, that the landlord will be responsible for compliance, and that you are aware of the full costs you will bear.

Expansion

As your business grows, you may need to expand your space. The time to find out about your options is before you sign the lease. Perhaps you can take over adjoining units when those leases expire.

Renewal

Location is a key to success for some businesses. If you spend five years building up a clientele, you do not want someone to take over your locale at the end of your lease. Therefore, you should have a renewal clause on your lease. This usually allows an increase in rent based on inflation.

Guaranty

Most landlords of commercial space will not rent to a small corporation without a personal guaranty of the lease. This is a very risky thing for a new business owner to do. The lifetime rent on a long-term commercial lease can be hundreds of thousands of dollars. If your business fails, the last thing you want to do is be personally responsible for several years of rent.

Where space is scarce or a location is hot, a landlord can get the guarantees he or she demands and there is nothing you can do about it (except perhaps set up an asset protection plan ahead of time). But when several units are vacant or the commercial rental market is soft, you can often negotiate out of the personal guaranty. If the lease is five years, maybe you can get away with a guaranty of just the first year. Give it a try.

Duty to Open

Some shopping centers have rules requiring all shops to be open certain hours. If you cannot afford to staff it the whole time required or if you have religious or other reasons that make this a problem, you should negotiate it out of the lease or find another location.

Sublease

At some point you may decide to sell your business. In many cases, your business' location is the most valuable aspect of it. For this reason, you should be sure that you have the right to either *assign* your lease or to *sublease* the property.

If this is impossible, one way around a prohibition is to incorporate your business before signing the lease and then when you sell the business, sell the stock. But some lease clauses prohibit the transfer of *any interest* in the business, so read the lease carefully.

BUYING A SPACE

If you are experienced with owning rental property, you will probably be more inclined to buy a site for your business. If you have no experience with real estate, you should probably rent and not take on the extra cost and responsibility of property ownership.

One reason to buy your site is that you can build up equity. Rather than pay rent to a landlord, you can pay off a mortgage and eventually own the property.

Separating the Ownership

One risk in buying a business site is that if the business gets into financial trouble the creditors may go after the building as well. For this reason, most people who buy a site for their business keep the ownership out of the business. For example, the business will be a corporation and the real estate will be owned personally by the owner or by a trust unrelated to the business.

Expansion

Before buying a site, you should consider the growth potential of your business. If it grows quickly, will you be able to expand at that site or will you have to move? Might the property next door be available for sale in the future if you need it? Can you get an option on it?

If the site is a good investment, whether or not your business is located on it, then by all means buy it. But if its main use is for your business, think twice.

Zoning

When you buy a site, you might be faced with some of the same concerns you would have if you were renting. You will want to make sure that the zoning permits the type of business you wish to start or that you can get a variance without a large expense or delay. Be aware that just because a business is now using the site does not mean that you can expand or remodel the business at that site. Some zoning laws allow businesses to be grandfathered in, but not expanded. Check with the zoning department and find out exactly what is allowed.

Signs Signs are another concern. Some cities have regulated signs and do not allow new or larger ones. Some businesses have used these laws to get publicity. A car dealer who was told to take down a large number of American flags on his lot filed a federal lawsuit and rallied the community behind him.

ADA Compliance ADA compliance is another concern when buying a commercial building. Find out from the building department if the building is in compliance or what needs to be done to put it in compliance. If you remodel, the requirements may be more strict.

> **NOTE:** *When dealing with public officials, keep in mind that they do not always know what the law is or accurately explain it. They often try to intimidate people into doing things that are not required by law. Read the requirements yourself and question the officials if they seem to be interpreting it wrong. Seek legal advice if officials refuse to reexamine the law or move away from an erroneous position.*

> **NOTE:** *Also consider that keeping public officials happy may be worth the price. If you are already doing something they have overlooked, do not make a big deal over a little thing they want changed, or they may subject you to a full inspection or audit.*

CHECK GOVERNMENTAL REGULATIONS

When looking for a site for your business, you should investigate the different government regulations in your area. For example, a location just outside the city or county limits might have a lower licensing fee, a lower sales tax rate, and less strict signage requirements.

Licensing Your Business

Some Massachusetts cities require you to obtain an occupational license. If you are in a city, you may need both a city and a state license. Businesses that do work in several cities sometimes must obtain a license from each city in which they do work.

City licenses are usually available at city hall. Be sure to find out if zoning allows your type of business before buying or leasing property. The licensing departments will check the zoning before issuing your license.

If you will be preparing or serving food, you will need to check with the local health department to be sure that the premises are in compliance with their regulations.

HOME BUSINESSES

Problems occasionally arise when persons attempt to start a business in their homes. Small new businesses cannot afford to pay rent for commercial space and cities often try to forbid business in residential areas. Getting an occupational license or advertising a fictitious name often gives notice to the city that a business is being conducted in a residential area.

Some people avoid the problem by starting their businesses without obtaining the necessary licenses or fictitious name filings, figuring that the penalties for not having done so (if they are caught) are less expensive than the cost of office space. Some also avoid zoning restrictions. If a person regularly parks commercial trucks and equipment on his or her property, has delivery trucks coming and going, or has employee cars parked along the street, there will probably be complaints from neighbors and the city will probably take legal action. But if a person's business consists merely of making phone calls out of the home and keeping supplies there, the problem may never become an issue.

If a problem does arise regarding a home business that does not disturb the neighbors, a good argument can be made that the zoning law that prohibits the business is unconstitutional. When zoning laws were first instituted, they were not meant to stop people from doing things in a residence that had historically been part of the life in a residence. Consider an artist. Should a zoning law prohibit a person from sitting in his home and painting pictures? If he sells them for a living is there a difference? Should the government be able to force him to rent commercial space just because he decides to sell the paintings he paints?

Similar arguments can be made for many home businesses. For hundreds of years people performed income-producing activities in their homes. (The authors are waiting for their city fathers to tell them to stop writing books in their home offices.) But court battles with a city are expensive and probably not worth the effort for a small business. The best course of action is to keep a low profile. Using a post office box for the business is sometimes helpful in diverting attention away from the residence.

STATE-REGULATED PROFESSIONS

The state requires licensing of certain professions and occupations. If you are in a regulated profession, you should be aware of the laws that apply to your profession. The following pages contain a list of many of these professions and the state laws covering them. You can make copies of these laws and related regulations at any law library.

You can also find these laws on the Internet at **www.mass.gov/ legis/laws/mgl/index.htm**.

If you do not think your profession is regulated, you should read through the list anyway. Some of those included may surprise you.

Regulated Professions in Massachusetts and the Statutes Governing Them
Citations are to Massachusetts General Laws (M.G.L.)

(If no sections are specified, the entire chapter cited applies.)

Profession	M.G.L. Chapter	Section(s)
Auctioneers	100	
Physicians and Surgeons	112	2–12CC
Physician Assistants	112	9C–9K
Podiatrists	112	13–22
Athletic Trainers and Occupational/Physical Therapists	112	23A–23Q
Respiratory Therapists	112	23R–23BB
Pharmacists	112	24–36
Sellers of Drugs	112	36A–42A
Dentists	112	43–53
Veterinarians	112	54–60
Architects	112	60A–60O
Optometrists	112	66–73B
Dispensing Opticians	112	3C–73M

Nurses	112	74–81C
Professional Engineers and Land Surveyors	112	81D–81T
Embalmers and Funeral Directors	112	82–87
Certified Public Accountants	112	87A–87E 1/2
Barbers	112	87F–87S
Cosmetologists	112	87T–87KK
Sanitarians	112	87LL–87OO
Real Estate Brokers and Salesmen	112	87PP–87DDD 1/2
Electrologists	112	87EEE–87OOO
Radio and Television Technicians	112	87PPP–87VVV
Certified Health Officers	112	87WWW–87ZZZ
Drinking Water Supply Facility Operators	112	87CCCC–87DDDD
Chiropractors	11	89–97
Landscape Architects	112	98–107
Nursing Home Administrators	112	108–117
Psychologists	112	118–129A
Social Workers	112	130–137
Speech-Language Pathologists and Audiologists	112	138–147
Acupuncturists	112	148–162

Allied Mental Health and Human Services Professionals	112	163–172
Real Estate Appraisers	112	173–195
Hearing Insturment Specialists	112	196–200
Nutritionists	112	201–210
Perfusionists	112	211–220
Home Inspectors	112	221–226
Labeling, Distribution, Sale, Storage, Transportation, Use, and Disposal of Pesticides	132B	
Attorneys	221	37–52
Financing Motor Vehicles	255B	
Certain Mortgage Brokers and Lenders	255E	

FEDERAL LICENSES

So far, there are few businesses that require federal registration. If you are in any of the types of businesses listed, check with the federal agency that regulates the business.

Radio or television stations or manufacturers of equipment emitting radio waves:

Federal Communications Commission
445 12th Street SW
Washington, DC 20554
www.fcc.gov

Manufacturers of alcohol, tobacco, or firearms:

Bureau of Alcohol, Tobacco, Firearms, and Explosives
Office of Public and Governmental Affairs
650 Massachusetts Avenue, NW
Room 8290
Washington, DC 20226
www.atf.treas.gov

Securities brokers and providers of investment advice:

SEC
100 F Street, NW
Washington, DC 20549
www.sec.gov

Manufacturers of drugs and processors of meat:

Food and Drug Administration
5600 Fishers Lane
Rockville, MD 20857
www.fda.gov

Interstate carriers:

Surface Transportation Board
1925 K Street, NW
Washington, DC 20423
www.stb.dot.gov

Exporters:

Bureau of Industry and Security
Department of Commerce
14th Street & Constitution Avenue, NW
Washington, DC 20220
www.bis.doc.gov

Contract Laws

As a business owner, you will need to know the basics of forming a simple contract for your transactions with both customers and vendors. There is a lot of misunderstanding about what the law is and people may give you erroneous information. Relying on it can cost you money. This chapter gives you a quick overview of the principles that apply to your transactions and the pitfalls to avoid. If you face more complicated contract questions, consult a law library or an attorney familiar with small business law.

TRADITIONAL CONTRACT LAW

One of the first things taught in law school is that a *contract* is not legal unless three elements are present: offer, acceptance, and consideration. During the rest of the semester in contracts class, the students dissect exactly what may be a valid offer, acceptance, and consideration. For your purposes, the important things to remember include the following.

✪ If you make an *offer* to someone, it may result in a binding contract, even if you change your mind or find out it was a bad deal for you.

✪   Unless an offer is *accepted* and both parties agree to the same terms, there is no contract.

✪   A contract does not always have to be in *writing*. Some laws require certain contracts to be in writing, but as a general rule an oral contract is legal. (The problem is proving that the contract existed.)

✪   Without *consideration* (the exchange of something of value or mutual promises), there is not a valid contract.

As mentioned, an entire semester is spent analyzing each of the three elements of a contract. The most important rules for the business owner are as follows.

✪   *An advertisement is not an offer.* Suppose you put an ad in the newspaper offering new IBM computers for $1,995 but there is a typo in the ad and it says $19.95? Can people come in and say *I accept, here's my $19.95*, thereby creating a legal contract? Fortunately, no. Courts have ruled that the ad is not an offer that a person can accept. It is an *invitation* to come in and make offers, which the business can accept or reject.

✪   *The same rule applies to the price tag on an item.* If someone switches price tags on your merchandise, or if you accidentally put the wrong price on it, you are not required by law to sell it at that price. However, many merchants honor a mistaken price, because refusing to do so would constitute bad will and probably lose a customer. If you intentionally put a lower price on an item, intending to require a buyer to pay a higher price, you may be in violation of bait and switch laws.

✪   *When a person makes an offer, several things may happen.* It may be *accepted*, creating a legal contract. It may be *rejected*. It may *expire* before it has been accepted, or it may be *withdrawn* before acceptance. A contract may expire either by a date made in the offer (e.g., *This offer remains open until noon on January 29, 2008*) or after a reasonable amount of time. What is reasonable is a legal question that a court must decide. If someone makes you an offer to sell goods, clearly you cannot come back five years later and accept. Can you accept a week later or a month later and create a legal contract? That depends on the type of goods and the circumstances.

- ✪ *A person accepting an offer cannot add any terms to it.* If you offer to sell a car for $1,000 and the other party says he or she accepts as long as you put new tires on it, there is no contract. An acceptance with changed terms is considered a rejection and a counteroffer.

- ✪ When someone rejects your offer and makes a counteroffer, *a contract can be created by your acceptance of the counteroffer.*

These rules can affect your business on a daily basis. Suppose you offer to sell something to one customer over the phone and five minutes later another customer walks in and offers you more for it. To protect yourself, you should call the first customer and withdraw your offer before accepting the offer of the second customer. If the first customer accepts before you have withdrawn your offer, you may be sued if you have sold the item to the second customer.

Exceptions There are a few exceptions to the basic rules of contracts. These exceptions include the following.

- ✪ *Consent to a contract must be voluntary.* If it is made under a threat, the contract is not valid. If a business refuses to give a person's car back unless he or she pays $200 for changing the oil, the customer could probably sue and get the $200 back.

- ✪ *Contracts to do illegal acts or acts against public policy are not enforceable.* If an electrician signs a contract to put some illegal wiring in a house, the customer could probably not force the electrician to do it because the court would refuse to require an illegal act.

- ✪ *If either party to an offer dies, the offer expires and cannot be accepted by the heirs.* If a painter is hired to paint a portrait and dies before completing it, his wife cannot finish it and require payment. However, a corporation does not die, even if its owners die. If a corporation is hired to build a house and the corporation's owner dies, that person's heirs may take over the corporation and finish the job and require payment.

✪ *Contracts made under misrepresentation are not enforceable.* For example, if someone tells you a car has thirty-five thousand miles on it, you agree to buy it, and you later discover it has one hundred thirty-five thousand miles, you may be able to rescind the contract for fraud and misrepresentation.

✪ *If there was a mutual mistake a contract may be rescinded.* For example, if both you and the seller thought the car had thirty-five thousand miles on it and both relied on that assumption, the contract could be rescinded. However, if the seller knew the car had one hundred thirty-five thousand miles on it, but you assumed it had thirty-five thousand and did not ask, you probably could not rescind the contract.

STATUTORY CONTRACT LAW

The previous section discussed the basics of contract law. These basics are not usually stated in a state's statutes, but are the legal principles decided by judges over hundreds of years. The legislatures in recent times have made numerous exceptions to these principles. In most cases, these laws have been passed when the legislature felt that traditional law was not fair. The important laws that affect contracts are the following.

Statute of Frauds   The *statute of frauds* states when a contract must be in writing to be valid. Some people believe a contract is not valid unless it is in writing, but that is not so. Only those types of contracts mentioned in the statute of frauds must be in writing. Of course, an oral contract is much harder to prove in court than one that is in writing.

In Massachusetts, some of the contracts that must be in writing, and the applicable statute sections, are as follows:

✪ sales of any interest in real estate (Mass. Gen. Laws, ch. 259, Sec. 1);

✪ guarantees of debts of another person (Mass. Gen. Laws, ch. 259, Sec. 1);

✪ agreements that take more than one year to complete (Mass. Gen. Laws, ch. 259, Sec. 1);

✪ promises by executors, administrators, or assignees in insolvency to pay damages from their own estates (Mass. Gen. Laws, ch. 259, Sec. 1);

✪ prenuptial agreements (Mass. Gen. Laws, ch. 259, Sec. 1);

✪ agreements concerning making or revoking a will or codicil or making a devise (Mass. Gen. Laws, ch. 259, Sec. 5, 5A);

✪ sales of goods over $500 (Mass. Gen. Laws, ch. 106, Sec. 2-201); and,

✪ sales of personal property of over $5,000 (Mass. Gen. Laws, ch. 106, Sec. 1-206).

Consumer Protection Law

Because of alleged unfair practices by some types of businesses, laws have been passed controlling transactions between consumers and certain businesses. Most notable among these are agreements arising from door-to-door solicitations. These agreements would cover:

the sale or lease of goods or the rendering of services, or both, primarily for personal, family, or household purposes of over $25 and which are consummated at a place other than the address of the seller or lessor.

These types of agreements may be canceled within three business days. Retail installment sales contracts may also be canceled within three business days. Motor vehicle retail installment sales contracts may be canceled under certain circumstances. These laws are described in more detail in the section on "Advertising Laws and Rules" in Chapter 12.

PREPARING YOUR CONTRACTS

Before you open your business, you should obtain or prepare the contracts or policies you will use in it. In some businesses, such as a restaurant, you may not need much. Perhaps you will want a sign near the entrance stating *Shirt and shoes required* or *Diners must be seated by 10:30 p.m.*

However, if you are a building contractor or run a similar business, you will need detailed contracts to use with your customers. If you do not clearly spell out your rights and obligations, you may end up in court and lose thousands of dollars in profits.

Of course, the best way to have an effective contract is to have an attorney who is experienced in the subject prepare one to meet the needs of your business. However, since this may be too expensive for your new operation, you may want to go elsewhere. Three sources for the contracts you will need are other businesses like yours, trade associations, and legal form books. You should obtain as many different contracts as possible, compare them, and decide which terms are most comfortable for you.

Insurance

There are not many laws requiring you to have insurance, but if you do not have insurance you may face liability that could ruin your business. You should be aware of the types of insurance available, and weigh the risks of a loss against the cost of policy.

Be aware that there can be a wide range of prices and coverage in insurance policies. Get at least three quotes from different insurance agents and ask each one to explain the benefits of his or her policy.

WORKERS' COMPENSATION

In general, if you have any employees, you are required by law to carry workers' compensation insurance.

The term *employee* is specifically defined in Massachusetts General Laws, Chapter 152. You should read this law carefully if you think you need to comply with it. For example, part-time workers, students, aliens, and illegal workers count as employees. However, under certain conditions, professional athletes, real estate agents, part-time domestic workers, seamen, taxi cab drivers, casual and seasonal workers, and door-to-door salespeople are not considered employees. Independent contractors are also not considered employees.

Even if you are not required to have workers' compensation insurance, you may still wish to carry it because it can protect you from litigation.

This insurance can be obtained from most insurance companies and, in many cases, is not expensive. If you have such coverage, you are protected against suits by employees or their heirs in case of an accident.

Failure to provide workers' compensation insurance when required is considered serious. It could result in a substantial fine, prison time, and an injunction against employing anyone. If a person is injured on a job, even if another employee caused it or the injured person contributed to his or her own injury, you may be required to pay for all resulting losses.

There are reporting requirements under workers' compensation law, so make sure you read and understand what your policy requires. Also, it is a misdemeanor to deduct the amount of the premiums from the employee's wages.

UNEMPLOYMENT INSURANCE

Massachusetts requires employers who employ one or more permanent, temporary, or part-time workers to provide information to the Department of Employment and Training (D.E.T.) regarding its employees. The D.E.T. will determine whether the employer must make unemployment insurance contributions. A sample **EMPLOYER STATUS REPORT (1110-A)** that provides this information is in Appendix A at page 215. A blank **EMPLOYER STATUS REPORT (1110-A)** is contained in Appendix B. (see form 11, p.257.)

The unemployment insurance system is a state system, administered by the Department of Employment and Training. Employers who fail to pay required contributions are subject to various civil and criminal penalties, which include up to $50,000 and five years in jail for certain infractions.

LIABILITY INSURANCE

Liability insurance can be divided into two main areas: coverage for injuries on your premises and by your employees, and coverage for injuries caused by your products.

Coverage for the first type of injury is usually very reasonably priced. Injuries in your business or by your employees (such as in an auto accident) are covered by standard premises or auto policies. But coverage for injuries by products may be harder to find and more expensive. In the current liability crisis, juries have awarded high judgments for accidents involving products that had little if any impact on the accident. The situation has become so bad that some entire industries have gone out of business or moved overseas.

Asset Protection

The best way to find out if insurance is available for your type of business is to check with other businesses. If there is a trade group for your industry, its newsletter or magazine may contain ads for insurers. If insurance is unavailable or unaffordable, you can go without and use a corporation and other asset protection devices to protect yourself from liability.

Umbrella Policy

As a business owner, you will be a more visible target for lawsuits even if there is little merit to them. Lawyers know that a *nuisance suit* is often settled for thousands of dollars. Because of your greater exposure, consider getting a personal *umbrella policy*. This is a policy that covers you for claims of up to one, two, or even five million dollars and is very reasonably priced.

HAZARD INSURANCE

One of the worst things that can happen to your business is a fire, flood, or other disaster. With lost customer lists, inventory, and equipment, many businesses have been forced to close after such a disaster.

The premium for such insurance is usually reasonable and could protect you from losing your business. You can even get business interruption insurance that will cover your losses while your business is getting back on its feet.

HOME BUSINESS INSURANCE

There is a special insurance problem for home businesses. Most homeowner and tenant insurance policies do not cover business activities. In fact, under some policies you may be denied coverage if you used your home for a business.

If you merely use your home to make business phone calls and send letters, you will probably not have a problem and not need extra coverage. But if you own equipment, or have dedicated a portion of your home exclusively to the business, you could have a problem. Check with your insurance agent for the options that are available to you.

If your business is a sole proprietorship, and you have, say, a computer that you use both personally and for your business, it would probably be covered under your homeowners' policy. But if you incorporate your business and buy the computer in the name of the corporation, coverage might be denied. If a computer is your main business asset, you could get a special insurance policy in the company name covering just the computer. One company that offers such a policy is Safeware, which can be reached at 800-800-1492.

AUTOMOBILE INSURANCE

If you or any of your employees will be using an automobile for business purposes, be sure that such use is covered. Sometimes a policy may include an exclusion for business use. Check to be sure your liability policy covers you if one of your employees causes an accident while running a business errand.

HEALTH INSURANCE

While new businesses can rarely afford health insurance for their employees, the sooner they can obtain it, the better chance they will have to find and keep good employees. Those starting a business usually need insurance for themselves (unless they have a working spouse who can cover the family), and they can sometimes get a better rate if they get a small business package. Many local chambers of commerce offer group health insurance plans to small businesses.

EMPLOYEE THEFT

If you fear employees may be able to steal from your business, you may want to have them *bonded*. This means that you pay an insurance company a premium to guarantee employees' honesty, and if they cheat you the insurance company pays you damages. This can cover all existing and new employees.

Health and Safety Laws

There are federal and state laws that relate to the health and safety of workers and customers. As a business owner you are liable under these laws and need to comply with them.

OSHA

The *Occupational Safety and Health Administration* (OSHA) is a good example of government regulation so severe it can strangle businesses out of existence. The point of the law is to place the duty on the employer to keep the workplace free from recognized hazards that are likely to cause death or serious bodily injury to workers.

If you have ten or fewer employees or if you are in certain types of businesses, you do not have to keep a record of employees' illnesses, injuries, and exposure to hazardous substances. If you have eleven or more employees, you do have to keep this record, which is called a *Log 300*. All employers are required to display a poster that you can get from OSHA.

Within forty-eight hours of an on-the-job death of an employee or an injury of five or more employees on the job, the area director of OSHA must be contacted.

For more information, you should write or call an OSHA office:

U.S. Department of Labor
200 Constitution Avenue, NW
Washington, DC 20210
Boston: 617-565-9860

You can also visit their website at **www.osha.gov** and obtain copies of their publications, *OSHA Handbook for Small Business* (OSHA 2209) and *OSHA Publications and Audiovisual Programs Catalog* (OSHA 2019). They also have a poster that is required to be posted in the workplace at **www.osha.gov/Publications/poster.html**.

Hazard Communication Standard

The *Hazard Communication Standard* requires that employees be made aware of the hazards in the workplace. (Title 29, Code of Federal Regulations (C.F.R.), Section (Sec.) 1910.1200.) It is especially applicable to those working with chemicals, but this can include even offices that use copy machines. Businesses using hazardous chemicals must have a comprehensive program for informing employees of the hazards and for protecting them from contamination.

For more information, you can contact OSHA at the previously mentioned address, phone number, or website. They can supply a copy of the regulation and a booklet called *OSHA 3084,* which explains the law.

EPA

The *Worker Protection Standard for Agricultural Pesticides* requires safety training, decontamination sites, and, of course, posters. The *Environmental Protection Agency* will provide information on compliance with this law. They can be reached at 800-490-9198 or their website at **www.epa.gov**. They can also be reached by mail at the following address.

Environmental Protection Agency
1200 Pennsylvania Avenue, NW
Washington, DC 20460

FDA

The *Pure Food and Drug Act of 1906* prohibits the misbranding or adulteration of food and drugs. It also created the *Food and Drug Administration* (FDA), which has promulgated tons of regulations and must give permission before a new drug can be introduced into the market. If you will be dealing with any food or drugs you should keep abreast of their policies. Their website is **www.fda.gov**, their small business site is **www.fda.gov/ora/fed_state/small_business**, and their local small business representative is:

FDA, Northeast Region
Small Business Representative
158-15 Liberty Avenue
Jamaica, NY 11433
718-662-5618

HAZARDOUS MATERIAL TRANSPORTATION

There are regulations that control the shipping and packing of hazardous materials. For more information, contact:

U.S. Department of Transportation
Pipeline and Hazardous Materials Safety Administration
Office of Contracts and Procurement, PHA-30
1200 New Jersey Avenue, SE
East Building, 2nd Floor
Washington, DC 20590
202-366-8553

For an organizational structure and phone contacts, visit **http://hazmat.dot.gov/contact/org/org&ct.htm**.

CPSC

The *Consumer Product Safety Commission* (CPSC) has a set of rules that cover the safety of products. The commission feels that because its rules cover products rather than people or companies, they apply to everyone producing such products. However, federal laws do not apply to small businesses that do not affect interstate commerce. Whether a small business would fall under a CPSC rule would depend on the size and nature of the business.

The CPSC rules are contained in the Code of Federal Regulations, Title 16 in the following parts. These can be found at most law libraries, some public libraries, and on the Internet at **www.gpoaccess.gov/nara/index.html**. Click on the "Code of Federal Regulations (CFR)" link, and follow the link to "Browse and/or search the CFR." The CPSC's site is at **http://cpsc.gov**.

Product Part

Antennas, CB and TV	1402
Architectural Glazing Material	1201
Articles Hazardous to Children Under 3	1501
Baby Cribs—Full Size	1508
Baby Cribs—Non-Full Size	1509
Bicycle Helmets	1203
Bicycles	1512
Carpets and Rugs	1630, 1631
Cellulose Insulation	1209, 1404
Cigarette Lighters	1210
Citizens Band Base Station Antennas	1204
Coal and Wood Burning Appliances	1406
Consumer Products Containing Chlorofluorocarbons	1401
Electrically Operated Toys	1505
Emberizing Materials Containing Asbestos (banned)	1305
Extremely Flammable Contact Adhesives (banned)	1302
Fireworks Devices	1507
Garage Door Openers	1211
Hazardous Lawn Darts (banned)	1306
Hazardous Substances	1500
Human Subjects	1028
Lawn Mowers—Walk-Behind	1205
Lead-Containing Paint (banned)	1303
Matchbooks	1202

Mattresses	1632
Pacifiers	1511
Patching Compounds Containing Asbestos (banned)	1304
Poisons	1700
Rattles	1510
Self-Pressurized Consumer Products	1401
Sleepwear—Children's	1615, 1616
Swimming Pool Slides	1207
Toys—Electrical	1505
Unstable Refuse Bins (banned)	1301

ADDITIONAL REGULATIONS

There are proposals for new laws and regulations every day. It would be impossible to include every conceivable one in this book. To be up to date on the laws that affect your type of business, you should belong to a trade association for your industry and subscribe to newsletters that cover your industry. Attending industry conventions is a good way to learn more and to discover new ways to increase your profits.

SMOKING

Massachusetts has laws that prohibit smoking in the following places:

- ✪   workplaces;

- ✪   work spaces;

- ✪   common work areas;

- ✪   classrooms;

- ✪   conference and meeting rooms;

- ✪   offices;

- ✪ elevators;

- ✪ hallways;

- ✪ medical facilities;

- ✪ cafeterias;

- ✪ employee lounges;

- ✪ staircases;

- ✪ restrooms;

- ✪ restaurants;

- ✪ cafes;

- ✪ coffee shops;

- ✪ food courts or concessions;

- ✪ supermarkets or retail food outlets;

- ✪ bars, taverns, or places where food or drink is sold to the public and consumed on the premise as part of a business required to collect state meals tax on the purchase;

- ✪ trains, airplanes, theatres, concert halls, exhibition halls, convention centers, auditoriums, arenas, or stadiums open to the public;

- ✪ schools, colleges, universities, museums, libraries, health care facilities, group child care centers, school-age child care centers, family child care centers, school age day or overnight camp buildings, or on premises where beano games are licensed;

- ✪ public transportation conveyances; and,

✪   airports, train stations, bus stations, transportation passenger terminals, or enclosed outdoor platforms.

There are a few complicated exceptions, which are described at **www.mass.gov/legis/laws/mgl/270-22.htm.**

Employment and Labor Laws

For small businesses, there are not many rules regarding whom you may hire or fire. Fortunately, the ancient law that an employee can be fired at any time (or may quit at any time) still prevails for small businesses. But in certain situations, and as you grow, you will come under a number of laws that affect your hiring and firing practices.

HIRING LAWS

One of the most important things to consider when hiring someone is that if you fire him or her, he or she may be entitled to unemployment compensation. If so, your unemployment insurance contributions will likely go up and it can cost you a lot of money. Therefore, only hire people whom you are sure you will keep, and avoid situations in which your former employees can collect unemployment.

One way this can be done is by hiring only part-time employees. The drawback to this is that you may not be able to attract the best employees. When hiring dishwashers or busboys, this may not be an issue, but when hiring someone to develop a software product, you do not want him or her to leave halfway through the development.

A better solution is to screen applicants and only hire those who you feel certain will succeed. Of course, this is easier said than done. Some people interview well but then turn out to be incompetent at the job.

The best record to look for is someone who has stayed a long time at each of his or her previous jobs. Next best is someone who has not stayed as long (for good reasons) but has always been employed. The worst type of hire would be someone who is or has been collecting unemployment compensation.

In the authors' experience, the intelligence of an employee is more important than his or her experience. An employee with years of typing experience may be fast but unable to figure out how to use your new computer. On the other hand, an intelligent employee can learn the equipment quickly and eventually gain speed. Of course, common sense is important in all situations.

The bottom line is that you cannot know if an employee will be able to fill your needs from a résumé and an interview. Once you have found someone who you think will work out, offer him or her a job with a ninety-day probationary period. If you are not completely satisfied with him or her after the ninety days, offer to extend the probationary period for ninety additional days rather than end the relationship immediately. Of course, all of this should be in writing.

Background Checks
Checking references is important, but beware that a former boss may be a good friend or even a relative. Some may consider it acceptable to exaggerate on résumés, but in recent years, some applicants have been found to be completely fabricating sections of their education and experience.

Polygraph Tests
Under the federal *Employee Polygraph Protection Act*, you cannot require an employee or prospective employee to take a polygraph test unless you are in the armored car, guard, or pharmaceutical businesses. Under Massachusetts law, employers may not use lie detector tests on any employee or applicant for employment. Applications must contain a written notice stating that lie detector testing is illegal.

Medical Examinations

Employers may conduct medical exams, at the employer's expense, only for the purpose of determining whether the employee is capable of performing the job with reasonable accommodation. Employers may not require AIDS/HIV testing as a condition of employment. Upon request, a copy of the medical report must be furnished to the employee.

Drug Tests

Under the ADA, drug testing can only be required of applicants who have been offered jobs conditioned upon passing the drug test. Massachusetts does not have a statute limiting or prohibiting drug testing, but drug tests would be susceptible to challenges under broad statutes such as privacy laws.

NEW HIRE REPORTING

A federal law was passed in 1996 that requires the reporting of new hires. This is the *Personal Responsibility and Work Opportunity Reconciliation Act of 1996* (PRWORA). It provides that such information must be reported by employers to their state government. Massachusetts has had a similar law since 1993.

Massachusetts law requires that within fourteen days of hiring a new employee, an employer must provide the state with information about the employee including his or her name, Social Security number, and address. This information can be submitted in several ways, including mail, fax, or over the Internet. There is a special form that must be used for this reporting; a sample completed form can be found on page 223 and the blank form appears on page 261. The form may be faxed to 617-376-3262 or mailed to:

Department of Revenue
P.O. Box 55141
Boston, MA 02205

You can call the Department of Revenue at 800-332-2733 or visit their website at **www.dor.state.ma.us** for more information about the program.

EMPLOYMENT AGREEMENTS

To avoid misunderstandings with employees, you should use an employment agreement or an employee handbook. These can spell out in detail the policies of your company and the rights of your employees. They can protect your trade secrets and spell out clearly that employment can be terminated at any time by either party.

While it may be difficult or awkward to ask an existing employee to sign such an agreement, an applicant hoping you will hire him or her will usually sign whatever is necessary to obtain the job. However, because of the unequal bargaining position, you should not use an agreement that would make you look bad if the matter ever went to court.

If having an employee sign an agreement is awkward, you can usually obtain the same rights by putting the company policies in an employee manual. Each existing and new employee should be given a copy of the manual, along with a letter stating that the rules apply to all employees and that by accepting or continuing employment at your company they agree to abide by the rules. Having an employee sign a receipt for the letter and manual is proof that he or she received it.

One danger of an employment agreement or handbook is that it may be interpreted to create a long-term employment contract. To avoid this, be sure that you clearly state in the agreement or handbook that the employment is *at will* and can be terminated at any time by either party for any or no reason.

Some other things to consider in an employment agreement or handbook are:

- ✪ what the salary and other compensation will be;

- ✪ what the hours of employment will be;

- ✪ what the probationary period will be;

- ✪ the sexual harassment policy;

- ✪ that the employee cannot sign any contracts binding the employer; and,

✪ that the employee agrees to arbitration rather than filing a lawsuit in the event of a dispute.

INDEPENDENT CONTRACTORS

One way to avoid problems with employees and taxes at the same time is to have all of your work done through *independent contractors*. This can relieve you of most of the burdens of employment laws and the obligation to pay Social Security and Medicare taxes for the workers.

An independent contractor is, in effect, a separate business that you pay to do a job. You pay them just as you pay any company from which you buy products or services. If the amount paid at the end of the year exceeds $600, you will issue an IRS Form 1099 instead of an IRS Form W-2.

This may seem too good to be true; and in some situations, it is. The IRS does not like independent contractor (IC) arrangements because it is too easy for the ICs to cheat on their taxes. To limit the use of ICs, the IRS has strict regulations on who may and may not be classified as an independent contractor. Also, companies that do not appear to pay enough in wages for their field of business are often audited.

The highest at-risk jobs are those that are not traditionally done by independent contractors. For example, you could not get away with hiring a secretary as an independent contractor. One of the most important factors considered in determining if a worker can be an independent contractor is the amount of *control* the company has over his or her work. If you need someone to paint your building and you agree to pay the painter a certain price to do it according to the painter's own methods and schedule, you can pay the painter as an independent contractor. But if you tell the painter when to work, how to do the job, and you provide the tools and materials, the painter will be classified as an employee.

If you just need some typing done and you take it to a typing service and pick it up when it is ready, you will be safe in treating them as independent contractors. But, if you need someone to come into your office to type on your machine at your schedule, you will probably be required to treat that person as an employee for tax purposes. The IRS has a form you can use in determining if a person is an employee or an independent contractor, called **DETERMINATION OF WORKER STATUS.** It is **IRS FORM SS-8.** (see form 9, p.249.)

Independent Contractors versus Employees

In deciding whether to make use of independent contractors or employees, you should weigh the following advantages and disadvantages.

Advantages of using ICs.

- ✪ *Lower taxes.* You do not have to pay Social Security, Medicare, unemployment, or other employee taxes.

- ✪ *Less paperwork.* You do not have to separate and then send federal withholding deposits or monthly employer returns to the state or federal government.

- ✪ *Less insurance.* You do not have to pay workers' compensation insurance and since the workers are not your employees, you do not have to insure against their possible liabilities.

- ✪ *More flexibility.* You can use ICs when you need them and not pay them when business is slow.

Disadvantages of using ICs.

- ✪ The IRS and state tax offices are strict about when workers may be qualified as ICs. They will audit companies whose use of ICs does not appear to be legitimate.

- ✪ If your use of ICs is found to be improper, you may have to pay back taxes and penalties and have problems with your pension plan.

- ✪ While employees usually cannot sue you for their injuries (if you have covered them with workers' compensation), ICs can sue you if their injuries were your fault.

✪ If you are paying someone to produce a creative work (writing, photography, artwork), you receive less rights to the work of an IC.

✪ You have less control over the work of an IC and less flexibility in terminating him or her if you are not satisfied that the job is being done the way you require.

✪ You have less loyalty from an IC who works sporadically for you and possibly others than from your own full-time employees.

For some businesses, the advantages outweigh the disadvantages. For others, they do not. Consider your business plans and the consequences from each type of arrangement. Keep in mind that it will be easier to start with ICs and switch to employees than to hire employees and have to fire them to hire ICs.

TEMPORARY WORKERS

Another way to avoid the hassles of hiring employees is to get workers from a temporary agency. In this arrangement, you may pay a higher amount per hour for the work, but the agency will take care of all the tax and insurance requirements.

Since these can be expensive and time-consuming, the extra per-hour cost may be well worth it. Whether temporary workers will work for you depends upon the type of business you are in and the tasks you need performed. For such jobs as sales management, you would probably want someone who will stay with you long-term and develop relationships with the buyers, but for order fulfillment, temporary workers might work out well.

Another advantage of temporary workers is that you can easily stop using those who do not work out well for you. Also, if you find one who is ideal, you may be able to hire him or her on a full-time basis.

In recent years, a new wrinkle has developed in the temporary worker area. Many large companies are beginning to use them because they are so much cheaper than paying the benefits demanded by full-time employees. For example, Microsoft Corp. has had as many as 6,000 temporary workers, some of whom worked for them for years. However, some of the temporary workers recently won a lawsuit declaring that they are really employees and are entitled to the same benefits as other employees (such as pension plans).

The law is not yet settled in this area as to what arrangements will result in a temporary worker being declared an employee. That will take several more court cases, some of which have already been filed. A few things you can do to protect yourself include the following.

❂ Be sure that all of your benefit plans make it clear that they do not apply to workers obtained through temporary agencies.

❂ Do not keep the same temporary workers for longer than a year.

❂ Do not list temporary workers in any employee directories or hold them out to the public as your employees.

❂ Do not allow them to use your business cards or stationery.

FIRING LAWS

In most cases, unless you have a contract with an employee for a set time period, you can fire him or her at any time for any or no reason. This is only fair, since the employee can quit at any time. This type of employment is called *at will*. You should make it clear when offering a job to someone that, upon acceptance, he or she will be an at-will employee. The exceptions to this are if you fired someone:

❂ based on illegal discrimination;

❂ for filing some sort of health or safety complaint; or,

❂ for refusing your sexual advances.

DISCRIMINATION LAWS

There are numerous federal laws forbidding discrimination based upon race, sex, pregnancy, color, religion, national origin, age, or disability. The laws apply to both hiring and firing, and to employment practices such as salaries, promotions, and benefits. Most of these laws only apply to an employer who has fifteen or more employees for twenty weeks of a calendar year or who has federal contracts or subcontracts. Therefore, you most likely will not be required to comply with the law immediately upon opening your business. However, there are similar state laws that may apply to your business.

One exception is the *Equal Pay Act,* which applies to employers with two or more employees and requires that women be paid the same as men in the same type of job.

Employers with fifteen or more employees are required to display a poster regarding discrimination. This poster is available from the *Equal Employment Opportunity Commission* (EEOC) by calling 866-4-USA-DOL or their website at **www.dol.gov/esa/regs/compliance/posters/eeo.htm**. Employers with 100 or more employees are required to file an annual report with the EEOC.

Discriminatory Interview Questions

When hiring employees, some questions are illegal or inadvisable to ask. The following questions should not be included on your employment application, or in your interviews, unless the information is somehow directly tied to the duties of the job.

- ✪ Do not ask about an applicant's citizenship or place of birth. But after hiring an employee you must ask about his or her right to work in this country.

- ✪ Do not ask a female applicant her maiden name. You can ask if she has been known by any other name in order to do a background check.

- ✪ Do not ask if applicants have children, plan to have them, or have child care. You can ask if an applicant will be able to work the required hours.

- ✪ Do not ask if the applicant has religious objections to working Saturday or Sunday. You can mention if the job requires such hours and ask whether the applicant can meet this job requirement.

○ Do not ask an applicant's age. You can ask if an applicant is 18 or over, or for a liquor-related job if he or she is 21 or over.

○ Do not ask an applicant's weight.

○ Do not ask if an applicant has AIDS or is HIV positive.

○ Do not ask if the applicant has filed a workers' compensation claim.

○ Do not ask about the applicant's previous health problems.

○ Do not ask if the applicant is married or whether his or her spouse would object to the job, hours, or duties.

○ Do not ask if the applicant owns a home, furniture, or car, as it is considered racially discriminatory.

○ Do not ask if the applicant was ever arrested. You can ask if the applicant was ever convicted of a crime.

ADA   Under the *Americans with Disabilities Act* (ADA) of 1990, employers who do not make *reasonable accommodations* for disabled employees will face fines of up to $100,000, as well as other civil penalties and civil damage awards.

While the goal of creating more opportunities for people with disabilities is a good one, the result of this law is to place all the costs of achieving this goal on businesses that are faced with disabled applicants. In fact, studies have shown that employers have hired fewer rather than more disabled people. It is theorized that this may be due to the expense of the reasonable accommodations or the fear of lawsuits by disabled employees.

The ADA currently applies to employers with fifteen or more employees. Employers who need more than fifteen employees might want to consider contracting with independent contractors to avoid problems with this law, particularly if the number of employees is only slightly larger than fifteen.

To find out how this law affects your business, see the ADA Technical Assistance Manual at **www.ada.gov/taman3.html.**

Tax benefits. There are three types of tax credits to help small business with the burden of these laws.

- ✪ Businesses can deduct up to $15,000 a year for making their premises accessible to the disabled and can depreciate the rest (Internal Revenue Code Sec. 190).

- ✪ Small businesses (under $1,000,000 in revenue and under thirty employees) can get a tax credit each year for 50% of the cost of making their premises accessible to the disabled, but this only applies to an amount between $250 and $10,500.

- ✪ Small businesses can get a credit of up to 40% of the first $6,000 of wages paid to certain new employees who qualify. See IRS form 8850 and instructions.

Records. To protect against potential claims of discrimination, all employers should keep detailed records showing reasons for hiring or not hiring applicants and for firing employees.

Massachusetts Law

Massachusetts has its own laws regarding discrimination in employment practices. Chapter 151B of the Massachusetts General Laws, which applies to employers with six or more employees, prohibits discrimination or classification based upon race, color, religion, sex, national origin, age, sexual orientation (excluding persons whose sexual orientation involves minor children as the sex object), ancestry, handicap, or marital status, unless based on a bona fide occupational qualification. It is also unlawful to require someone, as a condition of obtaining or keeping employment, to violate or forgo the practice of his creed or religion, including the observance of any particular holy day. Reasonable accommodation by the employer is required. An employer who violates these laws can be sued and be required to pay back pay, damages, and punitive damages.

SEXUAL HARASSMENT

What began as protection for employees who were fired or not promoted for failing to succumb to the sexual advances of their superiors has been expanded to outlaw nearly any sexual comments or references in the workplace.

In the 1980s, the *Equal Employment Opportunity Commission* (EEOC) interpreted *Title VII* of the *Civil Rights Act of 1964* to forbid sexual harassment. After that, the courts took over and reviewed all types of conduct in the workplace. The numerous lawsuits that followed began a trend toward expanding the definition of sexual harassment and favoring employees.

The EEOC has held the following in sexual harassment cases.

- ✪ The victim as well as the harasser may be a woman or a man.

- ✪ The victim does not have to be of the opposite sex.

- ✪ The harasser can be the victim's supervisor, an agent of the employer, a supervisor in another area, a co-worker, or a non-employee.

- ✪ The victim does not have to be the person harassed, but could be anyone affected by the offensive conduct.

- ✪ Unlawful sexual harassment may occur without economic injury to or discharge of the victim.

- ✪ The harasser's conduct must be unwelcome.

Some of the actions that have been considered harassment are:

- ✪ displaying sexually explicit posters in the workplace;

- ✪ requiring female employees to wear revealing uniforms;

- ✪ rating the sexual attractiveness of female employees as they pass male employees' desks;

- ✪ continued sexual jokes and innuendos;

- ✪ demands for sexual favors from subordinates;

- ✪ unwelcomed sexual propositions or flirtation;

- ✪ unwelcomed physical contact; and,

- ✪ whistling or leering at members of the opposite sex.

In 1993, the United States Supreme Court ruled that an employee can make a claim for sexual harassment even without proof of a specific injury. However, lower federal courts in more recent cases have dismissed cases in which no specific injury was shown. These new cases may indicate that the pendulum has stopped moving toward expanded rights for the employee.

On the other hand, another recent case ruled that an employer can be liable for the harassment of an employee by a supervisor, even if the employer was unaware of the supervisor's conduct, if the employer did not have a system in place to allow complaints against harassment. This area of law is still developing, and to avoid a possible lawsuit you should be aware of the things that could potentially cause liability and avoid them.

Some things a business can do to protect against claims of sexual harassment are:

- ✪ distribute a written policy against all kinds of sexual harassment to all employees (this is required in Massachusetts);

- ✪ encourage employees to report all incidents of sexual harassment;

- ✪ ensure there is no retaliation against those who complain;

- ✪ make clear that your policy is *zero tolerance*;

- ✪ explain that sexual harassment includes both requests for sexual favors and a work environment that some employees may consider hostile;

- ✪ allow employees to report harassment to someone other than their immediate supervisor in case that person is involved in the harassment; and,

- ✪ promise as much confidentiality as possible to complainants.

Massachusetts Law

Massachusetts requires all employers with six or more employees to adopt a written policy against sexual harassment. The written policy must include:

- ✪ a statement that sexual harassment in the workplace is unlawful;

- ✪ a statement that it is unlawful to retaliate against an employee for filing a complaint of sexual harassment or for cooperating in an investigation of a complaint for sexual harassment;

- ✪ a description and examples of sexual harassment;

- ✪ a statement of the range of consequences for employees who are found to have committed sexual harassment;

- ✪ a description of the process for filing internal complaints about sexual harassment and the work addresses and telephone numbers of the person or persons to whom complaints should be made; and,

- ✪ the identity of the appropriate state and federal employment discrimination enforcement agencies and directions as to how to contact them.

Employers must provide all new employees with a copy of the policy when they commence employment and must provide each employee with a copy annually. The law required the Massachusetts

Commission Against Discrimination to prepare a model policy that conforms with the federal and state requirements.

Common Law Although the federal and civil rights laws only apply to businesses with fifteen or more employees, and the Massachusetts laws to businesses with six or more employees, any employee could sue for sexual harassment in civil court. However, this is difficult, expensive, and would only be worthwhile when there were substantial damages.

WAGE AND HOUR LAWS

The *Fair Labor Standards Act* (FLSA) applies to all employers who are engaged in *interstate commerce* or in the production of goods for interstate commerce (anything that will cross the state line) and all employees of hospitals, schools, residential facilities for the disabled or aged, or public agencies. It also applies to all employees of enterprises that gross $500,000 or more per year.

Minimum Wage While many small businesses might not think they are engaged in interstate commerce, the laws have been interpreted so broadly that nearly any use of the mails, interstate telephone service, or other interstate services, however minor, is enough to bring a business under the law.

The federal wage and hour laws are contained in the *Federal Fair Labor Standards Act*. In 2007, Congress passed and President Bush signed the *Fair Minimum Wage Act of 2007*, raising the minimum wage to $5.85 an hour beginning July 24, 2007. It also provides that the minimum wage will rise to $6.55 per hour on July 24, 2008, and to $7.25 per hour on July 24, 2009. In certain circumstances, a wage of $4.25 may be paid to employees under 20 years of age for a ninety-day training period. For employees who regularly receive more than $30 a month in tips, the minimum wage is $2.13 per hour. But if the employee's tips do not bring him or her up to the full $5.85 minimum wage, then the employer must make up the difference.

Overtime The general rule is that employees who work more than forty hours a week must be paid time-and-a-half for hours worked over forty. But there are many exemptions to this general rule based on salary and position. These exceptions were completely revised in 2004, and an explanation of the changes, including a tutorial video, is available at **www.dol.gov/esa**. For answers to questions about the law, you can call the Department of Labor at 866-487-9243.

Exempt Employees

While nearly all businesses are covered, certain employees are exempt from the FLSA. Exempt employees include employees who are considered executives, administrative, managerial, professionals, computer professionals, and outside salespeople.

Whether one of these exceptions applies to a particular employee is a complicated legal question. Thousands of court cases have been decided on this issue but they have given no clear answers. In one case a person could be determined to be exempt because of his or her duties, but in another, a person with the same duties could be found not exempt.

One thing that is clear is that the determination is made on the employee's function, and not just the job title. You cannot make a secretary exempt by calling him or her a manager if most of the job duties are clerical. For more information, see the Department of Labor website at **www.dol.gov/esa/whd/flsa/index.htm.**

You can also obtain information on the Department of Labor's Employment Plan Guide at **www.dol.gov/asp/programs/guide.htm**.

Massachusetts Law

At the time of this publication, Massachusetts requires a minimum wage of $7.50 per hour, except in particular specified occupations, and is set to raise the minimum wage to $8.00 per hour on January 1, 2008. The Commissioner of Labor may set lower minimum rates for certain occupations, but may not set a rate lower than a specified amount per hour except for learners, apprentices, ushers, ticket sellers and takers, janitors, caretakers, golf caddies, and service people earning more than $20 a month in tips.

Most employees are entitled to time-and-a-half for hours worked over forty per week. Most employers must pay wages at least every two weeks, or pay no later than six days after the last day worked.

State, county, and certain municipal employees may not work more than eight hours a day, forty-eight hours a week, and six days a week, except in case of emergency.

Private employers must give employees in certain occupations twenty-four consecutive hours to rest every seven consecutive days. There are also restrictions on requiring employees to work on Sundays or holidays. Generally, employers must allow a thirty-minute meal break for each six hours of work.

PENSION AND BENEFIT LAWS

There are no laws requiring small businesses to provide any types of special benefits to employees. Such benefits are given to attract and keep good employees. With pension plans, the main concern is if you do start one it must comply with federal tax laws.

Holidays

There are no federal or Massachusetts laws that require that employees be given holidays off. You can require them to work Thanksgiving and Christmas and dock their pay or fire them for failing to show. Of course, you will not have much luck keeping employees with such a policy.

Most companies give full-time employees a certain number of paid holidays, such as: New Year's Day (January 1); Memorial Day (last Monday in May); Fourth of July; Labor Day (first Monday in September); Thanksgiving (fourth Thursday in November); and, Christmas (December 25). Some employers include other holidays such as Martin Luther King, Jr.'s birthday (January 15); President's Day; and, Columbus Day. If one of the holidays falls on a Saturday or Sunday, many employers give the preceding Friday or following Monday off. Massachusetts law says that legal holidays include the following (or the day following when any of said days occurs on Sunday):

New Year's Day	(January 1)
Martin Luther King, Jr.'s Day	(3rd Monday in January)
George Washington's birthday	(3rd Monday in February)
Patriot's Day	(3rd Monday in April)
Memorial Day	(last Monday in May)
Independence Day	(July 4)

Labor Day	(1st Monday in September)
Columbus Day	(2nd Monday in October)
Veteran's Day	(November 11)
Thanksgiving Day	(4th Thursday in November)
Christmas Day	(December 25)

With respect to Suffolk County only, Evacuation Day on March 17th (for certain purposes only) and Bunker Hill Day on June 17th, or the day following when said days occur on Sunday, are also legal holidays.

However, the fact that these are designated state holidays does not mean that private employers, other than owners of mills and factories, must observe them. In fact, not even the state government is closed on all of these days.

Sick Days   There is no federal or Massachusetts law mandating that an employee be paid for time that he or she is home sick. The situation seems to be that the larger the company, the more paid sick leave is allowed. Part-time workers rarely get sick leave and small business sick leave is usually limited for the simple reason that they cannot afford to pay for time that employees do not work.

Some small companies have an official policy of no paid sick leave, but when an important employee misses a day because he or she is clearly sick, it is paid.

Pension Plans and Retirement Accounts   Few small new businesses can afford to provide pension plans for their employees. The first concern of many small business owners is usually how the owner can shelter income in a pension plan without having to set up a pension plan for an employee. Under most pension plans, this is not allowed.

IRA. Anyone with $3,000 of earnings can put up to that amount in an individual retirement account (IRA). Unless the person or his or her spouse is covered by a company pension plan and has income over a certain amount, the amount put into the account is fully tax deductible.

ROTH IRA. Contributions to a Roth IRA are not tax deductible, but when the money is taken out, it is not taxable. People who expect to still have taxable income when they withdraw from their IRA can benefit from these.

SEP IRA, SAR-SEP IRA, SIMPLE IRA. With these types of retirement accounts, a person can put a much greater amount into a retirement plan and deduct it from his or her taxable income. Employees must also be covered by such plans, but certain employees are exempt so it is sometimes possible to use these for the owners alone. The best source for more information is a mutual fund company (such as Vanguard, Fidelity, Dreyfus, etc.) or a local bank, which can set up the plan and provide you with all the rules. These have an advantage over qualified plans (discussed later) since they do not have the high annual fees.

Qualified retirement plans. Qualified retirement plans are 401(k) plans, Keough plans, and corporate retirement plans. These are covered by ERISA, the *Employee Retirement Income Security Act*. ERISA is a complicated law meant to protect employee pension plans. Congress did not want employees who contributed to pension plans all their lives ending up with nothing when the plan went bankrupt. The law is complicated and the penalties are severe. However, many banks and mutual funds have created *canned plans* that can be used instead of drafting one from scratch. Still, the fees for administering them are steep. Check with a bank or mutual fund for details.

FAMILY AND MEDICAL LEAVE LAW
The *Family and Medical Leave Act of 1993* (FEML) requires an employee to be given up to twelve weeks of unpaid leave when:

- ✪ the employee or employee's spouse has a child;

- ✪ the employee adopts a child or takes in a foster child;

- ✪ the employee needs to care for an ill spouse, child, or parent; or,

- ✪ the employee becomes seriously ill.

The law only applies to employers with fifty or more employees. Also, the top 10% of an employer's salaried employees can be denied this leave because of the disruption in business their absence could cause.

Massachusetts Law

Massachusetts law requires employers with six or more employees to give up to eight weeks of maternity leave (but does not require pay during the period) for female employees for the purpose of giving birth or adopting a child under 18 years of age, or under 23 years of age if mentally or physically disabled, provided the employee gives at least two weeks' notice and intends to return to work. Notice of this provision must be posted in the workplace.

Employees of manufacturing, mechanical, or mercantile establishments must be given leave to vote in any election during the first two hours after the polls are open, upon request. The law also requires leave in certain circumstances for training for armed forces reserves, participation in Veteran's Day or Memorial Day exercises, and jury duty.

In August of 1998, a statute became effective in Massachusetts, entitled *An Act Providing Employee Leave for Certain Family Obligations*. The act, commonly referred to as the Small Necessities Leave Act (SNLA), is applicable only to employers who are covered by the federal Family and Medical Leave Act of 1993.

The SNLA grants an eligible employee up to twenty-four hours of leave during any twelve-month period, in addition to leave under the FMLA, to:

- ✪ participate in school activities directly related to the educational advancement of a son or daughter of the employee, such as parent/teacher conferences or interviewing for a new school;

- ✪ accompany the son or daughter of the employee to routine medical or dental appointments, such as checkups or vaccinations; or,

- ✪ accompany an elderly relative of the employee to routine medical or dental appointments or appointments for other professional services related to the elder's care, such as interviewing at nursing or group homes.

An elderly relative is defined as someone at least 60 years of age who is related by blood or marriage to the employee. A school is defined as a public or private elementary or secondary school, a Head Start program, or a state-licensed children's day care facility.

There are various options to employers for determining the twelve-month period and certain notice requirements.

CHILD LABOR LAWS

The Federal Fair Labor Standards Act also contains rules regarding the hiring of children. The basic rules are that children under 16 years old may not be hired at all except in a few jobs such as acting and newspaper delivery, and those under 18 may not be hired for dangerous jobs. Children may not work more than three hours a day/eighteen hours a week in a school week or more than eight hours a day/forty hours a week in a nonschool week. If you plan to hire children, you should check the Federal Fair Labor Standards Act, in Chapter 29, United States Code (29 USC) and also the related regulations found in Chapter 29 of the Code of Federal Regulations (29 C.F.R.).

Massachusetts Law

Massachusetts also has its own child labor laws. The following rules apply to child labor in Massachusetts in addition to federal laws.

- ✪ Persons under 18 generally may not work more than nine hours a day, forty-eight hours a week, or six days a week. In most cases, a child's hours of work each day must fall within a ten-consecutive-hour period. These rules do not apply to professional, executive, administrative, supervisory, and personal secretarial positions.

- ✪ Sixteen- and 17-year-olds can work only between 6 a.m. and 11:30 p.m., except in restaurants; they may also work in restaurants until midnight on Fridays, Saturdays, and during school vacations, except the last day of vacation; generally, they cannot work more than forty-eight hours a week, nine hours a day, or six days a week.

✪ Fourteen- and 15-year olds can work only between 7 a.m. and 7 p.m. during the school year, and between 7 a.m. and 9 p.m. during the summer, and not during school hours; generally, they cannot work more than eighteen hours a week, three hours a day on school days, eight hours a day on Saturdays, Sundays, and holidays, or six days a week.

✪ Children are allowed to work up to fifty-two hours per week in certain types of seasonal employment from June to October.

✪ Children under 18 may not work after 8 p.m. unless they are supervised by an adult, except at kiosks in enclosed shopping malls with securtiy.

✪ Children 14 or younger may work in agricultural labor for up to four hours a day or twenty-four hours a week, or more if related to the owner or operator of the farm.

✪ Children under 16 may not work on certain equipment and in certain hazardous, arduous, or corruptive occupations, or in occupations that may unduly interfere with their schooling.

Hazardous occupations. No persons under 18 years of age may work in the following occupations or use the following equipment:

✪ blast furnaces;

✪ hoisting machines;

✪ oiling or cleaning hazardous machinery in motion;

✪ polishing or buffing wheels;

✪ switch tending;

✪ gate tending;

✪   track repairing;

✪   brakeman, fireman, engineer, motorman, or conductor on railroad;

✪   fireman or engineer on boat;

✪   operating motor vehicles except in auto repair shop;

✪   gunpowder and other explosive manufacturing;

✪   manufacture of phosphorus or phosphorous matches;

✪   distillery, brewery, or other bottling, manufacturing, or packing of alcoholic beverages;

✪   logging or sawmilling;

✪   selling alcoholic beverages;

✪   at heights of more than thirty feet above the floor of a room or above ground or water level;

✪   operating, cleaning, or repairing elevators; or

✪   any job requiring possession or use of a firearm.

IMMIGRATION LAWS

There are strict penalties for any business that hires aliens who are not eligible to work. You must verify both the identity and the employment eligibility of anyone you hire by using the **EMPLOYMENT ELIGIBILITY VERIFICATION (FORM I-9)**. (see form 7, p.243.) Both you and the employee must fill out the form, and you must check an employee's identification cards or papers. Fines for hiring illegal aliens range from $250 to $2,000 for the first offense and up to $10,000 for the third offense. Failure to maintain the proper paperwork may result in a fine of up to $1,000. The law does not apply to independent contractors with whom you may contract, and it does not penalize you if the employee used fake identification.

There are also penalties that apply to employers of four or more persons for discriminating against eligible applicants because they appear foreign or because of their national origin or citizenship status.

Appendix B has a list of acceptable documentation, a blank form, and instructions. (see form 7, p.243.) The blank form can also be downloaded at **www.uscis.gov/i-9**.

For more information, call 800-357-2099. For the *Handbook for Employers: Instructions for Completing Form I-9*, check the United States Citizenship and Immigration Services (USCIS) website at **www.uscis.gov**.

Foreign Employees

If you wish to hire employees who are foreign citizens and are not able to provide the proper documentation, they must first obtain a work visa from USCIS.

Work visas for foreigners are not easy to get. Millions of people around the globe would like to come to the United States to work, but the laws are designed to keep most of them out to protect the jobs of American citizens.

Whether or not a person can get a work visa depends on whether there is a shortage of U.S. workers available to fill the job. For jobs requiring few or no skills, it is practically impossible to get a visa. For highly skilled jobs, such as nurses and physical therapists, and for people of exceptional ability, such as Nobel Prize winners and Olympic medalists, obtaining a visa is fairly easy.

There are several types of visas, and different rules for different countries. For example, the North American Free Trade Agreement (NAFTA) has made it easier for some types of workers to enter the United States from Canada and Mexico. For some positions, the shortage of workers is assumed by the USCIS. For others, a business must first advertise a position available in the United States. Only after no qualified persons apply can it hire someone from another country.

The visa system is complicated and subject to regular change. If you wish to hire a foreign worker, you should consult with an immigration specialist or a book on the subject.

Massachusetts Law   Massachusetts General Laws, Chapter 149, Section 19C makes it illegal to hire aliens who are not legally authorized to work.

HIRING OFF THE BOOKS

Because of the taxes, insurance, and red tape involved with hiring employees, some new businesses hire people "off the books." They pay them in cash and never admit they are employees. While the cash paid in wages would not be deductible, they consider this a smaller cost than compliance. Some even use off the books receipts to cover it.

Except when your spouse or child is giving you some temporary help, this is a terrible idea. Hiring people off the books can result in civil fines, loss of insurance coverage, and even criminal penalties. When engaged in dangerous work like roofing or using power tools, you are risking millions of dollars in potential liability if a worker is killed or seriously injured.

It may be more costly and time-consuming to comply with the employment laws, but if you are concerned about long-term growth with less risk, it is the wiser way to go.

FEDERAL CONTRACTS

Companies that do work for the federal government are subject to several laws.

The *Davis-Bacon Act* requires contractors engaged in U.S. government construction projects to pay wages and benefits that are equal to or better than the prevailing wages in the area.

The *McNamara-O'Hara Service Contract Act* sets wages and other labor standards for contractors furnishing services to agencies of the U.S. government.

The *Walsh-Healey Public Contracts Act* requires the Department of Labor to settle disputes regarding manufacturers supplying products to the U.S. government.

MISCELLANEOUS LAWS

In addition to the broad categories of laws affecting businesses, there are several other federal and state laws that you should be familiar with.

Federal Laws   Federal law regulates affirmative action, layoffs, unions, and informational posters.

Affirmative action. In most cases, the federal government does not yet tell employers who they must hire. This would be especially true for new small businesses. The only situation in which a small business would need to comply with affirmative action requirements would be if it accepted federal contracts or subcontracts. These requirements could include the hiring of minorities or Vietnam veterans.

Layoffs. Companies with one hundred or more full-time employees at one location are subject to the *Worker Adjustment and Retraining Notification Act*. This law requires a sixty-day notification prior to certain layoffs and has other strict provisions.

Unions. The *National Labor Relations Act of 1935* gives employees the right to organize a union or to join one. (29 U.S.C., Sec. 151 et seq.) There are things employers can do to protect themselves, but consult a labor attorney or a book on the subject before taking action that might be illegal and result in fines.

Poster laws. There are laws regarding what posters you are required to display. The following list should be of help.

✪ All employers must display the wage and hour poster available from:

U. S. Department of Labor
www.dol.gov/esa

✪ Employers with fifteen or more employees for twenty weeks of the year must display the sex, race, religion, and ethnic discrimination poster and the age discrimination poster available from:

EEOC
www.eeoc.gov/posterform.html

✪ Employers with federal contracts or subcontracts of $10,000 or more must display the sex, race, etc., discrimination poster mentioned previously plus a poster regarding Vietnam era veterans available from the local federal contracting office.

✪ Employers with government contracts subject to the *Service Contract Act* or the *Public Contracts Act* must display a notice to employees working on government contracts available from:

Employment Standards Division
www.dol.gov/esa

Massachusetts Law

Working conditions. Employers must provide proper ventilation, sanitation, lighting, and heat from October 15 to May 15. Industrial and construction workers must be provided drinking water. Fire exits must be accessible during working hours.

Personnel records. Employers must, upon written request of present and former employees, allow those persons to inspect and copy their personnel records.

Prevention of employment. No one may, by intimidation or force, prevent or seek to prevent a person from entering into or continuing in the employment of any person.

Coercion of agreement not to join a labor organization. No one may coerce or compel a person into an agreement not to join or become a member of a labor organization as a condition of securing employment or continuing employment.

Volunteer experience. Employment applications requiring the applicant to set forth experience history must contain a statement that the applicant may include in such history any verified work performed on a volunteer basis.

Seats. Employers must provide seats for employees and must allow their use when not engaged in active duties of employment and while at work unless sitting would interfere with the work or cause danger.

Advertising and Promotion Laws

Federal rules do not apply to every business. Small businesses that operate only within one state and do not use the postal service may be exempt. However, many of the federal rules are encompassed by Massachusetts' unfair trade practices laws. Therefore, a violation could be prosecuted by the state rather than the federal government.

ADVERTISING LAWS AND RULES

The federal government regulates advertising through the *Federal Trade Commission* (FTC). The rules are contained in the *Code of Federal Regulations* (C.F.R.). You can find these rules in most law libraries and many public libraries. If you plan any advertising that you think may be questionable, you might want to check the rules. If you question it, most likely the Washington bureaucrats have forbidden it.

Deceptive Pricing

When prices are being compared, it is required that actual and not inflated prices are used. For example, if an object would usually be sold for $7, you should not first offer it for $10 and then start offering it at 30% off. It is considered misleading to suggest that a discount from list price is a bargain if the item is seldom actually sold at list price. If most surrounding stores sell an item for $7, it is considered misleading to say it has a *retail value of $10* even if there are some stores elsewhere selling it at that price. (16 C.F.r. Part 233.)

Bait and Switch Advertising

Bait and switch advertising is placing an ad when you do not really want the respondents to buy the product offered, but to switch to another item. The factors used to determine if there was a violation are similar to those used by Massachusetts in applying its unfair trade practices laws. (16 C.F.R. Part 238.)

Use of free, half-off, and similar words. Use of words such as *free*, *1¢ sale*, and the like must not be misleading. This means that the *regular price* must not include a markup to cover the *free* item. The seller must expect to sell the product without the free item at some time in the future. (16 C.F.R. Part 251.)

Substantiation of Claims

The FTC requires that advertisers be able to substantiate their claims. Some information on this policy is contained on the Internet at **www.ftc.gov/bcp/guides/ad3subst.htm**. (16 C.F.R. Sec. 3.40 and 48 F.R. Page 10471 (1983).)

Endorsements

This rule forbids endorsements that are misleading. An example is a quote from a film review used in such a way as to change the substance of the review. It is not necessary to use the exact words of the person endorsing the product as long as the opinion is not distorted. If a product is changed, an endorsement that does not apply to the new version cannot be used. For some items, such as drugs, claims cannot be used without scientific proof. Endorsements by organizations cannot be used unless one is sure that the membership holds the same opinion. (16 C.F.R. Part 255.)

Unfairness

Any advertising practices that can be deemed to be *unfair* are forbidden by the FTC. An explanation of this policy is located on the Internet at **www.ftc.gov/bcp/policystmt/ad-unfair.htm**. (15 U.S.C. Sec. 45.)

Negative Option Plans

When a seller uses a sales system in which the buyer must notify the seller if he or she does not want the goods, the seller must provide the buyer with a form to decline the sale and at least ten days in which to decline. Bonus merchandise must be shipped promptly and the seller must promptly terminate shipment for any who so request after completion of the contract. (16 C.F.R. Part 425.)

Laser Eye Surgery

Under the laws governing deceptive advertising, the FTC and the FDA are regulating the advertising of laser eye surgery. Anyone involved in this area should obtain a copy of these rules. They are located on the Internet at **www.ftc.gov/bcp/guides/eyecare2.shtm**. (15 U.S.C. Sections 45, 52–57.)

Food and Dietary Supplements

Under the *Nutritional Labeling Education Act of 1990*, the FTC and the FDA regulate the packaging and advertising of food and dietary products. Anyone involved in this area should obtain a copy of these rules. They are located on the Internet at **www.ftc.gov/bcp/menus/resources/guidance/adv.shtm**. (21 U.S.C. Sec. 343.)

Jewelry and precious metals. The FTC has numerous rules governing the sale and advertising of jewelry and precious metals. Anyone in this business should obtain a copy of these rules. They are located on the Internet at **www.ftc.gov/bcp/guides/jewel-gd.shtm**. (61 C.F.R. Sec. 27212.)

Massachusetts Law

Massachusetts has unfair trade practices laws that provide for treble damages for consumers against businesses that have willfully or knowingly violated the law. Among the prohibited actions are the following.

✪ Advertising goods at less than cost plus sales tax for the purpose of injuring or destroying competition (with exceptions).

✪ Failure by a merchant to disclose any fact, the disclosure of which may have influenced the buyer not to enter into the transaction to start with.

✪ Failure by a merchant in advertising to disclose all material facts concerning the product or service that, if not disclosed, might directly or by implication mislead the consumer.

✪ Making any claim or representation that by any means has the capacity, tendency, or effect of deceiving buyers or prospective buyers as to the value or the past, present, common, or usual price of a product, or as to any reduction in price of a product, or any saving relating to a product.

✪   A statement or illustration in an advertisement that creates a false impression of the grade, quality, make, value, currency of model, size, color, usability, or origin of the product offered, or that may otherwise misrepresent the product in such a manner that later, on disclosure of the true facts, there is a likelihood that the buyer may be switched from the advertised product to another.

✪   Engaging in any act or practice to discourage the purchase of the advertised product as part of a bait scheme to sell another product.

✪   Car dealers forcing customers to purchase optional accessories installed by the dealer.

✪   Negligent misrepresentation of fact when the truth is reasonably capable of ascertainment. This might include the following things:

   •   misrepresenting the owner, manufacturer, distributor, source, or geographical origin of goods;

   •   misrepresenting the age, model, grade, style, or standard of goods;

   •   misrepresenting the sponsorship, endorsement, approval, or certification of goods or services;

   •   misrepresenting the affiliation, connection, or association of any goods or services;

   •   misrepresenting the nature, characteristics, standard ingredients, uses, benefits, warranties, guarantees, quantities, or qualities of goods or services;

   •   misrepresenting used, altered, deteriorated, or repossessed goods as new;

- disparaging goods, services, or businesses of another by false or misleading representation; or,

- advertising goods or services with intent not to sell them as advertised.

INTERNET SALES LAWS

There are not yet specific laws governing Internet transactions that are different from laws governing other transactions. The FTC feels that its current rules regarding deceptive advertising, substantiation, disclaimers, refunds, and related matters must be followed by Internet businesses and that consumers are adequately protected by them.

For some specific guidelines on Internet advertising, see the FTC's site at:

> www.ftc.gov/bcp/conline/pubs/buspubs/ruleroad.htm

HOME SOLICITATION LAWS

The Federal Trade Commission has rules governing door-to-door sales. It is a deceptive trade practice in any such sale to fail to furnish a receipt explaining the sale (in the language of the presentation). It is also deceptive not to give notice that there is a right to back out of the contract within three days, known as a *right of rescission*. The notice must be supplied in duplicate, must be in at least ten-point type, and must be captioned either *Notice of Right to Cancel* or *Notice of Cancellation*. The notice must be worded as follows on the next page.

NOTICE OF CANCELLATION

_____
Date

YOU MAY CANCEL THIS TRANSACTION, WITHOUT ANY PENALTY OR OBLIGATION, WITHIN THREE BUSINESS DAYS FROM THE ABOVE DATE.

IF YOU CANCEL, ANY PROPERTY TRADED IN, ANY PAYMENTS MADE BY YOU UNDER THE CONTRACT OR SALE, AND ANY NEGOTIABLE INSTRUMENT EXECUTED BY YOU WILL BE RETURNED TO YOU WITHIN 10 BUSINESS DAYS FOLLOWING RECEIPT BY THE SELLER OF YOUR CANCELLATION NOTICE, AND ANY SECURITY INTEREST ARISING OUT OF THE TRANSACTION WILL BE CANCELLED.

IF YOU CANCEL, YOU MUST MAKE AVAILABLE TO THE SELLER AT YOUR RESIDENCE, IN SUBSTANTIALLY AS GOOD CONDITION AS WHEN RECEIVED, ANY GOODS DELIVERED TO YOU UNDER THIS CONTRACT OR SALE; OR YOU MAY IF YOU WISH, COMPLY WITH THE INSTRUCTIONS OF THE SELLER REGARDING THE RETURN SHIPMENT OF THE GOODS AT THE SELLER'S EXPENSE AND RISK.

IF YOU DO MAKE THE GOODS AVAILABLE TO THE SELLER AND THE SELLER DOES NOT PICK THEM UP WITHIN 20 DAYS OF THE DATE OF YOUR NOTICE OF CANCELLATION, YOU MAY RETAIN OR DISPOSE OF THE GOODS WITHOUT ANY FURTHER OBLIGATION. IF YOU FAIL TO MAKE THE GOODS AVAILABLE TO THE SELLER, OR IF YOU AGREE TO RETURN THE GOODS AND FAIL TO DO SO, THEN YOU REMAIN LIABLE FOR PERFORMANCE OF ALL OBLIGATIONS UNDER THE CONTRACT.

TO CANCEL THIS TRANSACTION, MAIL OR DELIVER A SIGNED AND DATED COPY OF THIS CANCELLATION NOTICE OR ANY OTHER WRITTEN NOTICE, OR SEND A TELEGRAM, TO _____[name of seller], AT _____[address of seller's place of business] NOT LATER THAN MIDNIGHT OF _____ [date].

I HEREBY CANCEL THIS TRANSACTION.

_____   _____
(Buyer's signature)   (Date)

The seller must complete the notice and orally inform the buyer of the right to cancel. He or she cannot misrepresent the right to cancel, assign the contract until the fifth business day, nor include a confession of judgment in the contract. For more specific details, see the rules contained at 16 C.P.R. Part 429.

Massachusetts Law

Massachusetts also has laws allowing buyers to cancel certain transactions within three days and requiring the seller or lessor to give written notice of this right. Covered transactions are those that are:

- ✪ consumer transactions (sales, rental, lease);

- ✪ over $25 (including all charges, interest, etc.);

- ✪ primarily for personal, family, or household purposes; and,

- ✪ consummated other than at the seller's regular place of business.

Right to cancel. Any such sale previously described may be cancelled by the buyer by written notice postmarked any time before midnight of the third business day after the sales day.

Written agreement. Every such sale must be in writing and must contain the following notice in boldface type and at least ten-point size.

> **You may cancel this agreement if it has been signed by a party thereto at a place other than an address of the seller, which may be his main office or branch thereof, provided you notify the seller in writing at his main office or branch by ordinary mail posted, by telegram sent or by delivery, not later than midnight of the third business day following the signing of this agreement. See the attached notice of cancellation form for an explanation of this right.**

Attached to the notice must be a form in duplicate that is easily detachable, stating the same, in at least ten-point boldface type, as the federal notice reproduced on the previous page.

Seller's duty. All businesses conducting solicitation sales must:

- ✪ ensure that all employees have the required permits;

- ✪ register with the chief of police or other designated official of a town or city; and,

- ✪ notify the chief of police or other designated official in each town where sales are to be made.

TELEPHONE SOLICITATION LAWS

Phone calls. In 2003, the Federal Trade Commission issued new rules regulating telephone solicitation calls. The main provision of these rules allow consumers to be listed on a national *Do Not Call* registry, and any company that calls those on the list is subject to penalties. Other provisions:

- ✪ require disclosures of specific information;

- ✪ prohibit misrepresentations;

- ✪ limit when telemarketers may call consumers;

- ✪ require transmission of caller ID information;

- ✪ prohibit abandoned outbound calls, subject to a safe harbor;

- ✪ prohibit unauthorized billing;

- ✪ set payment restrictions for the sale of certain goods and services; and,

- ✪ require that specific business records be kept for two years.

For more information on these rules you can visit **https://telemarketing.donotcall.gov**.

Faxes. It is illegal under the act to send advertising faxes to anyone who has not consented to receiving such faxes or is an existing customer.

Massachusetts Law

In Massachusetts, with respect to telephone solicitations, the person calling must, before making any other statement except a greeting and before asking any questions, state the identity of the caller, the trade name of the person represented by the caller, and the kind of goods or services being offered for sale. Callers using automatic dialing systems may not call those who have given notice to their telephone company that they do not want to receive those calls.

Automatic dialing. All telephone customers have the right to notify the telephone company that they do not wish to receive telephone calls from an automatic dialing system. The phone company cannot charge for this service.

PRICING, WEIGHTS, AND LABELING

Beginning in 1994, all food products were required to have labels with information on the product's nutritional values such as calories, fat, and protein. For most products, the label must be in the required format so that consumers can easily compare products. However, if such a format will not fit on the product label, the information may be in another format that is easily readable.

Massachusetts Law

The rules also require metric measurement. Under these rules, metric measures do not have to be the first measurement on the container, but they must be included. Food items that are packaged as they are sold (such as delicatessen items) do not have to contain metric labels.

Massachusetts laws require every item in food stores and every grocery item in food departments to be individually marked with the correct selling price. Many items are exempted, provided that a conspicuous separate sign indicates the price and that the cashier can readily discern the price of each item.

Massachusetts also has voluminous statutes governing the labeling requirements for a variety of specific items, including the following:

- ✪ horse meat;
- ✪ potatoes;
- ✪ farm products;
- ✪ native fruits, vegetables, and turkeys;
- ✪ stuffed toys and furniture;
- ✪ furs;
- ✪ non-original paintings;
- ✪ sewing thread;
- ✪ poison;
- ✪ anti-freeze;
- ✪ electric appliances;
- ✪ hazardous substances;
- ✪ milk cans;
- ✪ canned-soaked goods;
- ✪ honey;
- ✪ gold;
- ✪ kosher food;
- ✪ vinegar;
- ✪ prescription drugs;

- ✪ artificial colorings and flavorings;
- ✪ preservatives;
- ✪ cosmetics;
- ✪ patent medicine or food containing drugs;
- ✪ frozen desserts;
- ✪ baking powder;
- ✪ livestock and poultry products;
- ✪ lard;
- ✪ processed or renovated butter;
- ✪ imitation butter and cheeses;
- ✪ margarine;
- ✪ milk and cream;
- ✪ bottled water;
- ✪ bakery products;
- ✪ molasses;
- ✪ flammable clothing and fabrics;
- ✪ fertilizers;
- ✪ seeds;
- ✪ shellfish;

✪ alcoholic beverages;   ✪ halibut;

✪ safety glazing materials;   ✪ unstable drugs;

✪ explosives;   ✪ imitation foods; and,

✪ maple syrup and maple syrup food products.

EMAIL ADVERTISING

The *Controlling the Assault of Nonsolicited Pornography and Marketing Act of 2003* (CANSPAM) has put numerous controls on how you can use email to solicit business for your company. Some of the prohibited activities under the act are:

✪   false or misleading information in an email;

✪   deceptive subject heading;

✪   failure to include a functioning return address;

✪   mailing to someone who has asked not to receive solicitations;

✪   failure to include a valid postal address;

✪   omitting an opt-out procedure;

✪   failure to clearly mark the email as advertising; and,

✪   including sexual material without adequate warnings.

Some of the provisions contain criminal penalties as well as civil fines.

For more information on the CANSPAM Act see:

www.ftc.gov/bcp/conline/pubs/buspubs/canspam.shtm

For text of the act plus other spam laws around the world see:

www.spamlaws.com

Payment and Collection

Depending on the business you are in, you may be paid by cash, checks, credit cards, or some sort of financing arrangement such as a promissory note and mortgage. Both state and federal laws affect the type of payments you collect and failure to follow the laws can cost you considerably.

CASH

Cash is probably the easiest form of payment and it is subject to few restrictions. The most important one is that you keep an accurate accounting of your cash transactions and that you report all of your cash income on your tax return. Recent efforts to stop the drug trade have resulted in some serious penalties for failing to report cash transactions and for money laundering. The laws are so sweeping that even if you deal in cash in an ordinary business, you may violate the law and face huge fines and imprisonment.

The most important law to be concerned with is the one requiring the filing of IRS Form 8300 for cash transactions of $10,000 or more. A transaction does not have to happen in one day. If a person brings you smaller amounts of cash that add up to $10,000 and the government can construe them as one transaction, the form must be filed. Under this law, *cash* also includes travelers' checks and money orders, but not cashiers' checks or bank checks. For more information, obtain IRS Form 8300 and instructions from the IRS.

CHECKS

It is important to accept checks in your business. While there is a small percentage that will be bad, most checks will be good and you will be able to accommodate more customers. To avoid having problems with checks, you should comply with the following rules.

Accepting Checks

A business cannot require a customer to provide a credit card number or expiration date in order to pay by check. (Massachusetts General Laws (Mass. Gen. Laws), Chapter (Ch.) 93, Section (Sec.) 105.) The business can request to see a card to establish that the customer is credit-worthy or for additional identification and can record the type of credit card and issuing company. However, the business cannot record the number of the card.

Bad Checks

Massachusetts has a fairly effective bad check collection process. If you follow the rules, you may be able to collect on a bad check. Call your local police department to find out how to proceed.

Be sure that you are able to identify the person who gave you the check. To do this, you should require identification and write down the sources of identification on the face of the check. Make sure the person signs the check!

Refunds after Cashing Checks

A popular scam is for a person to purchase something by using a check and then come back the next day demanding a refund. After making the refund, the business discovers the initial payment check bounced. Do not make refunds until checks clear!

CREDIT CARDS

In our buy-now, pay-later society, charge cards can add greatly to your sales potential, especially with large, discretionary purchases. For

MasterCard, Visa, and Discover, the fees are about 2%, and this amount is easily paid for by the extra purchases that the cards allow. American Express charges 4–5% and you may decide this is not worth paying since almost everyone who has an American Express card also has another card.

For businesses that have a retail outlet, there is usually no problem getting merchant status. Most commercial banks can handle it. Discover can also set you up to accept its card, as well as MasterCard and Visa, and they will wire the money into your bank account daily.

For mail-order businesses, especially those operating out of the home, it is much harder to get merchant status. This is because of the number of scams in which large amounts are charged, no products are shipped, and the company folds. One good thing about American Express is that they will accept mail-order companies operating out of the home.

Some companies open a small storefront (or share one) to get merchant status, then process mostly mail orders. The processors usually do not want to accept you if you will do more than 50% mail order, but if you do not have many complaints, you may be allowed to process mostly mail orders. Whatever you do, keep your charge customers happy so that they do not complain!

You might be tempted to try to run your charges through another business. This may be okay if you actually sell your products through them, but if you run your business charges through their account, the other business may lose its merchant status. For example, if you are selling books and running credit card charges through your friend's florist shop account, people who buy a book by mail from you and then have a charge on their credit card statement from a florist shop will probably call the credit card company saying that they never bought anything from the florist shop. Too many of these calls and your friend's account for her florist shop will be closed.

FINANCING LAWS

Some businesses can make sales more easily if they finance the purchases themselves. If the business has enough capital to do this, it can earn extra profits on the financing terms. Nonetheless, because of abuses, many consumer protection laws have been passed by both the federal and state governments.

Regulation Z   Two important federal laws regarding financing are called the *Truth in Lending Act* and the *Fair Credit Billing Act*. These are implemented by what is called *Regulation Z* (commonly known as *Reg. Z*), issued by the Board of Governors of the Federal Reserve System. It is contained in Title 12 of the Code of Federal Regulations, page 226. (12 C.F.R. p.226.) This is a very complicated law, and some have said that no business can be sure to be in compliance with it.

The regulation covers all transactions in which all four of the following conditions are met:

1.   credit is offered;

2   the offering of credit is regularly done;

3.   there is a finance charge for the credit or there is a written agreement with more than four payments; and,

4.   the credit is for personal, family, or household purposes.

It also covers credit card transactions where only the first two conditions are met. It applies to leases if the consumer ends up paying the full value and keeping the item leased. It does not apply to the following transactions:

✪   transactions with businesses or agricultural purposes;

✪   transactions with organizations such as corporations or the government;

✪   transactions of over $25,000 that are not secured by the consumer's dwelling;

✪   credit involving public utilities;

✪   credit involving securities or commodities; and,

✪   home fuel budget plans.

The way for a small business to avoid Reg. Z violations is to avoid transactions that meet the conditions or to make sure all transactions fall under the exceptions. This is easy for many businesses. Instead of extending credit to customers, accept credit cards and let the credit card company extend the credit. However, if your customers usually do not have credit cards or if you are in a business, such as used car sales, which often extends credit, consult a lawyer knowledgeable about Reg. Z or get a copy of the laws for yourself at:

www.cardreport.com/laws/tila/tila.html

Massachusetts Law

Massachusetts also has extensive laws regarding financing arrangements. The laws govern disclosure, cancellation provisions, and limitations on interest rates. Anyone engaged in installment sales in Massachusetts should carefully review the latest version of Massachusetts General Laws, Chapter 255D, Retail Installment Sales and Services. Chapter 255B, Retail Installment Sales of Motor Vehicles, may also be relevant.

In addition to these acts, Massachusetts forbids discrimination in granting credit based upon age, sex, sexual orientation, marital status, race, color, religion, national origin, children, handicap, or the fact that all or part of one's income comes from an assistance program.

USURY

Usury is the charging of an illegally high rate of interest. In Massachusetts, the maximum rate of interest you may charge is 20%, unless you notify the attorney general and keep adequate records (what constitutes adequate records is not explained in the law).

COLLECTIONS

The *Fair Debt Collection Practices Act of 1977* bans the use of deception, harassment, and other unreasonable acts in the collection of debts. It has strict requirements whenever someone is collecting a debt for someone else (that is, they do not apply if you are collecting your own debt). If you are in the collection business (*i.e.*, you are in the business of collecting debts owed to others), you must get a copy of this law.

The Federal Trade Commission has issued some rules that prohibit deceptive representations such as pretending to be in the motion picture industry, the government, or a credit bureau, or using questionnaires that do not say that they are for the purpose of collecting a debt. (16 C.F.R. Part 237.)

Massachusetts Law

The *Unfair Debt Collection Practices Law* applies to debts owed by persons (not corporations) for transactions that were for personal, family, or household purposes. (Mass. Gen. Law., Ch. 93, Sec. 49.) The law forbids:

○ using instruments that simulate judicial process;

○ communicating with third parties about the debt without permission of the debtor;

○ communicating with the debtor after being notified that communications should be directed to the debtor's attorney; and,

○ harassing or embarrassing the debtor.

Business Relations Laws

At both the federal and state levels, there exist many laws regarding how businesses relate to one another. Some of the more important ones are discussed in this chapter.

THE UNIFORM COMMERCIAL CODE

The *Uniform Commercial Code* (UCC) is a set of laws regulating numerous aspects of doing business. A national group drafted this set of uniform laws to avoid having a patchwork of different laws around the fifty states. Although some states modified some sections of the laws, the code is basically the same in most of the states. In Massachusetts, the UCC is contained in chapter 106 of Massachusetts General Laws. Each chapter is concerned with a different aspect of commercial relations such as sales, warranties, bank deposits, commercial paper, and bulk transfers.

Businesses that wish to know their rights in all types of transactions should obtain a copy of the UCC and become familiar with it. It is especially useful in transactions between merchants. However, the meaning is not always clear from a reading of the statutes. In many law schools, students spend a full semester studying each chapter of this law.

COMMERCIAL DISCRIMINATION

The *Robinson-Patman Act of 1936* prohibits businesses from injuring competition by offering the same goods at different prices to different buyers. This means that the large chain stores should not be getting a better price than your small shop. It also requires that promotional allowances must be made on proportionally the same terms to all buyers.

As a small business, you may be a victim of a Robinson-Patman Act violation, but fighting a much larger company in court would probably be too expensive for you. Your best bet, if an actual violation has occurred, would be to see if you could get the government to prosecute it. For more information on what constitutes a violation, see the Federal Trade Commission and the Department of Justice's joint site at **www.ftc.gov/bc/compguide/index.htm**.

Massachusetts Law

Massachusetts' *Unfair Sales Act* makes unlawful the advertising, offer for sale, and sale of merchandise at less than cost with the *intent to injure competitors or destroy competition*.

RESTRAINING TRADE

One of the earliest federal laws affecting business is the *Sherman Antitrust Act of 1890*. The purpose of the law was to protect competition in the marketplace by prohibiting monopolies. For example, one large company might buy out all of its competitors and then raise prices to astronomical levels. In recent years, this law was used to break up AT&T.

Examples of some things that are prohibited are:

- ✪ agreements between competitors to sell at the same prices;

- ✪ agreements between competitors on how much will be sold or produced;

- ✪ agreements between competitors to divide up a market;

- ✪ refusing to sell one product without a second product; and,

❂ exchanging information among competitors that results in similarity of prices.

As a new business, you probably will not be in a position to violate the act, but you should be aware of it in case a larger competitor tries to put you out of business. A good place to find information on the act is at **www.lawmall.com/sherman.act.**

Massachusetts Law

Massachusetts antitrust laws are substantially identical to federal laws. Where federal laws do not apply because interstate commerce is not involved, the Massachusetts laws would apply to business activities in Massachusetts.

INTELLECTUAL PROPERTY PROTECTION

As a business owner, you should know enough about intellectual property law to protect your own creations and to keep from violating the rights of others. Intellectual property is that which is the product of human creativity, such as writings, designs, inventions, melodies, and processes. They are things that can be stolen without being physically taken. For example, if you write a book, someone can steal the words from your book without stealing a physical copy of it.

As the Internet grows, intellectual property is becoming more valuable. Smart business owners are those who will take the action necessary to protect their company's intellectual property. Additionally, business owners should know intellectual property law to be sure that they do not violate the rights of others. Even an unknowing violation of the law can result in stiff fines and penalties.

The following are the types of intellectual property and the ways to protect them.

Patent

A *patent* is protection given to new and useful inventions, discoveries, and designs. To be entitled to a patent, a work must be completely new and *unobvious*. A patent is granted to the first inventor who files for the patent. Once an invention is patented, no one else can make use of that invention, even if he or she discovers it independently after a lifetime of research. A patent protects an invention for seventeen years and protects designs for three-and-a-half, seven, or fourteen years. Patents cannot be renewed. The patent application must clearly explain how to make the invention so that when the patent expires, others will be able to freely make and use the invention. Patents are registered with the United States Patent and Trademark Office (USPTO). Examples of things that would be patentable would be mechanical devices or new drug formulas.

Copyright

A *copyright* is protection given to *original works of authorship*, such as written works, musical works, visual works, performance works, or computer software programs. A copyright exists from the moment of creation, but one cannot register a copyright until it has been fixed in tangible form. Also, one cannot copyright titles, names, or slogans. A copyright currently gives the author and his or her heirs exclusive right to the work for the life of the author plus seventy years. Copyrights first registered before 1978 last for ninety-five years. This was previously seventy-five years but was extended twenty years to match the European system. Copyrights are registered with the Register of Copyrights at the Library of Congress. Examples of works that would be copyrightable are books, paintings, songs, poems, plays, drawings, and films.

Trademark

A *trademark* is protection given to a name or symbol that is used to distinguish one person's goods or services from those of others. It can consist of letters, numerals, packaging, labeling, musical notes, colors, or a combination of these. If a trademark is used on services, as opposed to goods, it is called a *service mark*. A trademark lasts indefinitely if it is used continuously and renewed properly. Trademarks are registered with the United States Patent and Trademark Office and with individual states. This is explained further in Chapter 3.

Trade Secrets

A *trade secret* is some information or process that provides a commercial advantage and is protected by keeping it a secret. Examples of trade secrets may be a list of successful distributors, the formula for Coca-Cola, or some unique source code in a computer program. Trade secrets are not registered anywhere, but are protected by the fact that they are not disclosed. They are protected only for as long as they are kept secret. If you independently discover the formula for Coca-Cola tomorrow, you can freely market it. (But you cannot use the trademark *Coca-Cola* on your product to market it.)

Massachusetts law. Massachusetts law provides that stealing trade secrets constitutes larceny. Penalties include fines of up to $25,000 and/or imprisonment.

Nonprotectable Creations

Some things are just not protectable. Such things as ideas, systems, and discoveries are not allowed any protection under any law. If you have a great idea, such as selling packets of hangover medicine in bars, you cannot stop others from doing the same thing. If you invent a new medicine, you can patent it; if you pick a distinctive name for it, you can register it as a trademark; if you create a unique picture or instructions for the package, you can copyright them. You cannot stop others from using your basic business idea of marketing hangover medicine in bars.

Notice the subtle differences between the protective systems available. If you invent something two days after someone else does, you cannot even use it yourself if the other person has patented it. But if you write the same poem as someone else and neither of you copied the other, both of you can copyright the poem. If you patent something, you can have the exclusive rights to it for the term of the patent, but you must disclose how others can make it after the patent expires. However, if you keep it a trade secret, you have exclusive rights as long as no one learns the secret.

Endless Laws

The Commonwealth of Massachusetts and the federal government have numerous laws and rules that apply to every aspect of every type of business. There are laws governing even such things as exploding golf balls and selling baby food at flea markets.

Some activities are covered by both state and federal laws. In such cases, you must obey the stricter of the rules. In addition, more than one agency of the state or federal government may have rules governing your business. Each of these may have the power to investigate violations and impose fines or other penalties.

Penalties for violations of these laws can range from a warning to a criminal fine and even jail time. In some cases, employees can sue for damages. It is your duty to learn which laws apply to your business or to risk these penalties.

Very few people in business know the laws that apply to their businesses. If you take the time to learn them, you can become an expert in your field and avoid problems with regulators. You can also fight back if one of your competitors uses some illegal method to compete with you.

The laws and rules that affect the most businesses are explained in this section. Following that is a list of more specialized laws. You should read through this list and see which ones may apply to your business. Then go to your public library or law library and read them. Some may not apply to your phase of the business, but if any of them do apply, make copies to keep on hand.

No one could possibly know all the rules that affect business, much less comply with them all. The Interstate Commerce Commission alone has forty trillion (that is forty million million or 40,000,000,000,000) rates on its books telling the transportation industry what it should charge! But if you keep up with the important rules, you will stay out of trouble and have a greater chance of success.

FEDERAL LAWS

The federal laws that are most likely to affect small businesses are rules of the Federal Trade Commission (FTC). The FTC has some rules that affect many businesses, such as the rules about labeling, warranties, and mail order sales.

Other rules affect only certain industries. If you sell goods by mail, you should send for the booklet, *A Business Guide to the Federal Trade Commission's Mail Order Rule*. If you are going to be involved in a certain industry, such as those listed as follows, or are using warranties or your own labeling, you should ask for the FTC's latest information on the subject. The address is:

Federal Trade Commission
Consumer Response Center
600 Pennsylvania Avenue, NW
Washington, DC 20580

The rules of the FTC are contained in the Code of Federal Regulations (C.F.R.) in Chapter 16. Some of the industries covered are:

Industry	**Part**
Adhesive Compositions	235
Aerosol Products Used for Frosting Cocktail Glasses	417
Automobiles (New car fuel economy advertising)	259
Barber Equipment and Supplies	248
Binoculars	402
Business Opportunities and Franchises	436
Cigarettes	408
Decorative Wall Paneling	243
Dog and Cat Food	241
Dry Cell Batteries	403
Extension Ladders	418
Fallout Shelters	229
Feather and Down Products	253
Fiber Glass Curtains	413
Food (Games of Chance)	419
Funerals	453
Gasoline (Octane posting)	306
Gasoline	419
Greeting Cards	244
Home Entertainment Amplifiers	432
Home Insulation	460
Hosiery	22
Household Furniture	250
Jewelry	23
Ladies' Handbags	247
Law Books	256
Light Bulbs	409
Luggage and Related Products	24
Mail Order Insurance	234
Mail Order Merchandise	435
Men's and Boys' Tailored Clothing	412
Metallic Watch Band	19
Mirrors	21
Nursery	18
Ophthalmic Practices	456
Photographic Film and Film Processing	242
Private Vocational and Home Study Schools	254
Radiation Monitoring Instruments	232
Retail Food Stores (Advertising)	424
Shell Homes	230

Shoes	231
Sleeping Bags	400
Tablecloths and Related Products	404
Television Sets	410
Textile Wearing Apparel	423
Textiles	236
Tires	228
Used Automobile Parts	20
Used Lubricating Oil	406
Used Motor Vehicles	455
Waist Belts	405
Watches	245
Wigs and Hairpieces	252

Some other federal laws that affect businesses are as follows:

○ *Alcohol Administration Act*

○ *Child Protection and Toy Safety Act (1969)*

○ *Clean Water Act*

○ *Comprehensive Smokeless Tobacco Health Education Act (1986)*

○ *Consumer Credit Protection Act (1968)*

○ *Consumer Product Safety Act (1972)*

○ *Energy Policy and Conservation Act*

○ *Environmental Pesticide Control Act of 1972*

○ *Fair Credit Reporting Act (1970)*

○ *Fair Packaging and Labeling Act (1966)*

○ *Flammable Fabrics Act (1953)*

○ *Food, Drug, and Cosmetic Act*

- ✪ *Fur Products Labeling Act (1951)*

- ✪ *Hazardous Substances Act (1960)*

- ✪ *Hobby Protection Act*

- ✪ *Insecticide, Fungicide, and Rodenticide Act*

- ✪ *Magnuson-Moss Warranty Act*

- ✪ *Poison Prevention Packaging Act of 1970*

- ✪ *Solid Waste Disposal Act*

- ✪ *Textile Fiber Products Identification Act*

- ✪ *Toxic Substance Control Act*

- ✪ *Wool Products Labeling Act (1939)*

- ✪ *Nutrition Labeling and Education Act of 1990*

- ✪ *Food Safety Enforcement Enhancement Act of 1997*

MASSACHUSETTS LAWS

Massachusetts has numerous laws regulating specific types of businesses or certain activities of businesses. The following is a list of those laws that are most likely to affect small businesses. If you are running a type of business that is not mentioned here, or using some sales technique that could come under government regulation, check the indexes to the Massachusetts General Laws and the Massachusetts Code of Regulations. Since these indexes are not well done, you should look up every possible synonym or related word to be sure not to miss anything. You can find the laws online at **www.mass.gov/legis/laws/ mgl/index.htm** (not an official version, but fairly accurate nonetheless).

Citations refer to Massachusetts General Laws (Mass. Gen. Laws). If no sections are cited, the entire chapter cited applies.

	Chapter(s)	Section(s)
Acupuncturists	112	148–162
Adoption agencies	210	
Adulteration and misbranding of food and drugs	94	185–196
Agents, consignees and factors	104	
Agricultural and other seeds	128	84–101
Alcoholic liquors	138	
Allied mental health and human services professionals	112	163–172
Ambulances and EMTs	111C	
Anti-freeze solutions	94	303G–303M
Antitrust act	93	
Apples	94	100–105
	128	102–115
Architects	112	60A–60O
Assignment of wages	154	
Athletic trainers	112	23F
Auctioneers	100	
Audiologists	112	138–147
Bakeries and bakery products	94	2–10
Baking powder	94	2–10
Bank deposits and collections	106	4-101–4-504
Barbers	112	87F–87S
Bells, whistles, and gongs	149	175
Brokers	112	87UU
Butter, cheese, and lard	94	49–63
Cancelation of agreements	93	48–48A
Canned goods and molasses	94	154–156
Carriers of property by motor vehicle	159B	
Cemeteries	114	
Certain business corporations	156D	
Certified health officers	112	87WWW–87ZZZ
Certified public accountants	112 8	7A–87E 1/2
Chiropractors	112	89–97
Cinematographers operating in public buildings	143	75
Clinical laboratories	111D	
Coal, coke, charcoal, and kindling wood	94	238–249F
Cold storage	94	66–73
Collection agencies	93	24–28
Commercial drivers	90F	

	Chapter(s)	Section(s)
Commercial feeds	128	51–63
Commercial fertilizers	128	64–83
Commercial paper	106	3-101–3-805
Consignment of fine art	104A	
Consumer credit reporting	93	50–68
Consumer privacy in commercial transactions	93	104, 105
Cosmetologists	112	87T–87KK
Cranberries	94	115–117
Credit services organizations	93	68A–68E
Credit slips	93	14S
Day care providers	28A	
Debt collection	93	49
Demonstration sheep farms	128	9–11
Dentists	112	43–53
Discrimination against handicapped persons	93	102, 103
Discrimination based on race, color, religious creed, national origin, ancestry, or sex	151B	
Discrimination in employment on account of age	149	24A–24J
Discriminatory wage rates based on sex	149	105A–105C
Dishonored checks	93	40A
Dispensing opticians	112	73C–73M
Eggs	94	89–92A
Electric appliances	94	314–318
Electricians	141	
Electrologists	112	87EEE–87OOO
Embalmers and funeral directors	112	82–87
Emergency medical care	111C	
Employment of aliens	149	19C
Engineers	112	81D–81T
Enrichment of bread and flour	94	10H–10K
Equipment dealers	93G	
False advertisement for help or employment	149	21
Farm products	94	117A–117F
Fish	94	77A–88D
Foresters	132	47–50
Frozen desserts and frozen dessert mix	94	65G–65U
Frozen food	94	73A
Fruits, vegetables, and nuts	94	96–99B
Fuel oils	94	303F

	Chapter(s)	Section(s)
Furs	94	277A
Gasoline dealers	93E	1–9
Grain and meal	94	219–224
Hay	94	236
Hazardous substances	94B	
Hazardous substances disclosure by employers	111F	
Hazardous waste site cleanup professionals	21A	19C
Health and safety	149	106–142
Health clubs	93	78–88
Hearing aids	93	71–75
Hearing instrument specialists	112	196–200
Heating oils	94	249H
Herring, alewives, etc.	130	93–96
Home improvement contractors	142A	
Home inspectors	112	221–226
Horse and dog racing meetings	128A	
Hospitals, clinics, and dispensaries	111	50–57D
Ice	94	157–162
Imported goods	94	277B
Inland fisheries and game	131	
Inspection and sale of meat	94	146–153A
Insurance agents	175	
Insurance premium finance agencies	255C	
Junkyards	140B	
Kennel operators	140	137A
Kosher foods	94	156
Labels, trademarks, and trade names	110	
Land surveyors	112	81D–81T
Landscape architects	112	98–107
Laundries and dry cleaning establishments	93	18A, 18B
Liability of employers to employees for injuries not resulting in a death	153	
Lime and lime casks	94	262–268
Limited partnerships	109	
Lobsters	130	37–51A
Manufacturers and sellers of upholstered furniture, bedding, or stuffed toys or filling for same	94	271
Maple syrup and maple syrup food products	128	36C
Marine fish and fisheries	130	

	Chapter(s)	Section(s)
Marking of packages containing food	94	181–184E
Maternity leave	149	105D
Measurement of lumber	96	
Measuring of leather	95	
Meats, poultry, and fish	94	92B
Methyl or wood alcohol	94	303A–303E
Milk and cream	94	12–48D
Milk control	94A	
Minimum fair wages	151	
Mining stocks	93	15–18
Mortgage transactions	93	70
Motion picture distributors	93F	1–4
Motor vehicle damage repair shops	100A	
Motor vehicle manufacturers, distributors, and dealers	93B	1–15
Multi-level distribution companies	93	69
Nails	94	278–282
Noisome trades	111	143–154
Non-alcoholic beverages	94	10A–10G
Nuisances	111	122–131
Nurses	112	74–81C
Nursing home administrators	112	108–117
Nursing homes	93	76
Nutritionists	112	201–210
Occupational therapists	112	23G
Occupational therapy assistants	112	23H
Operators of drinking water supply facilities	112	87CCCC–87DDDD
Operators of hoisting machinery not run by stead	146	53–55
Operators of security systems businesses	147	57–61
Optometrists	112	66–73B
Outdoor advertising adjacent to interstate and primary highway systems	93	D 1–7
Outdoor advertising signs and devices within public view	93	29–33
Paintings	94	277C
Partnerships	108A	
Perfusionists	112	211–220
Pesticides	132B	
Petroleum products	94	295A–295W

	Chapter(s)	Section(s)
Pharmacists	112	24–36
Physical therapists	112	23J
Physical therapy assistants	112	23J
Physicians and surgeons	112	12CC
Physicians assistants	112	9C–9K
Pick-your-own farming operations	128	2E
Pilots	103	
Plant closings	151	A 71A–71H
Plumbers	142	
Podiatrists	112	13–22
Potatoes	94	117G–117L
Professional corporations	156A	
Prohibition of certain discrimination by businesses	151E	
Psychologists	112	118–137
Public warehouses	105	
Radio and television technicians	112	87PPP–87VVV
Real estate brokers and salesmen	112	87PP–87DDD1/2
Real estate appraisers	112	173–195
Registration and protection of trademarks	110B	
Regulation of business practices for consumers protection	93A	1–11
Removal, termination or fire sales	93	28A–28F
Rental agreements for personal property used primarily for household or family use	93	90–94
Research institutions using dogs or cats for experimentation	140	174D
Respiratory therapists	112	23R–23BB
Retail clothing stores dressing room surveillance	93	89
Retail drug stores	112	37–42A
Retail trade reporting agencies	93	49A
Sales	106	2-101–2-725
Sales by weight	94	176–180
Sales financiers	255B	2
Sanitarians	112	87LL–87OO
Sausages	94	142–143A
Scallops	130	92
School bus operators	90	8–8A 1/2
Secured transactions	106	9-101–9-507
Self-service storage facilities	105A	
Sellers of ammunitions	140	122B

	Chapter(s)	Section(s)
Sellers of milk or cream to other than consumers	94	41A
Shellfish	130	52–75
Shipping and seamen	102	1–4
Slaughter houses	94	118–139G
Slot machines	94	283, 284
Social workers	112	130–137
Solicitation of business on public sidewalks	93	40
Speech language pathologists	112	138–147
Stables	111	155–158
	128	2B
Striped bass	130	100A–100B
Surveying of land	97	
Taking of trade secrets	93	42
Tanning facilities	111	207–214
Thread	94	285–288
Timothy or herdsgrass seed	94	237
Trade schools	93	20A–21G
Trading stamp companies	93	14L–14R
Transient vendors, hawkers, and peddlers	101	
Turpentine, paints, and linseed oil	94	289–295
Unemployment benefits	151A	22–37
Unemployment compensation contributions	151A	13–21
Unfair sales	93	14E–14K
Unsolicited merchandise	93	43
Upholstered furniture, bedding, and stuffed toys	94	270–277
Vending machines	94	308–313
Veterinarians	112	54–60
Victuallers and innkeepers	140	2–21
Video rentals	93	106
Vinegar	94	163–171
Waiver of consumer rights	93	101
Warehouse receipts, bills of lading, other documents of title	106	7-101–7-603
Weekly payment of wages	149	148–159B
Weighers of beef	94	140–141
Weights and measures	98	
Wholesale food processing and distribution	94	305C
Wholesale sale, distribution or delivery of drugs or medicines	112	36A–36D

	Chapter(s)	Section(s)
Wood and bark	94	296–303
Workers' compensation	152	

Your Business and the Internet

The Internet has opened up a world of opportunities for businesses. It was not long ago that getting national visibility cost a fortune. Today, a business can set up a web page for a few hundred dollars, and with some clever publicity and a little luck, millions of people around the world will see it.

This new world has new legal issues and new liabilities. Not all of them have been addressed by laws or by the courts. Before you begin doing business on the Internet, you should know the existing rules and the areas where legal issues exist.

DOMAIN NAMES

A domain name is the address of your website. For example, **www.apple.com** is the domain name of Apple Computer, Inc. The last part of the domain name, the ".com" (or "dot com") is the top-level domain, or TLD. Dot com is the most popular, but others are currently available in the United States, including ".net" and ".org." (Originally, ".net" was only available to network service providers and ".org" only to nonprofit organizations, but regulations have eliminated those requirements.)

It may seem like most words have been taken as a dot-com name, but if you combine two or three short words or abbreviations, a nearly unlimited number of possibilities are available. For example, if you have a business dealing with automobiles, most likely someone has already registered automobile.com and auto.com. You can come up with all kinds of variations, using adjectives or your name, depending on your type of business:

autos4u.com	joesauto.com	autobob.com
myauto.com	yourauto.com	onlyautos.com
greatauto.com	autosfirst.com	usautos.com
greatautos.com	firstautoworld.com	4autos.com

When the Internet first began, some individuals realized that major corporations would soon want to register their names. Since the registration was easy and cheap, people registered names they thought would ultimately be used by someone else.

At first, some companies paid high fees to buy their names from the registrants. One company, Intermatic, filed a lawsuit instead of paying. The owner of the domain name the company wanted had registered numerous domain names, such as britishairways.com and ussteel.com. The court ruled that since Intermatic owned a trademark on the name, the registration of its name by someone else violated that trademark, and that Intermatic was entitled to it.

Since then, people have registered names that are not trademarks, such as CalRipkin.com, and have attempted to charge the individuals with those names to buy their domain. In 1998, Congress passed the *Anti-Cybersquatting Consumer Protection Act*, making it illegal to register a domain with no legitimate need to use it.

This law helped a lot of companies protect their names, but then some companies started abusing it and tried to stop legitimate users of names similar to theirs. This is especially likely against small companies. An organization that has been set up to help small companies protect their domains is the Domain Name Rights Coalition. Its website is **www.netpolicy.com**. Some other good information on domain names can be found at **www.bitlaw.com/internet/ domain.html**.

Registering a domain name for your own business is a simple process. There are many companies that offer registration services. For a list of those companies, visit the site of the Internet Corporation for Assigned Names and Numbers (ICANN) at **www.icann.org**. You can link directly to any member's site and compare the costs and registration procedures required for the different top-level domains.

WEB PAGES

There are many new companies eager to help you set up a website. Some offer turnkey sites for a low, flat rate, while custom sites can cost tens of thousands of dollars. If you have plenty of capital, you may want to have your site handled by one of these professionals. However, setting up a website is a fairly simple process, and once you learn the basics, you can handle most of it in-house.

If you are new to the Web, you may want to look at **www.learnthenet.com** and **www.webopedia.com**, which will familiarize you with the Internet jargon and give you a basic introduction to the Web.

Site Set Up

There are seven steps to setting up a website: site purpose, design, content, structure, programming, testing, and publicity. Whether you do it yourself, hire a professional site designer, or employ a college student, the steps toward creating an effective site are the same.

Before beginning your own site, you should look at other sites, including those of major corporations and of small businesses. Look at the sites of all the companies that compete with you. Look at hundreds of sites and click through them to see how they work (or do not work).

Site purpose. To know what to include on your site, you must decide what its purpose will be. Do you want to take orders for your products or services, attract new employees, give away samples, or show off your company headquarters? You might want to do several of these things.

Site design. After looking at other sites, you can see that there are numerous ways to design a site. It can be crowded, or open and airy; it can have several windows (frames) open at once or just one; and, it can allow long scrolling or just click-throughs.

You will have to decide whether the site will have text only; text plus photographs and graphics; or, text plus photos, graphics, and other design elements, such as animation or Java script. Additionally, you will begin to make decisions about colors, fonts, and the basic graphic appearance of the site.

Site content. You must create the content for your site. For this, you can use your existing promotional materials, new material just for the website, or a combination of the two. Whatever you choose, remember that the written material should be concise, free of errors, and easy for your target audience to read. Any graphics (including photographs) and written materials not created by you require permission. You should obtain such permission from the lawful copyright holder in order to use any copyrighted material. Once you know your site's purpose, look, and content, you can begin to piece the site together.

Site structure. You must decide how the content (text plus photographs, graphics, animation, etc.) will be structured—what content will be on which page, and how a user will link from one part of the site to another. For example, your first page may have the business name and then choices to click on, such as "about us," "opportunities," or "product catalog." Have those choices connect to another page containing the detailed information, so that a user will see the catalog when he or she clicks on "product catalog." Your site could also have an option to click on a link to another website related to yours.

Site programming and setup. When you know nothing about setting up a website, it can seem like a daunting task that will require an expert. However, programming here means merely putting a site together. There are inexpensive computer programs available that make it very simple.

Commercial programs such as Microsoft FrontPage, Dreamweaver, Pagemaker, Photoshop, MS Publisher, and PageMill allow you to set up web pages as easily as laying out a print publication. These programs will convert the text and graphics you create into HTML, the programming language of the Web. Before you choose web design software and design your site, you should determine which web hosting service you will use. Make sure that the design software you use is compatible with the host server's system. The web host is the provider who will give you space on their server and who may provide other services to you, such as secure order processing and analysis of your site to see who is visiting and linking to it.

If you have an America Online (AOL) account, you can download design software and a tutorial for free. You do not have to use AOL's design software in order to use this service. You are eligible to use this site whether you design your own pages, have someone else do the design work for you, or use AOL's templates. This service allows you to use your own domain name and choose the package that is appropriate for your business.

If you have used a page layout program, you can usually get a simple web page up and running within a day or two. If you do not have much experience with a computer, you might consider hiring a college student to set up a web page for you.

Site testing. Some of the website setup programs allow you to thoroughly check your new site to see if all the pictures are included and all the links are proper. There are also websites you can go to that will check out your site. Some even allow you to improve your site, such as by reducing the size of your graphics so they download faster. Use a major search engine listed on page 164 to look for companies that can test your site before you launch it on the Web.

Site publicity. Once you set up your website, you will want to get people to look at it. Publicity means getting your site noticed as much as possible by drawing people to it.

The first thing to do to get noticed is to be sure your site is registered with as many search engines as possible. These are pages that people use to find things on the Internet, such as Yahoo and Google. They do not automatically know about you just because you created a website. You must tell them about your site, and they must examine and catalog it.

For a fee, there are services that will register your site with numerous search engines. If you are starting out on a shoestring, you can easily do it yourself. While there are hundreds of search engines, most people use a dozen or so of the bigger ones. If your site is in a niche area, such as genealogy services, then you would want to be listed on any specific genealogy search engines. Most businesses should be mainly concerned with getting on the biggest ones.

By far the biggest and most successful search engine today is Google (**www.google.com**). Some of the other big ones are:

www.altavista.com   www.hotbot.com

www.excite.com   www.lycos.com

www.fastsearch.com   www.metacrawler.com

www.go.com   www.northernlight.com

www.goto.com   www.webcrawler.com

Most of these sites have a place to click to "add your site" to their system. Some sites charge hundreds of dollars to be listed. If your site contains valuable information that people are looking for, you should be able to do well without paying these fees.

Getting Your Site Known   A *meta tag* is an invisible subject word added to your site that can be found by a search engine. For example, if you are a pest control company, you may want to list all the scientific names of the pests you control and all the treatments you have available, but you may not need them to be part of the visual design of your site. List these words as meta tags when you set up your page so people searching for those words will find your site.

Some companies thought that a clever way to get viewers would be to use commonly searched names, or names of major competitors, as meta tags to attract people looking for those big companies. For example, a small delivery service that has nothing to do with UPS or FedEx might use those company names as meta tags so people looking for them would find the smaller company. While it may sound like a good idea, it has been declared illegal trademark infringement. Today many companies have computer programs scanning the Internet for improper use of their trademarks.

Once you have made sure that your site is passively listed in all the search engines, you may want to actively promote your site. However, self-promotion is seen as a bad thing on the Internet, especially if its purpose is to make money.

Newsgroups are places on the Internet where people interested in a specific topic can exchange information. For example, expectant mothers have a group where they can trade advice and experiences. If you have a product that would be great for expectant mothers, that would be a good place for it to be discussed. However, if you log into the group, and merely announce your product, suggesting people order it from your website, you will probably be *flamed* (sent a lot of hate mail).

If you join the group, however, and become a regular, and in answer to someone's problem, mention that you "saw this product that might help," your information will be better received. It may seem unethical to plug your product without disclosing your interest, but this is a procedure used by many large companies. They hire buzz agents to plug their products all over the Internet and create positive buzz for the products. So, perhaps it has become an acceptable marketing method and consumers know to take plugs with a grain of salt. Let your conscience be your guide.

Keep in mind that Internet publicity works both ways. If you have a great product and people love it, you will get a lot of business. If you sell a shoddy product, give poor service, and do not keep your customers happy, bad publicity on the Internet can kill your business. Besides being an equalizer between large and small companies, the Internet can be a filtering mechanism between good and bad products.

Spamming   Sending unsolicited email advertising (called *spam*) started out as a mere breach of Internet etiquette (*netiquette*) but has now become a state and federal crime. The ability to reach millions of people with advertising at virtually no cost was too good for too many businesses to pass up and this resulted in the clogging of most users' email boxes and near shut down of some computer systems. Some people ended up with thousands of offers every day.

To prevent this, many states passed anti-spamming laws and Congress passed the *CAN-SPAM Act*. This law:

- ✪ bans misleading or false headers on email;

- ✪ bans misleading subject lines;

- ✪ requires allowing recipients to opt out of future mailings;

- ✪ requires the email to be identified as advertising; and,

- ✪ requires the email to include a valid physical address.

Each violation can result in up to an $11,000 fine, and the fines can be raised if advertisers violate other rules such as not harvesting names and not using permutations of existing names. More information can be found on the Federal Trade Commission's website (**www.ftc.gov**).

Advertising   Advertising on the Internet has grown in recent years. At first, small, thin rectangular ads appeared at the top of websites; these are called *banner ads*. Lately they have grown bigger, can appear anywhere on the site, and usually blink or show a moving visual.

The fees can be based on how many people view an ad, how many click on it, or both. Some larger companies, such as Amazon.com, have affiliate programs in which they will pay a percentage of a purchase if a customer comes from your site to theirs and makes a purchase. For sites that have thousands of visitors, the ads have been profitable—some sites reportedly make over $100,000 a year.

Example:
One financially successful site is Manolo's Shoe Blog (**http://shoeblogs.com**). It is written by a man who loves

shoes, has a great sense of humor, and writes in endearing broken English. Because he is an expert in his field, his suggestions are taken by many readers who click through to the products and purchase them.

LEGAL ISSUES

Before you set up a web page, you should consider the many legal issues associated with it.

Jurisdiction   *Jurisdiction* is the power of a court in a particular location to decide a particular case. Usually, you have to have been physically present in a jurisdiction or have done business there before you can be sued there. Since the Internet extends your business's ability to reach people in faraway places, there may be instances when you could be subject to legal jurisdiction far from your own state (or country). There are a number of cases that have been decided in this country regarding the Internet and jurisdiction, but very few cases have been decided on this issue outside of the United States.

In most instances, U.S. courts use the pre-Internet test—whether you have been present in another jurisdiction or have had enough contact with someone in the other jurisdiction. The fact that the Internet itself is not a "place" will not shield you from being sued in another state when you have shipped your company's product there, have entered into a contract with a resident of that state, or have defamed a foreign resident with content on your website.

According to the court, there is a spectrum of contact required between you, your website, and consumers or audiences. (*Zippo Manufacturing Co. v. Zippo Dot Com, Inc.*, 952 F. Supp. 1119 (W.D. Pa 1997).) The more interactive your site is with consumers, the more you target an audience for your goods in a particular location, and the farther you reach to send your goods out into the world, the more it becomes possible for someone to sue you outside of your own jurisdiction—so weigh these risks against the benefits when constructing and promoting your website.

The law is not even remotely final on these issues. The American Bar Association, among other groups, is studying this topic in detail. At present, no final, global solution or agreement about jurisdictional issues with websites exists.

One way to protect yourself from the possibility of being sued in a faraway jurisdiction would be to state on your website that those using the site or doing business with you agree that "jurisdiction for any actions regarding this site" or your company will be in your home county.

For extra protection, you can have a preliminary page that must be clicked before entering your website. However, this may be overkill for a small business with little risk of lawsuits. If you are in any business for which you could have serious liability, you should review some competitors' sites and see how they handle the liability issue. They often have a place to click for a "legal notice" or "disclaimer" on their first page.

You may want to consult with an attorney to discuss the specific disclaimer you will use on your website, where it should appear, and whether you will have users of your site actively agree to this disclaimer or just passively read it. However, these disclaimers are not enforceable everywhere in the world. Until there is global agreement on jurisdictional issues, this may remain an area of uncertainty for some time to come.

Libel   *Libel* is any publication that injures the reputation of another. This can occur in print, writing, pictures, or signs. All that is required for publication is that you transmit the material to at least one other person. When putting together your website, you must keep in mind that it is visible to millions of people all over the planet and that if you libel a person or company, you may have to pay damages. Many countries do not have the freedom of speech that we do, and a statement that is not libel in the United States may be libelous elsewhere. If you are concerned about this, alter the content of your site or check with an attorney about libel laws in the country you think might take action against you.

Copyright Infringement   It is so easy to copy and borrow information on the Internet that it is easy to infringe copyrights without even knowing it. A copyright exists for a work as soon as the creator creates it. There is no need to register the copyright or to put a copyright notice on it. Therefore, practically everything on the Internet belongs to someone.

Some people freely give their works away. For example, many people have created web artwork (gifs and animated gifs) that they freely allow people to copy. There are numerous sites that provide hundreds or thousands of free gifts that you can add to your web pages. Some require you to acknowledge the source and some do not. You should always be sure that the works are free for the taking before using them.

Linking and Framing

One way to violate copyright laws is to improperly link other sites to yours, either directly or with framing. Linking is when you provide a link that takes the user to the linked site. Framing occurs when you set up your site so that when you link to another site, your site is still viewable as a frame around the linked site.

While many sites are glad to be linked to others, some, especially providers of valuable information, object. Courts have ruled that linking and framing can be copyright violations. One rule that has developed is that it is usually okay to link to the first page of a site, but not to link to some valuable information deeper within the site. The rationale for this is that the owner of the site wants visitors to go through the various levels of his or her site (viewing all the ads) before getting the information. By linking directly to the information, you are giving away his or her product without the ads.

The problem with linking to the first page of a site is that it may be a tedious or difficult task to find the needed page from there. Many sites are poorly designed and make it nearly impossible to find anything.

If you wish to link to another page, the best solution is to ask permission. Email the webmaster or other person in charge of the site, if an email address is given, and explain what you want to do. If he or she grants permission, be sure to print out a copy of his or her email for your records.

Privacy

Since the Internet is such an easy way to share information, there are many concerns that it will cause a loss of individual privacy. The two main concerns arise when you post information that others consider private, and when you gather information from customers and use it in a way that violates their privacy.

While public actions of politicians and celebrities are fair game, details about their private lives are sometimes protected by law, and details about persons who are not public figures are often protected. The laws in each state are different, and what might be allowable in one state could be illegal in another. If your site will provide any personal information about individuals, you should discuss the possibility of liability with an attorney.

Several well-known companies have been in the news lately for violations of their customers' privacy. They either shared what the customer was buying or downloading, or looked for additional information on the customer's computer. To let customers know that you do not violate certain standards of privacy, you can subscribe to one of the privacy codes that have been created for the Internet. These allow you to put a symbol on your site guaranteeing to your customers that you follow the code.

The following are the websites of two organizations that offer this service and their fees at the time of this publication.

www.privacybot.com $100

www.bbbonline.com $200–$7,000

Protecting Yourself The easiest way to protect yourself personally from the various possible types of liability is to set up a corporation or limited liability company to own the website. This is not foolproof protection since, in some cases, you could be sued personally as well, but it is one level of protection.

COPPA If your website is aimed at children under the age of 13, or if it attracts children of that age, then you are subject to the federal *Children Online Privacy Protection Act of 1998* (COPPA). This law requires such websites to:

- ✪ give notice on the site of what information is being collected;

- ✪ obtain verifiable parental consent to collect the information;

- ✪ allow the parent to review the information collected;

✪   allow the parent to delete the child's information or to refuse to allow the use of the information;

✪   limit the information collected to only that necessary to participate on the site; and,

✪   protect the security and confidentiality of the information.

HIRING A WEBSITE DESIGNER

If you hire someone to design your website, you should make sure of what rights you are buying. Under copyright law, when you hire someone to create a work, you do not get all rights to that work unless you clearly spell that out in a written agreement.

For example, if your designer creates an artistic design to go on your website, you may have to pay extra if you want to use the same design on your business cards or letterhead. Depending on how the agreement is worded, you may even have to pay a yearly fee for the rights.

If you spend a lot of money promoting your business and a logo or design becomes important to your image, you would not want to have to pay royalties for the life of your business to someone who spent an hour or two putting together a design. Whenever you purchase a creative work from someone, be sure to get a written statement of what rights you are buying. If you are not receiving all rights for all uses for all time, you should think twice about the purchase.

If the designer also is involved with hosting your site, you should be sure you have the right to take the design with you if you move to another host. You should get a backup of your site on a CD in case it is ever lost or you need to move it to another site.

FINANCIAL TRANSACTIONS

The existing services for sending money over the Internet, such as PayPal, usually offer more risk and higher fees than traditional credit card processing. Under their service agreements, you usually must agree that they can freeze your account at any time and can take money out of your bank account at any time. Some do not offer an appeal process. Before signing up for any of these services, you should read their service agreement carefully and check the Internet for other peoples' experiences with them. For example, for PayPal you can check **www.nopaypal.com**.

For now, the easiest way to exchange money on the Internet is through traditional credit cards. Because of concerns that email can be abducted in transit and read by others, most companies use a secure site in which customers are guaranteed that their card data is encrypted before being sent.

When setting up your website, you should ask the provider if you can be set up with a secure site for transmitting credit card data. If they cannot provide it, you will need to contract with another software provider. Use one of the major search engines listed on page 164 to look for companies that provide credit card services to businesses on the Internet.

As a practical matter, there is very little to worry about when sending credit card data by email. If you do not have a secure site, another option is to allow purchasers to fax or phone in their credit card data. However, keep in mind that this extra step will lose some business unless your products are unique and your buyers are very motivated.

The least effective option is to provide an order form on the site that can be printed out and mailed in with a check. Again, your customers must be really motivated or they will lose interest after finding out this extra work is involved.

FTC RULES

Because the Internet is an instrument of interstate commerce, it is a legitimate subject for federal regulation. The Federal Trade Commission (FTC) first said that all of its consumer protection rules applied to the Internet, but lately it has been adding specific rules and issuing publications. The following publications are available from the FTC website at **www.ftc.gov/bcp/menus/business/adv.shtm** or by mail from:

Federal Trade Commission
CRC-240
Washington, DC 20580

✪   *A Businessperson's Guide to Federal Warranty Law*

✪   *A Dealer's Guide to the Used Car Rule*

✪   *Ads for Business Opportunities: How To Detect Deception*

✪   *Advertising Consumer Leases*

✪   *Frequently Asked Advertising Questions: A Guide for Small Business*

✪   *Advertising and Marketing on the Internet: Rules of the Road*

✪   *Advertising Retail Electricity and Natural Gas*

✪   *Big Print. Little Print. What's the Deal?*

✪   *A Business Guide to the Federal Trade Commission's Mail or Telephone Order Merchandise Rule*

✪   *Complying With the Appliance Labeling Rule: Labeling Light Bulbs*

✪   *Complying with the Appliance Labeling Rule: A Guide for Retailers*

✪   *Complying with the Environmental Marketing Guides*

✪   *Complying With the Funeral Rule*

✪   *Complying with the Made In the USA Standard*

✪   *Dietary Supplements: An Advertising Guide for Industry*

✪   *Dot Com Disclosures*

✪   *Down...But Not Out: Advertising and Labeling of Feather and Down Products*

✪   *Environmental Marketing Claims*

- ✪   *Good Pricing Practices? SCAN DO*

- ✪   *How to Comply with the FTC Fuel Rating Rule*

- ✪   *In The Loupe: Advertising Diamonds, Gemstones and Pearls*

- ✪   *Making Environmental Marketing Claims on Mail*

- ✪   *Red Flag: Bogus Weight Loss Claims*

- ✪   *Offering Layaways*

- ✪   *Screening Advertisements: A Guide for the Media*

- ✪   *Writing Readable Warranties*

- ✪   *Voluntary Guidelines for Providers of Weight Loss Products*

FRAUD

Because the Internet is somewhat anonymous, it is a tempting place for those with fraudulent schemes to look for victims. As a business consumer, you should exercise caution when dealing with unknown or anonymous parties on the Internet.

The U.S. Department of Justice, the FBI, and the National White Collar Crime Center jointly launched the Internet Crime Complaint Center (IC3). If you suspect that you are the victim of fraud online, whether as a consumer or a business, you can report incidents to the IC3 on their website, **www.ic3.gov**. The IC3 is currently staffed by FBI agents and representatives of the National White Collar Crime Center, and will work with state and local law enforcement officials to prevent, investigate, and prosecute high-tech and economic crime online.

Bookkeeping and Accounting

It is beyond the scope of this book to explain all the intricacies of setting up a business' bookkeeping and accounting systems. But the important thing to realize is that if you do not set up an understandable bookkeeping system, your business will undoubtedly fail.

Without accurate records of where your income is coming from and where it is going, you will be unable to increase your profits, lower your expenses, obtain needed financing, or make the right decisions in all areas of your business. The time to decide how you will handle your bookkeeping is when you open your business, not a year later when it is tax time.

INITIAL BOOKKEEPING

If you do not understand business taxation, you should pick up a good book on the subject, as well as the IRS tax guide for your type of business (proprietorship, partnership, or corporation).

The IRS tax book for small businesses is Publication 334, *Tax Guide for Small Businesses*. There are also instruction booklets for each type of business form: Schedule C for proprietorships, Form 1120 or 1120S for C corporations and S corporations, and 1165 for partnerships and businesses that are taxed like partnerships (LLCs, LLPs).

Keep in mind that the IRS does not give you the best advice for saving on taxes and does not give you the other side of contested issues. You need a private tax guide or advisor for that.

The most important thing to do is to set up your bookkeeping so that you can easily fill out your monthly, quarterly, and annual tax returns. The best way to do this is to get copies of the returns, note the categories that you will need to supply, and set up your book-keeping system to arrive at those totals. For example, for a sole proprietorship you will use *Schedule C* to report business income and expenses to the IRS at the end of the year. Use the categories on that form to sort your expenses. To make your job especially easy, every time you pay a bill, put the category number on the check.

ACCOUNTANTS

Your new business will most likely not be able to afford hiring an accountant right off to handle your books. That is good. Doing your own bookkeeping and tax preparation will force you to learn about business accounting and taxation. The worst way to run a business is to know nothing about the tax laws and turn everything over to an accountant at the end of the year to find out what is due.

You should know the basics of tax law before making basic decisions such as whether to buy or rent equipment or premises. You should understand accounting so you can time your financial affairs appro-priately. If your business needs to buy supplies, inventory, or equip-ment and provides goods or services throughout the year, you need to at least have a basic understanding of the system within which you are working.

Once you can afford an accountant, you should weigh the cost against your time and the risk that you will make an error. Even if you think you know enough to do your own corporate tax return, you should still take it to an accountant one year to see if you have been missing any deductions. You might decide that the money saved is worth the cost of the accountant's services.

COMPUTER PROGRAMS

Today, every business should keep its books by computer. There are inexpensive programs such as Quicken that can instantly provide you with reports of your income and expenses and the right figures to plug into your tax returns.

Most programs even offer a tax program each year that will take all of your information and print it out on the current year's tax forms.

TAX TIPS

Using these tax tips for small businesses can help you save money.

- ✪ Usually when you buy equipment for a business, you must amortize the cost over several years. That is, you do not deduct it all when you buy it, but instead take, say, 25% of the cost off your taxes each year for four years. (The time is determined by the theoretical usefulness of the item.) However, small businesses are allowed to write off the entire cost of a limited amount of items under Internal Revenue Code, Section 179. If you have income to shelter, use it.

- ✪ Owners of S corporations do not have to pay Social Security or Medicare taxes on the part of their profits that is not considered salary. As long as you pay yourself a reasonable salary, other money you take out is not subject to these taxes.

- ✪ You should not neglect to deposit withholding taxes for your own salary or profits. Besides being a large sum to come up with at once in April, there are penalties that must be paid for failure to do so.

- ✪ Do not fail to keep track of and remit your employees' withholding. You will be personally liable for them even if you are a corporation.

- ✪ If you keep track of the use of your car for business, you can deduct mileage. (The amount can go up or down each year.) You may be able to depreciate your car if you use it for business for a considerable amount of time.

✪ If your business is a corporation and you designate the stock as *section 1244 stock* and the business fails, you are able to get a much better deduction for the loss.

✪ By setting up a retirement plan, you can exempt up to 20% of your salary from income tax. (see Chapter 11.) Do not use money you might need later. There are penalties for taking it out of the retirement plan.

✪ When you buy things that will be resold or made into products that will be resold, you do not have to pay sales taxes on those purchases. (see Chapter 20.)

Paying Federal Taxes

There are several different categories of taxes your business may be subject to. Income tax, Social Security withholding, excise tax, and unemployment taxes are just a few that may apply to your business.

FEDERAL INCOME TAX

How you pay your taxes will depend upon the type of business entity you start. The manner in which each type of business pays taxes is as follows:

Proprietorship   A proprietor reports profits and expenses on a Schedule C, attaches it to the usual IRS Form 1040, and pays tax on all the net income of the business. IRS Form ES-1040 must be filed each quarter along with payment of one-quarter of the amount of income tax and Social Security taxes estimated to be due for the year.

Partnership   The partnership files a return showing the income and expenses but pays no tax. Each partner is given a form showing his or her share of the profits or losses and reports these on Schedule E, which is attached to IRS Form 1040. Each quarter, IRS Form ES-1040 must be filed by each partner along with payment of one-quarter of the amount of income tax and Social Security taxes estimated to be due for the year.

C-Corporation

A regular corporation is a separate taxpayer and pays tax on its profits after deducting all expenses, including officers' salaries. If dividends are distributed, they are paid out of after-tax dollars, and the shareholders pay tax a second time on the dividends they receive. If a corporation needs to accumulate money for investment, it may be able to do so at lower tax rates than the shareholders. But if all profits will be distributed to shareholders, the double-taxation may be excessive unless all income is paid as salaries. C corporations file IRS Form 1120.

S-Corporation

A small corporation has the option of being taxed like a partnership. If IRS Form 2553 is filed by the corporation and accepted by the Internal Revenue Service, the S corporation will only file an informational return listing profits and expenses. Each shareholder will be taxed on a proportional share of the profits (or be able to deduct a proportional share of the losses). Unless a corporation will make a large profit that will not be distributed, S-status is usually best in the beginning. An S corporation files IRS Form 1120S and distributes IRS Form K-1 to each shareholder. If any money is taken out by a shareholder that is not listed as wages subject to withholding, then the shareholder will usually have to file IRS Form ES-1040 each quarter along with payment of the estimated withholding on the withdrawals.

Limited Liability Companies and Partnerships

Limited liability companies and limited liability partnerships are allowed by the IRS to elect to be taxed either as a partnership or a corporation. LLCs that elect to be taxed as corporations can also elect to be taxed as S corporations. To make this election, you file IRS Form 8832, *Entity Classification Election*, with the IRS. However, you need not file IRS Form 8832 if you wish to be treated under the *default rules*. These rules provide, among other things, that a *domestic eligible entity* will be treated as a partnership if it has two or more members.

Tax Workshops and Booklets

The IRS conducts workshops to inform businesses about the tax laws. (Do not expect an in-depth study of the loopholes.) For information about any of these programs, contact the Taxpayer Education Coordinator at:

JFK Federal Building
15 New Sudbury St., Room 76C
Boston, MA 02203
800-829-1040
617-565-4325 (Boston only)

FEDERAL WITHHOLDING, SOCIAL SECURITY, AND MEDICARE TAXES

If you need basic information on business tax returns, the IRS publishes a rather large booklet that answers most questions and is available free of charge. Call or write them and ask for Publication No. 334. If you have any questions, look up their toll-free number in the phone book under United States Government/Internal Revenue Service. If you want more creative answers and tax saving information, find a good local accountant. But to get started, you will need the following.

Employer Identification Number

If you are a sole proprietor with no employees, you can use your Social Security number for your business. If you are a corporation, a partnership, or a proprietorship with employees, you must obtain an *Employer Identification Number*. This is done by filing an **APPLICATION FOR EMPLOYER IDENTIFICATION NUMBER (IRS FORM SS-4)** (form 8, p.247). It usually takes a week or two to receive. You will need this number to open bank accounts for the business, so you should file this form as soon as you decide to go into business. A sample, filled-in form and instructions are included in Appendix A. (see form 3, p.211.)

You can also get your EIN immediately online at the following website: **https://www4.irs.gov/modiein/individual/index.jsp.**

Employee's Withholding Allowance Certificate

You must have each employee fill out an **EMPLOYEE'S WITHHOLDING ALLOWANCE CERTIFICATE (IRS FORM W-4)** (form 10, p.255) to calculate the amount of federal taxes to be deducted and to obtain their Social Security numbers. (The number of allowances on this form is used with IRS Circular E, Publication 15, to figure out the exact deductions.) A sample, filled-in form is included in Appendix A. (see form 4, p.213.)

Federal Tax Deposit Coupons

After taking withholdings from employees' wages, you must deposit them at a bank that is authorized to accept such funds. If at the end of any month you have over $1,000 in withheld taxes (including your contribution to FICA), you must make a deposit prior to the 15th of the following month. If on the 3rd, 7th, 11th, 15th, 19th, 22nd, or 25th of any month you have over $3,000 in withheld taxes, you must make a deposit within three banking days. The deposit is made using the coupons in the IRS Form 8109 booklet.

Businesses that make $50,000 or more a year in federal tax deposits are required to use electronic filing.

Estimated Tax Payment Voucher

Sole proprietors and partners usually take draws from their businesses without the formality of withholding. However, they are still required to make deposits of income and FICA taxes each quarter. If more than $500 is due in April on a person's 1040 form, then not enough money was withheld each quarter and a penalty is assessed unless the person falls into an exception. The quarterly withholding is submitted on IRS Form 1040-ES on April 15th, June 15th, September 15th, and January 15th each year. If these days fall on a weekend then the due date is the following Monday. The worksheet with IRS Form 1040-ES can be used to determine the amount to pay.

NOTE: *One of the exceptions to the rule is that if you withhold the same amount as last year's tax bill, then you do not have to pay a penalty. This is usually a lot easier than filling out the IRS Form 1040-ES worksheet.*

Employer's Quarterly Tax Return

Each quarter you must file IRS Form 941 reporting your federal withholding and FICA taxes. If you owe more than $1,000 at the end of a quarter, you are required to make a deposit at the end of any month that you have $1,000 in withholding. The deposits are made to the Federal Reserve Bank or an authorized financial institution on Form 501. Most banks are authorized to accept deposits. If you owe more than $3,000 for any month, you must make a deposit at any point in the month in which you owe $3,000. After you file the **APPLICATION FOR EMPLOYER INDENTIFICATION NUMBER (IRS FORM SS-4)**, the 941 forms will be sent to you automatically if you checked the box saying that you expect to have employees.

At the end of each year, you are required to issue an IRS Form W-2 to each employee. This form shows the amount of wages paid to the employee during the year as well as the amounts withheld for taxes, Social Security, Medicare, and other purposes.

If you pay at least $600 to a person other than an employee (such as independent contractors), you are required to file an IRS Form 1099 for that person. Along with the 1099s, you must file an IRS Form 1096, which is a summary sheet.

Many people are not aware of this law and fail to file these forms. They are required for such things as services, royalties, rents, awards, and prizes that you pay to individuals (but not corporations). The rules for this are quite complicated, so you should either obtain *Package 1099* from the IRS or consult your accountant.

Earned Income Credit

Persons who are not liable to pay income tax may have the right to a check from the government because of the *Earned Income Credit*. You are required to notify your employees of this. You can satisfy this requirement with one of the following:

❂   a W-2 Form with the notice on the back;

❂   a substitute for the W-2 Form with the notice on it;

❂   a copy of Notice 797; or,

❂   a written statement with the wording from Notice 797.

A Notice 797 can be obtained by calling the IRS at 800-829-3676.

FEDERAL EXCISE TAXES

Excise taxes are taxes on certain activities or items. Most federal excise taxes have been eliminated since World War II, but a few still remain.

Some of the things that are subject to federal excise taxes are tobacco and alcohol, gasoline, tires and inner tubes, some trucks and trailers, firearms, ammunition, bows, arrows, fishing equipment, the use of highway vehicles of over 55,000 pounds, aircraft, wagering, telephone and teletype services, coal, hazardous wastes, and vaccines. If you are involved with any of these, you should obtain the IRS publication No. 510, *Information on Excise Taxes*.

FEDERAL UNEMPLOYMENT COMPENSATION TAXES

You must pay federal unemployment taxes if you paid wages of $1,500 in any quarter or if you had at least one employee for twenty calendar weeks. The federal tax amount is 0.8% of the first $7,000 of wages paid to each employee. If more than $100 is due by the end of any quarter (if you paid $12,500 in wages for the quarter), then IRS Form 508 must be filed with an authorized financial institution or the Federal Reserve Bank in your area. You will receive IRS Form 508 when you obtain your employer identification number.

At the end of each year, you must file IRS Form 940 or IRS Form 940EZ. This is your annual report of federal unemployment taxes. You will receive an original form from the IRS.

Paying Massachusetts Taxes

In addition to federal taxes, the Commonwealth of Massachusetts imposes certain taxes of its own.

SALES AND USE TAX

If you will be selling or renting goods or services at retail, you must collect *Massachusetts Sales and Use Tax*. The sales and use tax rate is 5%. Certain items are exempt from sales tax, such as clothing items under $175 and food not bought for immediate consumption. Some services, such as doctors' and lawyers' services and newspaper advertising, are not taxed, but most others are.

The sales tax also applies to meals (it is also called the *Meals Tax*). *Meals* for this purpose is defined as any food or beverage that has been prepared for immediate consumption, including take-out. The meals tax return is similar to the sales tax return. Returns are due monthly.

First, you must obtain a tax number by filling out an Application for Original Registration (TA-1) and paying a small fee. Form TA-1 can no longer be filed on paper. It must be filed online at **https://wfb.dor.state.ma.us/webfile/business/public/webforms/ Login/Login.aspx**. For more details about the tax, see **www.mass.gov/ Ador/docs/dor/Publ/PDFS/sales_use_07.pdf**.

If your sales and use tax liability (excluding meals tax) is reasonably expected to be over $1,200 for the year, you must file monthly returns and pay the taxes due for each month by the twentieth day of the next month. If your liability is under $100, you can file and pay annually; and if it is between $100 and $1,200, you can file and pay quarterly.

Once you file your Form TA-1, you will have to start filing returns whether you have any sales or not. Any business registering after September 1, 2003, is required to file all returns electronically.

One reason to get a tax number early is to exempt your purchases from tax. When you buy a product that you will resell, or use as part of a product that you will sell, you are exempt from paying tax on it. You need to submit a *Resale Certificate* to the seller to get the exemption. This form must contain your sales and use tax registration number.

If you will only be selling items wholesale or out of state, you might think that you do not need a tax number or do not need to submit returns, but you will need to be registered to obtain the tax number to exempt your purchases.

If you have any sales before you get your monthly tax return forms, you should calculate the tax anyway and submit it. Otherwise, you will be charged a penalty regardless of whether or not it was your fault that you did not have the forms.

After you obtain your tax number, you will be required to collect sales tax on all purchases.

If you sell to someone who claims to be exempt from sales and use taxes (for example, if they plan to resell merchandise they have purchased from you), then they must present to you the previously mentioned Resale Certificate.

Income Tax Withholding   All employers are required to withhold a portion of their employees' wages for state income tax purposes. If the withheld amount is less than $100 annually, the return is due annually. If the withheld amount is between $101 and $1,200 annually, the return is due quarterly. If the amount withheld is between $1,201 and $25,000 annually, the return is due monthly. If the withheld amount is over $25,000 annually, the return periods vary but can be required weekly.

Room Occupancy Tax

Individuals operating hotels, motels, lodging houses, or private clubs offering sleeping accommodations must pay a room occupancy tax of 5.7% on rooms rented for $15 or more per day to persons occupying the rooms for ninety consecutive days or less. Returns are due monthly.

Cigarette and Tobacco Tax

The state also imposes taxes on the sale of cigarettes, smoking tobacco, and cigars. Returns are due monthly.

CORPORATE EXCISE (INCOME) TAX

Massachusetts taxes corporations based on their Massachusetts income and their tangible and intangible property. The minimum tax (even for S corporations) is $456 per year. Estimated tax payments must be made during the year if your liability will be over $1,000 for the year.

The corporate income tax rate is 9.5% on income attributable to Massachusetts. Contact the Massachusetts Department of Revenue for more information.

UNEMPLOYMENT COMPENSATION TAXES

You are not liable to pay unemployment compensation taxes until you have had an employee work a part of a day in any thirteen calendar weeks or paid $1,500 in wages in a quarter. But once you reach that point, you are liable for all back taxes. The rate varies according to your employment record. The tax is paid on the first $10,800 of wages of each employee.

If you anticipate having an employee for thirteen weeks or when you have had an employee work for thirteen weeks, you should file an **EMPLOYERS STATUS REPORT** (form 11, p.257). A sample, filled-in form may be found on page 215. You will be sent quarterly returns to complete.

The Department of Revenue's website at **www.dor.state.ma.us** has a wealth of information, instructions, and forms to assist the business owner in complying with the state's tax requirements. Many of the returns can be filed electronically. You can see a list of online state tax forms by clicking on the "For Tax Professionals" tab, and then selecting the "Tax Forms" link under "Current Year Tax Information."

Out-of-State Taxes

At present, companies are only required to collect sales taxes for states in which they *do business*. Exactly what business is enough to trigger taxation is a legal question and some states try to define it as broadly as possible.

If you have an office in a state, you are doing business there, and any goods shipped to consumers in that state are subject to sales taxes. If you have a full-time employee working in the state most of the year, many states will consider you doing business there. In some states, attending a two-day trade show is enough business to trigger taxation for the entire year for every order shipped to the state.

NOTE: *One loophole that often works is to be represented at shows by persons who are not your employees.*

Because the laws are different in each state, you will have to do some research on a state-by-state basis to find out how much business you can do in a state without being subject to that state's taxation. You can request a state's rules from its department of revenue, but keep in mind that what a department of revenue wants the law to be is not always what the courts will rule that it is.

BUSINESS TAXES

Being subject to a state's income or other business taxes is even worse than being bound to a state's sales taxes. For example, California charges every company doing business in the state a minimum $800 a year fee and charges income tax on a portion of the company's worldwide income. Doing a small amount of business in the state is clearly not worth getting mired in California taxation.

For this reason, some trade shows have been moved from the state and this has resulted in a review of the tax policies and some *safe-harbor* guidelines to advise companies on what they can do without becoming subject to taxation. Write to the department of revenue of any state with which you have business contacts to see what might trigger your taxation.

INTERNET TAXES

State revenue departments are drooling at the prospect of taxing commerce on the Internet. Theories have already been proposed that if websites are available to state residents, it means a company is doing business in that state. Fortunately, Congress has passed a moratorium on taxation of the Internet.

CANADIAN TAXES

The Canadian government expects American companies that sell goods by mail order to Canadians to collect taxes for them and file returns with Revenue Canada, its tax department. Those that receive an occasional unsolicited order are not expected to register, and Canadian customers who order things from the United States pay the tax plus a $5 fee upon receipt of the goods. Nonetheless, companies that solicit Canadian orders are expected to be registered if their worldwide income is $30,000 or more per year. In some cases, a company may be required to post a bond and to pay for the cost of Canadian auditors visiting its premises and auditing its books! You may notice that some companies decline to accept orders from Canada for these reasons.

The End...and the Beginning

If you have read through this whole book, you know more about the rules and laws for operating a Massachusetts business than most people in business today. However, after learning about all the governmental regulations, you may become discouraged. You are probably wondering how you can keep track of all the laws and how you will have any time left to make money after complying with the laws. It is not that bad. People are starting businesses every day and they are making money—lots of money.

The regulations that exist right now are enough to strangle some businesses. One way to avoid problems with the government is to keep a low profile and avoid open confrontation. The important thing is that you know the laws and the penalties for violations before making your decision. Knowing the laws will also allow you to use the loopholes in the laws to avoid violations.

Glossary

A

authorized shares. When a corporation is formed, it is divided into parts called shares. A certain number of shares are authorized by filing organizational documents with the state. The number authorized may be changed later by a shareholders' vote and amendment to the organizational documents. The corporation may not at any time issue a number of shares greater than the number authorized. The shares issued, also called *outstanding* or *issued and outstanding*, at any point in time comprise the entire ownership of the company. In theory, there could be only one share authorized and issued, owned by one person, which would comprise 100% of the ownership of the company.

More often, the corporation is formed with multiple shares authorized, which can range from a small number (often 275 shares, especially in Massachusetts) to a large number (50,000,000 shares or more). The right number of shares to choose depends on several factors—for example, the number of current owners and potential owners, and the fees charged by each state for authorizing shares. Not all authorized shares need be issued—some, or most, can be reserved for future use (for example, an IPO).

B

business certificate. A filing that must be made with a town or city clerk by persons and entities doing business under a name other than their true legal name, also called a *trade name* or *fictitious name*.

buy-sell agreement. An agreement among shareholders governing the sale or other transfer of shares. It usually includes what happens if a shareholder working for the corporation leaves the job, is fired, dies, or becomes disabled. Buy-sell agreements can also include voting agreements regarding the voting of shares and other corporate governance provisions.

C

C corporation. One of the types of entities under which you may do business and achieve the protections of limited liability so that only the assets of the entity, not those of its owners, can be used to satisfy liabilities and obligations incurred by that business. C corporations may have unlimited numbers of shareholders. Publicly traded companies are C corporations.

copyright. The legal right granted to an author, composer, playwright, publisher, or distributor to exclusive publication, production, sale, or distribution of a literary, musical, dramatic, or artistic work. This allows the copyright's owner to prevent (a) a copier from using the copy or copies and (b) compensatory damages under certain conditions.

corporation. A body that is granted a charter recognizing it as a separate legal entity having its own rights, privileges, and liabilities distinct from those of its members. Corporations are entities created by the state in which they are formed. There are no *federal* corporations; each one is registered and created by a state. Once a corporation is established, it may be registered to do business in other states. Doing business through a corporation is one way to protect the owners' personal assets.

D

domain name.   A series of letters used to name organizations, computers, and addresses on the Internet. Every computer on the Internet has an *address,* which is a series of numbers much like a telephone number. (In technical jargon that address is called the *IP* address. IP stands for Internet Protocol.) The Domain Name System allows the use of more familiar names to reference those computers. There cannot be duplicate names. Each name is linked by the registration system to the unique string of numbers used to identify the computers. Once a name is taken, someone else cannot use it unless the first party relinquishes the name.

E

employee.   A worker who is subject to the supervision and control of management with respect to the manner and means of work done.

F

fictitious name.   *See* business certificate.

G

general partnership.   *See* partnership.

I

independent contractor.   A person who works on his or her own, rather than as an employee. If management has the right to supervise and control the manner and means of work done by an individual, that individual is normally called an *employee.* If a worker controls his or her own work methods, works for more than one entity, sets his or her own hours, and provides his or her own equipment, the person will usually be deemed an *independent contractor*. Taxes are collected and paid differently with respect to employees versus independent contractors.

initial public offering (IPO). The first time a corporation offers its stock to the public (*goes public*). This is different from a *private placement*, in which stock or other securities may be offered to a limited number of individuals, or individuals who meet certain criteria.

L

limited. One of the words that many states allow in a corporation's name as an indication that the company is of limited liability status. All states require corporations to use a word such as corporation, incorporated, or limited to indicate to the public that the entity is a limited liability entity.

limited liability company (LLC). A legal entity with characteristics of both a corporation and a partnership. The tax treatment of an LLC is similar to that of a partnership—that is, the income is not taxed at the entity level, but at the equity owner level. But the LLC also has the benefit of limited liability, meaning that the owners are not personally liable for the business's debts and obligations. Its limited liability protection is similar to that of a corporation.

limited liability entity. An entity whose equity owners are not personally liable for the entity's debts and obligations, such as a corporation, LLC, or LLP.

limited liability partnership (LLP). An entity similar to a partnership, but in which the personal liability of each partner is limited. Devised to allow partnerships of lawyers and other professionals to limit their personal liability without losing the partnership structure. Does not protect against malpractice or professional responsibility.

limited partnership. A legal entity that is somewhat similar to a partnership. In a limited partnership, there are one or more general partner(s), who do not enjoy limited liability status, and one or more limited partners, who do. The limited partners cannot participate in the running of the entity's business or their limited liability status will be jeopardized.

M

Massachusetts Commission Against Discrimination (MCAD). State agency responsible for enforcing the state's anti-discrimination laws.

Massachusetts Department of Revenue (DOR). The state agency responsible for collecting state taxes, enforcing state tax laws, and educating the public about state tax requirements.

N

noncompete. A contract restricting the right of a person to compete against another, usually a former employer. Also used by buyers of businesses to keep the business seller from competing.

nonprofit corporation. A corporation formed under a separate set of laws than those for business corporations, usually used by churches, condominium associations, and other groups not seeking profits.

P

partnership. An arrangement between two or more persons who agree to pool talent and money and share profits or losses, for the purpose of undertaking some sort of business.

patent. A property right granted by the government to an inventor to exclude others from making, using, offering for sale, or selling the invention in a territory or importing the invention into the territory for a limited time in exchange for public disclosure of the invention when the patent is granted.

piercing the corporate veil. A legal remedy that can be used to obtain assets of a company's shareholders or equity owners to satisfy a judgment against the company. With it, the equity owners of a corporation or limited liability company are held personally liable for the company's debts and liabilities. A court will only allow the piercing of the veil in limited circumstances. Some of the factors that may lead a court to pierce the veil are the commingling of personal and company assets, failure to observe company formalities, failing to hold oneself out to the public as a limited liability entity, undercapitalization, use of company assets for personal purposes, and failure to make legally required filings.

private placement. An offer and sale of securities by an entity to a limited number or category of persons.

professional corporation. A corporation owned and run by certain professionals such as accountants, lawyers, and doctors. Most states allow certain professionals to incorporate only as a professional corporation. Although the corporation does have limited liability status, it does not protect the professionals from malpractice liability nor does it alter professional responsibility or privilege.

proprietorship. A business owned and run by one person, and not incorporated or otherwise enjoying limited liability protection.

S

S corporation. A corporation that has made an official election under federal law to be treated similarly to a partnership for purposes of tax law. The tax attributes of the corporation flow through to its equity owners and are taxed only at the owner level. This is called *flow-through* taxation. In certain states, a state-level filing is also required for the corporation to receive the same tax treatment at the state level.

service mark. Same thing as a trademark, except that it identifies and distinguishes the source of a service rather than a product.

shareholders' agreement. *See* buy-sell agreement.

T

territory. Area covered by a contract, covenant, license, right, or the like, such as a noncompete or patent.

trade name. *See* business certificate.

trademark. Any word, name, symbol, or device, or any combination, used, or intended to be used, in commerce to identify and distinguish the goods of one manufacturer or seller from goods manufactured or sold by others, and to indicate the source of the goods, e.g., a brand name.

U

Uniform Commercial Code (UCC). A set of laws adopted by almost every state in the United States (with variations), governing sales of goods, secured transactions, and other commercial matters.

usury. Interest charged at a rate that is excessive or higher than that allowed by law.

Appendix A: Sample, Filled-In Forms

The following forms may be photocopied or removed from this book. Some of the tax forms explained in this book are not included here because you should use original returns provided by the IRS or the Massachusetts Department of Revenue. Be sure to check with the proper authorities in case there are any additional requirements.

FORM 1: TRADEMARK/SERVICE MARK APPLICATION 203

FORM 2: EMPLOYMENT ELIGIBILITY VERIFICATION (FORM I-9). 207

FORM 3: APPLICATION FOR EMPLOYER IDENTIFICATION NUMBER
       (IRS FORM SS-4) 211

FORM 4: EMPLOYEE'S WITHHOLDING ALLOWANCE CERTIFICATE
       (IRS FORM W-4) 213

FORM 5: EMPLOYER STATUS REPORT (1110-A) 215

FORM 6: NEW HIRE AND INDEPENDENT CONTACTOR
       REPORTING FORM (FORM NHR). 223

TM
SM

The Commonwealth of Massachusetts
William Francis Galvin
Secretary of the Commonwealth
One Ashburton Place, Boston, Massachusetts 02108-1512

Filing Fee $50.00 per class
5 year registration period

FORM MUST BE TYPED

Trademark / Service Mark Application
(General Laws Chapter 110H, Section 3)

FORM MUST BE TYPED

All information must be completed or this document will not be accepted for filing.

(1) Applicant's name and business address:

   a) Individual: _____
                      Last   *First*   *Middle*

   Business address: _____
                      Number   *Street*

                        City   *State*   *Zip*

or

   b) Business Organization:_ Johnny's Boats, Inc. _____

   Business address: _____1_____Beach Drive_____
                      Number   *Street*

        _____Norwalk_____MA_____000000____
                      City   *State*   *Zip*

(2) If applicant is a business, identify type (check box), and if applicable, state and date of organization:

☐ corporation   ☐ limited liability company   ☐ limited partnership   ☐ partnership   ☐ sole proprietor

☐ other _____
                             (indicate entity type)

   a) State of incorporation or organization: _____MA_____   b) Date of incorporation or organization: _6/1/2007_

(3) If applicant is a partnership, state the names of the general partners:

(4) Applicant is seeking to register (check box):

☑ Trademark   ☐ Service Mark

(5) The mark is (complete one of the following):

a) **Words only** - If the mark is only words, the words in the mark are (include type style if it is claimed as part of the mark):

Johnny's Boats

b) **Design Only** - If the mark is a design only, describe the design (include colors if they are claimed as part of the mark):

c) **Words and Design** - State the words in the mark (include color and type style if they are claimed as part of the mark) and describe the design:

Boats

(6) Describe briefly the goods or services used in connection with the mark:

12 Vehicles

(7) For each class provide the number and class in which such goods or services fall (see attached classification schedule): *(An application may include multiple classes)*

(8) Describe briefly how the mark is used in connection with such goods or services:

a) The mark is used by displaying it (check box):

☑ on documents, wrappers, or articles delivered with the goods
☐ in advertisements of the services
☐ in connection with the services rendered
☐ other

b) If other, describe briefly how the mark is used:

(9) The trademark or service-mark has been used by the applicant, or the applicant's predecessor in business, since

_____1/1/2007_____ and in the Commonwealth of Massachusetts since_____1/1/2007_____.
(month, day, year) *(month, day, year)*
(If first use of the mark anywhere was in Massachusetts, use the same date for both.).

(10) a) Has the applicant or predecessor in interest filed an application for the same mark or portions of the same mark with the U.S. Patent and Trademark Office? ☐ Yes ☑ No

b) If yes, for each application, provide (using additional pages if necessary):

Filing date _____ and serial number _____ .
(month, day, year)

c) What is the status of the application (check box)? ☐ awaiting examination ☐ refusal (office action) issued
☐ approved for publication ☐ registered
☐ abandoned/withdrawn

d) If finally refused, or not resulted in a registration, give reason: _____

(11) Attach a sample showing the mark as actively used. The sample specimen may not be larger than 3" x 3".

The applicant is the owner of the mark. The mark is in use, and, to the knowledge of the person verifying the application, no other person has registered, either federally or in this state, or has the right to use such mark either in the identical form thereof or in such near resemblance thereto as to be likely, when applied to the goods or services of such other person, to cause confusion, or to cause mistake, or to deceive.

I, _____John Longshoreman_____ , state that I am the applicant or a lawfully authorized
(Name of Applicant / Authorized Representative)

representative of the applicant and declare under penalty of perjury that the foregoing application is true and correct.

Executed on: _June 1, 2007_____
(Month, Day, Year)

Signature: *John Longshoreman*_____

COMMONWEALTH OF MASSACHUSETTS

William Francis Galvin
Secretary of the Commonwealth
One Ashburton Place, Boston, Massachusetts 02108-1512

Trademark / Service Mark Application
(General Laws Chapter 110H, Section 3)

Registered with

WILLIAM FRANCIS GALVIN
Secretary of the Commonwealth

on:

_____ , 20 _____

Trademark Section
One Ashburton Place, Rm. 1717
Boston, MA 02108

Contact Information

John Longshoreman's Lawyer
_____
Name

57 River Street
_____
Mailing Address

Wellesley   MA   00000
_____
City/town   *State*   *ZIP*

111-222-3333   rrr@jjjj.com
_____
Telephone   *Email*

Department of Homeland Security
U.S. Citizenship and Immigration Services

OMB No. 1615-0047; Expires 03/31/07

Employment Eligibility Verification

INSTRUCTIONS

PLEASE READ ALL INSTRUCTIONS CAREFULLY BEFORE COMPLETING THIS FORM.

Anti-Discrimination Notice. It is illegal to discriminate against any individual (other than an alien not authorized to work in the U.S.) in hiring, discharging, or recruiting or referring for a fee because of that individual's national origin or citizenship status. It is illegal to discriminate against work eligible individuals. Employers **CANNOT** specify which document(s) they will accept from an employee. The refusal to hire an individual because of a future expiration date may also constitute illegal discrimination.

Section 1- Employee.

All employees, citizens and noncitizens, hired after November 6, 1986, must complete Section 1 of this form at the time of hire, which is the actual beginning of employment. **The employer is responsible for ensuring that Section 1 is timely and properly completed.**

Preparer/Translator Certification. The Preparer/Translator Certification must be completed if Section 1 is prepared by a person other than the employee. A preparer/translator may be used only when the employee is unable to complete Section 1 on his/her own. However, the employee must still sign Section 1 personally.

Section 2 - Employer.

For the purpose of completing this form, the term "employer" includes those recruiters and referrers for a fee who are agricultural associations, agricultural employers or farm labor contractors.

Employers must complete Section 2 by examining evidence of identity and employment eligibility within three (3) business days of the date employment begins. If employees are authorized to work, but are unable to present the required document(s) within three business days, they must present a receipt for the application of the document(s) within three business days and the actual document(s) within ninety (90) days. However, if employers hire individuals for a duration of less than three business days, Section 2 must be completed at the time employment begins. **Employers must record: 1)** document title; **2)** issuing authority; **3)** document number, **4)** expiration date, if any; and **5)** the date employment begins. Employers must sign and date the certification. Employees must present original documents. Employers may, but are not required to, photocopy the document(s) presented. These photocopies may only be used for the verification process and must be retained with the I-9. **However, employers are still responsible for completing the I-9.**

Section 3 - Updating and Reverification.

Employers must complete Section 3 when updating and/or reverifying the I-9. Employers must reverify employment eligibility of their employees on or before the expiration date recorded in Section 1. Employers **CANNOT** specify which document(s) they will accept from an employee.

- If an employee's name has changed at the time this form is being updated/reverified, complete Block A.

- If an employee is rehired within three (3) years of the date this form was originally completed and the employee is still eligible to be employed on the same basis as previously indicated on this form (updating), complete Block B and the signature block.

- If an employee is rehired within three (3) years of the date this form was originally completed and the employee's work authorization has expired **or** if a current employee's work authorization is about to expire (reverification), complete Block B and:

- examine any document that reflects that the employee is authorized to work in the U.S. (see List A **or** C),

- record the document title, document number and expiration date (if any) in Block C, and

- complete the signature block.

Photocopying and Retaining Form I-9. A blank I-9 may be reproduced, provided both sides are copied. The Instructions must be available to all employees completing this form. Employers must retain completed I-9s for three (3) years after the date of hire or one (1) year after the date employment ends, whichever is later.

For more detailed information, you may refer to the Department of Homeland Security (DHS) Handbook for Employers, (Form M-274). You may obtain the handbook at your local U.S. Citizenship and Immigration Services (USCIS) office.

Privacy Act Notice. The authority for collecting this information is the Immigration Reform and Control Act of 1986, Pub. L. 99-603 (8 USC 1324a).

This information is for employers to verify the eligibility of individuals for employment to preclude the unlawful hiring, or recruiting or referring for a fee, of aliens who are not authorized to work in the United States.

This information will be used by employers as a record of their basis for determining eligibility of an employee to work in the United States. The form will be kept by the employer and made available for inspection by officials of the U.S. Immigration and Customs Enforcement, Department of Labor and Office of Special Counsel for Immigration Related Unfair Employment Practices.

Submission of the information required in this form is voluntary. However, an individual may not begin employment unless this form is completed, since employers are subject to civil or criminal penalties if they do not comply with the Immigration Reform and Control Act of 1986.

Reporting Burden. We try to create forms and instructions that are accurate, can be easily understood and which impose the least possible burden on you to provide us with information. Often this is difficult because some immigration laws are very complex. Accordingly, the reporting burden for this collection of information is computed as follows: **1)** learning about this form, 5 minutes; **2)** completing the form, 5 minutes; and **3)** assembling and filing (recordkeeping) the form, 5 minutes, for an average of 15 minutes per response. If you have comments regarding the accuracy of this burden estimate, or suggestions for making this form simpler, you can write to U.S. Citizenship and Immigration Services, Regulatory Division, 111 Massachuetts Avenue, N.W., Washington, DC 20529. OMB No. 1615-0047.

NOTE: This is the 1991 edition of the Form I-9 that has been rebranded with a current printing date to reflect the recent transition from the INS to DHS and its components.

EMPLOYERS MUST RETAIN COMPLETED FORM I-9
PLEASE DO NOT MAIL COMPLETED FORM I-9 TO ICE OR USCIS

Form I-9 (Rev. 05/31/05)Y

Department of Homeland Security
U.S. Citizenship and Immigration Services

OMB No. 1615-0047; Expires 03/31/07

Employment Eligibility Verification

Please read instructions carefully before completing this form. The instructions must be available during completion of this form. **ANTI-DISCRIMINATION NOTICE:** It is illegal to discriminate against work eligible individuals. Employers CANNOT specify which document(s) they will accept from an employee. The refusal to hire an individual because of a future expiration date may also constitute illegal discrimination.

Section 1. Employee Information and Verification. To be completed and signed by employee at the time employment begins.

Print Name: Last	First	Middle Initial	Maiden Name
Simpson	Bart		

Address (Street Name and Number)	Apt. #	Date of Birth (month/day/year)
1 Pleasant Street		04/22/1960

City	State	Zip Code	Social Security #
Springfield	MA	11111	222-44-3333

I am aware that federal law provides for imprisonment and/or fines for false statements or use of false documents in connection with the completion of this form.

I attest, under penalty of perjury, that I am (check one of the following):

- [X] A citizen or national of the United States
- [ ] A Lawful Permanent Resident (Alien #) A _____
- [ ] An alien authorized to work until _____

(Alien # or Admission #) _____

Employee's Signature	Date (month/day/year)

Preparer and/or Translator Certification. (To be completed and signed if Section 1 is prepared by a person other than the employee.) I attest, under penalty of perjury, that I have assisted in the completion of this form and that to the best of my knowledge the information is true and correct.

Preparer's/Translator's Signature	Print Name

Address (Street Name and Number, City, State, Zip Code)	Date (month/day/year)

Section 2. Employer Review and Verification. To be completed and signed by employer. Examine one document from List A OR examine one document from List B and one from List C, as listed on the reverse of this form, and record the title, number and expiration date, if any, of the document(s).

List A	OR	List B	AND	List C
Document title: Passport				
Issuing authority: Passport Agency PTB				
Document #: 123456789				
Expiration Date (if any): 03/01/2011				
Document #:				
Expiration Date (if any):				

CERTIFICATION - I attest, under penalty of perjury, that I have examined the document(s) presented by the above-named employee, that the above-listed document(s) appear to be genuine and to relate to the employee named, that the employee began employment on (month/day/year) _____ and that to the best of my knowledge the employee is eligible to work in the United States. (State employment agencies may omit the date the employee began employment.)

Signature of Employer or Authorized Representative	Print Name	Title
	Margaret Thatcher	President

Business or Organization Name	Address (Street Name and Number, City, State, Zip Code)	Date (month/day/year)
Boston Hot Dogs, Inc.	12 Main St., Wellesley, MA 22222	06/01/2007

Section 3. Updating and Reverification. To be completed and signed by employer.

A. New Name (if applicable)	B. Date of Rehire (month/day/year) (if applicable)

C. If employee's previous grant of work authorization has expired, provide the information below for the document that establishes current employment eligibility.

Document Title:	Document #:	Expiration Date (if any):

I attest, under penalty of perjury, that to the best of my knowledge, this employee is eligible to work in the United States, and if the employee presented document(s), the document(s) I have examined appear to be genuine and to relate to the individual.

Signature of Employer or Authorized Representative	Date (month/day/year)

NOTE: This is the 1991 edition of the Form I-9 that has been rebranded with a current printing date to reflect the recent transition from the INS to DHS and its components.

Form I-9 (Rev. 05/31/05)Y Page 2

LISTS OF ACCEPTABLE DOCUMENTS

LIST A		LIST B		LIST C
Documents that Establish Both Identity and Employment Eligibility	**OR**	**Documents that Establish Identity**	**AND**	**Documents that Establish Employment Eligibility**

LIST A — Documents that Establish Both Identity and Employment Eligibility

1. U.S. Passport (unexpired or expired)

2. Certificate of U.S. Citizenship (Form N-560 or N-561)

3. Certificate of Naturalization (Form N-550 or N-570)

4. Unexpired foreign passport, with *I-551 stamp or* attached *Form I-94* indicating unexpired employment authorization

5. Permanent Resident Card or Alien Registration Receipt Card with photograph (Form I-151 or I-551)

6. Unexpired Temporary Resident Card (Form I-688)

7. Unexpired Employment Authorization Card (Form I-688A)

8. Unexpired Reentry Permit (Form I-327)

9. Unexpired Refugee Travel Document (Form 1-571)

10. Unexpired Employment Authorization Document issued by DHS that contains a photograph (Form I-688B)

OR

LIST B — Documents that Establish Identity

1. Driver's license or ID card issued by a state or outlying possession of the United States provided it contains a photograph or information such as name, date of birth, gender, height, eye color and address

2. ID card issued by federal, state or local government agencies or entities, provided it contains a photograph or information such as name, date of birth, gender, height, eye color and address

3. School ID card with a photograph

4. Voter's registration card

5. U.S. Military card or draft record

6. Military dependent's ID card

7. U.S. Coast Guard Merchant Mariner Card

8. Native American tribal document

9. Driver's license issued by a Canadian government authority

For persons under age 18 who are unable to present a document listed above:

10. School record or report card

11. Clinic, doctor or hospital record

12. Day-care or nursery school record

AND

LIST C — Documents that Establish Employment Eligibility

1. U.S. social security card issued by the Social Security Administration *(other than a card stating it is not valid for employment)*

2. Certification of Birth Abroad issued by the Department of State *(Form FS-545 or Form DS-1350)*

3. Original or certified copy of a birth certificate issued by a state, county, municipal authority or outlying possession of the United States bearing an official seal

4. Native American tribal document

5. U.S. Citizen ID Card *(Form I-197)*

6. ID Card for use of Resident Citizen in the United States *(Form I-179)*

7. Unexpired employment authorization document issued by DHS *(other than those listed under List A)*

Illustrations of many of these documents appear in Part 8 of the Handbook for Employers (M-274)

This page intentionally blank

Form **SS-4**
(Rev. July 2007)
Department of the Treasury
Internal Revenue Service

Application for Employer Identification Number

(For use by employers, corporations, partnerships, trusts, estates, churches, government agencies, Indian tribal entities, certain individuals, and others.)

► See separate instructions for each line.   ► Keep a copy for your records.

OMB No. 1545-0003

EIN

Type or print clearly.

1	Legal name of entity (or individual) for whom the EIN is being requested Hound Dogs, Inc.	
2	Trade name of business (if different from name on line 1)	**3** Executor, administrator, trustee, "care of" name
4a	Mailing address (room, apt., suite no. and street, or P.O. box) 1 Always Underfoot Road	**5a** Street address (if different) (Do not enter a P.O. box.)
4b	City, state, and ZIP code (if foreign, see instructions) Middletown, MA 44444	**5b** City, state, and ZIP code (if foreign, see instructions)
6	County and state where principal business is located Middlesex, MA	
7a	Name of principal officer, general partner, grantor, owner, or trustor Ollie D. Goofball	**7b** SSN, ITIN, or EIN 444-55-2222

8a Is this application for a limited liability company (LLC) (or a foreign equivalent)? . . . . ☐ Yes ☒ No

8b If 8a is "Yes," enter the number of LLC members . . . . ►

8c If 8a is "Yes," was the LLC organized in the United States? . . . . ☐ Yes ☐ No

9a **Type of entity** (check only one box). **Caution.** If 8a is "Yes," see the instructions for the correct box to check.

☐ Sole proprietor (SSN) _____
☐ Partnership
☒ Corporation (enter form number to be filed) ► 1120S _____
☐ Personal service corporation
☐ Church or church-controlled organization
☐ Other nonprofit organization (specify) ► _____
☐ Other (specify) ►

☐ Estate (SSN of decedent) _____
☐ Plan administrator (TIN) _____
☐ Trust (TIN of grantor) _____
☐ National Guard   ☐ State/local government
☐ Farmers' cooperative   ☐ Federal government/military
☐ REMIC   ☐ Indian tribal governments/enterprises
Group Exemption Number (GEN) if any ►

9b If a corporation, name the state or foreign country (if applicable) where incorporated

State	Foreign country
MA	

10 **Reason for applying** (check only one box)

☒ Started new business (specify type) ► _____ Corporation
☐ Hired employees (Check the box and see line 13.)
☐ Compliance with IRS withholding regulations
☐ Other (specify) ►

☐ Banking purpose (specify purpose) ► _____
☐ Changed type of organization (specify new type) ► _____
☐ Purchased going business
☐ Created a trust (specify type) ► _____
☐ Created a pension plan (specify type) ►

11 Date business started or acquired (month, day, year). See instructions. 1/1/2008

12 Closing month of accounting year December

13 Highest number of employees expected in the next 12 months (enter -0- if none).

Agricultural	Household	Other
0	0	4

14 Do you expect your employment tax liability to be $1,000 or less in a full calendar year? ☐ Yes ☒ No (If you expect to pay $4,000 or less in total wages in a full calendar year, you can mark "Yes.")

15 First date wages or annuities were paid (month, day, year). **Note.** If applicant is a withholding agent, enter date income will first be paid to nonresident alien (month, day, year) . . . . ►

16 Check **one** box that best describes the principal activity of your business.
☐ Construction ☐ Rental & leasing ☐ Transportation & warehousing ☐ Health care & social assistance ☐ Wholesale-agent/broker
☐ Real estate   ☐ Manufacturing   ☐ Finance & insurance   ☒ Other (specify) Dog Breeding ☐ Wholesale-other ☐ Retail
☐ Accommodation & food service

17 Indicate principal line of merchandise sold, specific construction work done, products produced, or services provided.
Dog Breeding and Sales

18 Has the applicant entity shown on line 1 ever applied for and received an EIN? ☐ Yes ☒ No
If "Yes," write previous EIN here ►

Third Party Designee	Complete this section **only** if you want to authorize the named individual to receive the entity's EIN and answer questions about the completion of this form.
	Designee's name Ollie D. Goofball, owner
	Address and ZIP code

Designee's telephone number (include area code)
( )
Designee's fax number (include area code)
( )

Under penalties of perjury, I declare that I have examined this application, and to the best of my knowledge and belief, it is true, correct, and complete.

Name and title (type or print clearly) ► Ollie D. Goofball

Applicant's telephone number (include area code)
( )

Signature ► *Ollie D. Goofball*   Date ►

Applicant's fax number (include area code)
( )

For Privacy Act and Paperwork Reduction Act Notice, see separate instructions.   Cat. No. 16055N   Form **SS-4** (Rev. 7-2007)

Do I Need an EIN?

File Form SS-4 if the applicant entity does not already have an EIN but is required to show an EIN on any return, statement, or other document.[1] See also the separate instructions for each line on Form SS-4.

IF the applicant...	AND...	THEN...
Started a new business	Does not currently have (nor expect to have) employees	Complete lines 1, 2, 4a–8a, 8b–c (if applicable), 9a, 9b (if applicable), and 10–14 and 16–18.
Hired (or will hire) employees, including household employees	Does not already have an EIN	Complete lines 1, 2, 4a–6, 7a–b (if applicable), 8a, 8b–c (if applicable), 9a, 9b (if applicable), 10–18.
Opened a bank account	Needs an EIN for banking purposes only	Complete lines 1–5b, 7a–b (if applicable), 8a, 8b–c (if applicable), 9a, 9b (if applicable), 10, and 18.
Changed type of organization	Either the legal character of the organization or its ownership changed (for example, you incorporate a sole proprietorship or form a partnership)[2]	Complete lines 1–18 (as applicable).
Purchased a going business[3]	Does not already have an EIN	Complete lines 1–18 (as applicable).
Created a trust	The trust is other than a grantor trust or an IRA trust[4]	Complete lines 1–18 (as applicable).
Created a pension plan as a plan administrator[5]	Needs an EIN for reporting purposes	Complete lines 1, 3, 4a–5b, 9a, 10, and 18.
Is a foreign person needing an EIN to comply with IRS withholding regulations	Needs an EIN to complete a Form W-8 (other than Form W-8ECI), avoid withholding on portfolio assets, or claim tax treaty benefits[6]	Complete lines 1–5b, 7a–b (SSN or ITIN optional), 8a, 8b–c (if applicable), 9a, 9b (if applicable), 10, and 18.
Is administering an estate	Needs an EIN to report estate income on Form 1041	Complete lines 1–6, 9a, 10–12, 13–17 (if applicable), and 18.
Is a withholding agent for taxes on non-wage income paid to an alien (i.e., individual, corporation, or partnership, etc.)	Is an agent, broker, fiduciary, manager, tenant, or spouse who is required to file Form 1042, Annual Withholding Tax Return for U.S. Source Income of Foreign Persons	Complete lines 1, 2, 3 (if applicable), 4a–5b, 7a–b (if applicable), 8a, 8b–c (if applicable), 9a, 9b (if applicable), 10 and 18.
Is a state or local agency	Serves as a tax reporting agent for public assistance recipients under Rev. Proc. 80-4, 1980-1 C.B. 581[7]	Complete lines 1, 2, 4a–5b, 9a, 10 and 18.
Is a single-member LLC	Needs an EIN to file Form 8832, Classification Election, for filing employment tax returns, or for state reporting purposes[8]	Complete lines 1–18 (as applicable).
Is an S corporation	Needs an EIN to file Form 2553, Election by a Small Business Corporation[9]	Complete lines 1–18 (as applicable).

[1] For example, a sole proprietorship or self-employed farmer who establishes a qualified retirement plan, or is required to file excise, employment, alcohol, tobacco, or firearms returns, must have an EIN. A partnership, corporation, REMIC (real estate mortgage investment conduit), nonprofit organization (church, club, etc.), or farmers' cooperative must use an EIN for any tax-related purpose even if the entity does not have employees.

[2] However, do not apply for a new EIN if the existing entity only (a) changed its business name, (b) elected on Form 8832 to change the way it is taxed (or is covered by the default rules), or (c) terminated its partnership status because at least 50% of the total interests in partnership capital and profits were sold or exchanged within a 12-month period. The EIN of the terminated partnership should continue to be used. See Regulations section 301.6109-1(d)(2)(iii).

[3] Do not use the EIN of the prior business unless you became the "owner" of a corporation by acquiring its stock.

[4] However, grantor trusts that do not file using Optional Method 1 and IRA trusts that are required to file Form 990-T, Exempt Organization Business Income Tax Return, must have an EIN. For more information on grantor trusts, see the Instructions for Form 1041.

[5] A plan administrator is the person or group of persons specified as the administrator by the instrument under which the plan is operated.

[6] Entities applying to be a Qualified Intermediary (QI) need a QI-EIN even if they already have an EIN. See Rev. Proc. 2000-12.

[7] See also Household employer on page 4 of the instructions. Note. State or local agencies may need an EIN for other reasons, for example, hired employees.

[8] Most LLCs do not need to file Form 8832. See Limited liability company (LLC) on page 4 of the instructions for details on completing Form SS-4 for an LLC.

[9] An existing corporation that is electing or revoking S corporation status should use its previously-assigned EIN.

Form W-4 (2007)

Purpose. Complete Form W-4 so that your employer can withhold the correct federal income tax from your pay. Because your tax situation may change, you may want to refigure your withholding each year.

Exemption from withholding. If you are exempt, complete **only** lines 1, 2, 3, 4, and 7 and sign the form to validate it. Your exemption for 2007 expires February 16, 2008. See Pub. 505, Tax Withholding and Estimated Tax.

Note. You cannot claim exemption from withholding if (a) your income exceeds $850 and includes more than $300 of unearned income (for example, interest and dividends) and (b) another person can claim you as a dependent on their tax return.

Basic instructions. If you are not exempt, complete the **Personal Allowances Worksheet** below. The worksheets on page 2 adjust your withholding allowances based on itemized deductions, certain credits, adjustments to income, or two-earner/multiple job situations. Complete all worksheets that apply. However, you may claim fewer (or zero) allowances.

Head of household. Generally, you may claim head of household filing status on your tax return only if you are unmarried and pay more than 50% of the costs of keeping up a home for yourself and your dependent(s) or other qualifying individuals.

Tax credits. You can take projected tax credits into account in figuring your allowable number of withholding allowances. Credits for child or dependent care expenses and the child tax credit may be claimed using the **Personal Allowances Worksheet** below. See Pub. 919, How Do I Adjust My Tax Withholding, for information on converting your other credits into withholding allowances.

Nonwage income. If you have a large amount of nonwage income, such as interest or dividends, consider making estimated tax payments using Form 1040-ES, Estimated Tax

for Individuals. Otherwise, you may owe additional tax. If you have pension or annuity income, see Pub. 919 to find out if you should adjust your withholding on Form W-4 or W-4P.

Two earners/Multiple jobs. If you have a working spouse or more than one job, figure the total number of allowances you are entitled to claim on all jobs using worksheets from only one Form W-4. Your withholding usually will be most accurate when all allowances are claimed on the Form W-4 for the highest paying job and zero allowances are claimed on the others.

Nonresident alien. If you are a nonresident alien, see the Instructions for Form 8233 before completing this Form W-4.

Check your withholding. After your Form W-4 takes effect, use Pub. 919 to see how the dollar amount you are having withheld compares to your projected total tax for 2007. See Pub. 919, especially if your earnings exceed $130,000 (Single) or $180,000 (Married).

Personal Allowances Worksheet (Keep for your records.)

A	Enter "1" for **yourself** if no one else can claim you as a dependent	**A** _____
B	Enter "1" if: { You are single and have only one job; or / You are married, have only one job, and your spouse does not work; or / Your wages from a second job or your spouse's wages (or the total of both) are $1,000 or less. }	**B** _1_
C	Enter "1" for your **spouse**. But, you may choose to enter "-0-" if you are married and have either a working spouse or more than one job. (Entering "-0-" may help you avoid having too little tax withheld.)	**C** _____
D	Enter number of **dependents** (other than your spouse or yourself) you will claim on your tax return	**D** _____
E	Enter "1" if you will file as **head of household** on your tax return (see conditions under **Head of household** above) .	**E** _____
F	Enter "1" if you have at least $1,500 of **child or dependent care expenses** for which you plan to claim a credit . .	**F** _____
	(**Note.** Do **not** include child support payments. See Pub. 503, Child and Dependent Care Expenses, for details.)	
G	**Child Tax Credit** (including additional child tax credit). See Pub 972, Child Tax Credit, for more information.	
	If your total income will be less than $57,000 ($85,000 if married), enter "2" for each eligible child.	
	If your total income will be between $57,000 and $84,000 ($85,000 and $119,000 if married), enter "1" for each eligible child plus "1" **additional** if you have 4 or more eligible children.	**G** _1_
H	Add lines A through G and enter total here. (**Note.** This may be different from the number of exemptions you claim on your tax return.)	**H** _2_

For accuracy, complete all worksheets that apply. {	If you plan to **itemize or claim adjustments to income** and want to reduce your withholding, see the **Deductions and Adjustments Worksheet** on page 2.	
	If you have **more than one job** or are **married and you and your spouse both work** and the combined earnings from all jobs exceed $40,000 ($25,000 if married) see the **Two-Earners/Multiple Jobs Worksheet** on page 2 to avoid having too little tax withheld.	
	If **neither** of the above situations applies, **stop here** and enter the number from line H on line 5 of Form W-4 below.	

- - - - - - - - - - Cut here and give Form W-4 to your employer. Keep the top part for your records. - - - - - - - - - -

Form **W-4**	**Employee's Withholding Allowance Certificate**	OMB No. 1545-0074
Department of the Treasury Internal Revenue Service	**Whether you are entitled to claim a certain number of allowances or exemption from withholding is subject to review by the IRS. Your employer may be required to send a copy of this form to the IRS.**	2007

1 Type or print your first name and middle initial.	Last name	**2** Your social security number
Iris I.	Rich	003 04 0005

Home address (number and street or rural route)	**3** [X] Single [ ] Married [ ] Married, but withhold at higher Single rate.
4 Everlonging Lane	**Note.** If married, but legally separated, or spouse is a nonresident alien, check the "Single" box.
City or town, state, and ZIP code	**4** If your last name differs from that shown on your social security card, check here. You must call 1-800-772-1213 for a replacement card. [ ]
Emerald City, MA 00098	

5	Total number of allowances you are claiming (from line **H** above **or** from the applicable worksheet on page 2)	**5** 2
6	Additional amount, if any, you want withheld from each paycheck	**6** $ 0
7	I claim exemption from withholding for 2007, and I certify that I meet **both** of the following conditions for exemption.	
	Last year I had a right to a refund of **all** federal income tax withheld because I had **no** tax liability **and**	
	This year I expect a refund of **all** federal income tax withheld because I expect to have **no** tax liability.	
	If you meet both conditions, write "Exempt" here	**7**

Under penalties of perjury, I declare that I have examined this certificate and to the best of my knowledge and belief, it is true, correct, and complete.

Employee's signature
(Form is not valid unless you sign it.) ▶

Date ▶

8 Employer's name and address (Employer: Complete lines 8 and 10 only if sending to the IRS.)	**9** Office code (optional)	**10** Employer identification number (EIN)
Duz Notpaywell, Inc., 2 Scratch Blvd., Dearth, MA 33333	33	2222222

For Privacy Act and Paperwork Reduction Act Notice, see page 2. Cat. No. 10220Q   Form **W-4** (2007)

Form W-4 (2007)

Deductions and Adjustments Worksheet

Note. Use this worksheet *only* if you plan to itemize deductions, claim certain credits, or claim adjustments to income on your 2007 tax return.

1 Enter an estimate of your 2007 itemized deductions. These include qualifying home mortgage interest, charitable contributions, state and local taxes, medical expenses in excess of 7.5% of your income, and miscellaneous deductions. (For 2007, you may have to reduce your itemized deductions if your income is over $156,400 ($78,200 if married filing separately). See *Worksheet 2* in Pub. 919 for details.) . . | **1** | $ _____

2 Enter: { $10,700 if married filing jointly or qualifying widow(er)
              $ 7,850 if head of household
              $ 5,350 if single or married filing separately } . . . . | **2** | $ _____

3 **Subtract** line 2 from line 1. If zero or less, enter "-0-" . . . . | **3** | $ _____

4 Enter an estimate of your 2007 adjustments to income, including alimony, deductible IRA contributions, and student loan interest | **4** | $ _____

5 **Add** lines 3 and 4 and enter the total. (Include any amount for credits from *Worksheet 8* in Pub. 919) . | **5** | $ _____

6 Enter an estimate of your 2007 nonwage income (such as dividends or interest) . . . . | **6** | $ _____

7 **Subtract** line 6 from line 5. If zero or less, enter "-0-" . . . . | **7** | $ _____

8 **Divide** the amount on line 7 by $3,400 and enter the result here. Drop any fraction . . | **8** | _____

9 Enter the number from the **Personal Allowances Worksheet,** line H, page 1 . . . . | **9** | _____

10 **Add** lines 8 and 9 and enter the total here. If you plan to use the **Two-Earners/Multiple Jobs Worksheet,** also enter this total on line 1 below. Otherwise, **stop here** and enter this total on Form W-4, line 5, page 1 | **10** | _____

Two-Earners/Multiple Jobs Worksheet (See *Two earners/multiple jobs* on page 1.)

Note. Use this worksheet *only* if the instructions under line H on page 1 direct you here.

1 Enter the number from line H, page 1 (or from line 10 above if you used the **Deductions and Adjustments Worksheet**) | **1** | _____

2 Find the number in **Table 1** below that applies to the **LOWEST** paying job and enter it here. **However,** if you are married filing jointly and wages from the highest paying job are $50,000 or less, do not enter more than "3." . . . . | **2** | _____

3 If line 1 is **more than or equal to** line 2, subtract line 2 from line 1. Enter the result here (if zero, enter "-0-") and on Form W-4, line 5, page 1. **Do not** use the rest of this worksheet . . . . | **3** | _____

Note. If line 1 is *less than* line 2, enter "-0-" on Form W-4, line 5, page 1. Complete lines 4–9 below to calculate the additional withholding amount necessary to avoid a year-end tax bill.

4 Enter the number from line 2 of this worksheet . . . . . . | **4** | _____

5 Enter the number from line 1 of this worksheet . . . . . . | **5** | _____

6 Subtract line 5 from line 4 . . . . | **6** | _____

7 Find the amount in **Table 2** below that applies to the **HIGHEST** paying job and enter it here . . . . | **7** | $ _____

8 **Multiply** line 7 by line 6 and enter the result here. This is the additional annual withholding needed . . | **8** | $ _____

9 Divide line 8 by the number of pay periods remaining in 2007. For example, divide by 26 if you are paid every two weeks and you complete this form in December 2006. Enter the result here and on Form W-4, line 6, page 1. This is the additional amount to be withheld from each paycheck . . . . | **9** | $ _____

Table 1				Table 2			
Married Filing Jointly		**All Others**		**Married Filing Jointly**		**All Others**	
If wages from **LOWEST** paying job are—	Enter on line 2 above	If wages from **LOWEST** paying job are—	Enter on line 2 above	If wages from **HIGHEST** paying job are—	Enter on line 7 above	If wages from **HIGHEST** paying job are—	Enter on line 7 above
$0 - $4,500	0	$0 - $6,000	0	$0 - $65,000	$510	$0 - $35,000	$510
4,501 - 9,000	1	6,001 - 12,000	1	65,001 - 120,000	850	35,001 - 80,000	850
9,001 - 18,000	2	12,001 - 19,000	2	120,001 - 170,000	950	80,001 - 150,000	950
18,001 - 22,000	3	19,001 - 26,000	3	170,001 - 300,000	1,120	150,001 - 340,000	1,120
22,001 - 26,000	4	26,001 - 35,000	4	300,001 and over	1,190	340,001 and over	1,190
26,001 - 32,000	5	35,001 - 50,000	5				
32,001 - 38,000	6	50,001 - 65,000	6				
38,001 - 46,000	7	65,001 - 80,000	7				
46,001 - 55,000	8	80,001 - 90,000	8				
55,001 - 60,000	9	90,001 - 120,000	9				
60,001 - 65,000	10	120,001 and over	10				
65,001 - 75,000	11						
75,001 - 95,000	12						
95,001 - 105,000	13						
105,001 - 120,000	14						
120,001 and over	15						

Massachusetts Department of
Workforce
Development
Division of Unemployment Assistance

EMPLOYER STATUS REPORT

Complete And Return This Form Within 10 days To:
Division of Unemployment Assistance
Status Department - 5th Floor
19 Staniford Street
Boston, MA 02114-2589

PLEASE TYPE OR PRINT CLEARLY IN INK.

CALL (617) 626-5075 FOR ASSISTANCE.

Fax: (617) 727-8221

**THIS FORM IS FOR USE
BY NEW AND EXISTING EMPLOYERS**

FOR DIVISION USE ONLY

Emp. No.: _____ Subj. Date: _____

Reason: _____ Qtr.: _____ 13th Wk.: _____

No. Employees: _____ Area: _____

Rate Yr: _____ NAICS: _____ Aux: _____

Org.: _____ %Transfer _____

Deter. By: _____

Pred. No.: _____

Pred. Date: _____

Pred. Cd.: _____

ESR Status: _____

Leasing Code: _____

Employer Type: _____

	Workforce Training Yr./Rate	Contribution Yr./Rate
1.		1.
2.		2.
3.		3.
4.		4.
5.		5.

SECTION I   ALL FIELDS REQUIRED

1. Name of employing unit: **Make My Day, Inc.**   2. Trade name: **N/A**

3. List **ALL** business locations in Massachusetts. If more than one, attach a separate sheet.
12 Eastwood Dr.   **Clinton**   **MA**   **12345**
No.   Street (do not use P.O. box number)   City   State   Zip Code

4. Mailing address: **12 Eastwood Dr. Clinton MA**   5. Payroll Records Address: **Same**

6. Business phone: **(890) 123-4567**   7. Federal Identification #: **20-45676666**

8. Owner, partners or officers:

Name (Required)	S.S.A. No. (Required)	Home address	Title	Are officers compensated for their services?
Tough Guy	**234-56-7890**	**12 Eastwood Dr MA**	**President**	[X] Yes [ ] No
				[ ] Yes [ ] No
				[ ] Yes [ ] No

9. Type of organization: [ ] Sole Proprietor   [ ] Partnership   [X] Corporation   [ ] Other (specify) _____
   [ ] Trust   [ ] LLC (single member)   [ ] LLC (corp.)   [ ] LLC (partnership)

   If corporation: date incorporated **1/05/07**   state incorporated **MA**

10. First date of employment in Massachusetts: **1/12/07** 11. Describe nature of your company's business/industry: **Sales**

12. Name your principle commodity, product or service **Paintball Guns**

13. Are you a client of an employee leasing company?   [ ] Yes   [X] No
    Please attach a copy of your contract.   If Yes Name and Address of Leasing Company.

14. Are you liable for federal unemployment tax?   [ ] Yes   [X] No   First date of liability : _____

15. If your main activity in Massachusetts is to provide support services to other locations of your company, please check appropriate box:

    [ ] Headquarters   [ ] Research   [ ] Warehouse   [ ] Computer Center   [ ] Other (specify) _____

16. Do you hold an exemption from federal income taxes as a non-profit organization described under section 501 (c)(3) of the Internal Revenue Code?   [ ] Yes   [X] No   If Yes, please attach a copy of your exemption with this report.

17. Have you previously been subject to the Massachusetts Unemployment Insurance Law?   [ ] Yes   [X] No
    If yes, give DUA Account Number _____   Name _____

Form 1110-A Rev. 10-04-06   Commonwealth of Massachusetts

SECTION II PLEASE REFER TO INSTRUCTIONS TO COMPLETE THIS FORM

You must answer **"yes"** *if any of the following apply: You acquired* **All** *or* **Part** *of another business or organization operating in MA; you were part of a merger with (or consolidation of) a business operating in MA; you changed your Federal Identification Number; you have had a relationship with or are a "spin-off" of a company registered with MA DUA; you changed organizational structure. This includes any changes from one business type to another (examples include—but not limited to—changes from a sole proprietorship to corporation, LLC, LLP, etc., or from a corporation to a sole proprietor, partnership, LLP Trust, etc).*

1. Have you undergone any type of organizational change? ☐ Yes ☒ No If no proceed to Section III

2. What was the nature of the organizational change in Massachusetts?
   ☐ Acquisition ☐ Merger ☐ Consolidation ☐ Transfer of Employees only
   ☐ Other (please explain) _____

3. What is the date of the business transfer or organizational change? (mm/dd/yy) _____

4. Predecessor DUA account number: _____ 5. Predecessor FEIN _____

6. Name of predecessor: _____

7. Did you acquire the assets of the predecessor's business? ☐ Yes ☐ No

8. Did you acquire all or part of the predecessor's business? ☐ All ☐ Part

   If part, please explain: _____

9. Please check major assets acquired:

   ☐ Place of business ☐ Workforce ☐ License

   ☐ Customers ☐ Goodwill ☐ Franchise rights

   ☐ Trade name ☐ Stock ☐ Other

   ☐ Accounts receivable ☐ Tools, fixtures, equipment, furniture

10. Did you continue the operation of business that you acquired? ☐ Yes ☐ No

11. Brief summary of business reason(s) for this acquisition _____

12. Will the predecessor remain in business in Massachusetts?

    ☐ Yes If yes, list the present Massachusetts location of the predecessor. _____

    If yes, state the number of employees to remain with predecessor in Massachusetts after the date of succession. _____

    ☐ No If no, please give the date of the predecessor's final payroll. (mm/dd/yy) _____

13. Has the predecessor employer filed all quarterly reports and paid all contributions, interest, and penalties due to this Agency?

    ☐ Yes ☐ No ☐ Unknown

SECTION III PLEASE SELECT WHICH EMPLOYMENT TYPE LISTED BELOW BEST DESCRIBES YOUR BUSINESS

1. **DOMESTIC EMPLOYERS** (Services performed in the home such as: gardener, personal care attendant, baby sitter, housekeeper, etc.)

   Did you pay $1,000 or more in cash remuneration in any calendar quarter during the current or preceding calendar year for domestic services? ☐ Yes ☐ No

2. **AGRICULTURAL EMPLOYERS** (Services performed on a farm including stock, dairy, poultry, fruit, fur bearing animals, and truck farms, plantations, ranches, nurseries, ranges, orchards, greenhouses, and other similar structures that are used primarily for raising of agricultural and horticultural commodities.)

   Did you pay $20,000 or more in cash remuneration for agricultural services during any calendar quarter of the current or preceding calendar year? ☐ Yes ☐ No

   Did you employ 10 or more individuals on some day in each of 20 calendar weeks, not necessarily consecutive, in either the current or preceding calendar year? ☐ Yes ☐ No

   If you do not meet the agricultural requirements but have a farm-based retail operation that includes the sale of items other than those produced on your farm, you are <u>not</u> an agricultural employer. Please proceed to question #3 (all other employers).

3. ALL OTHER MASSACHUSETTS EMPLOYERS

Did you pay wages of $1,500 or more in any calendar quarter in either the current or preceding calendar year? ☒ Yes ☐ No

Did you employ one or more individuals on some day in each of 13 weeks, not necessarily consecutive, in either the current or preceding calendar quarter? ☒ Yes ☐ No

4. OUT-OF-STATE EMPLOYERS

Did you have a MASSACHUSETTS payroll in excess of $200? ☐ Yes ☐ No

5. PLEASE DO NOT SUBMIT UNTIL YOU ARE ABLE TO DOCUMENT ACTUAL GROSS WAGES PAID PER THE ABOVE REPORTING CRITERIA

List below the number of individuals in your employment in Massachusetts within each calendar week. Include full and part-time employees, also paid officers, if corporation. An individual sole proprietor or a partner should not be counted as an employee. Show total Massachusetts payroll for each calendar quarter.

This application cannot be processed with estimated or anticipated future wages. If this application is not completed in full it will be returned to you for the required information (i.e.: number of employees, dates of employment, gross wages).

RECORD OF MASSACHUSETTS EMPLOYMENT

	CURRENT CALENDAR YEAR	PRECEDING CALENDAR YEAR	PRECEDING CALENDAR YEAR
	Enter Year 2007	Enter Year _____	Enter Year _____
	Total Wages 1st QTR 25000 2nd QTR _____	Total Wages 1st QTR _____ 2nd QTR _____	Total Wages 1st QTR _____ 2nd QTR _____

	JANUARY		APRIL	JANUARY		APRIL	JANUARY		APRIL	
Week Ending	19	26								
Number Employed	4	4								

	FEBRUARY				MAY	FEBRUARY				MAY	FEBRUARY				MAY
Week Ending	02	09	16	23											
Number Employed	4	5	5	5											

	MARCH					JUNE	MARCH					JUNE	MARCH					JUNE
Week Ending	02	09	16	23	30													
Number Employed	4	5	5	5	5													

	Total Wages 3rd QTR _____ 4th QTR _____	Total Wages 3rd QTR _____ 4th QTR _____	Total Wages 3rd QTR _____ 4th QTR _____

	JULY	OCTOBER	JULY	OCTOBER	JULY	OCTOBER
Week Ending						
Number Employed						

	AUGUST	NOVEMBER	AUGUST	NOVEMBER	AUGUST	NOVEMBER
Week Ending						
Number Employed						

	SEPTEMBER	DECEMBER	SEPTEMBER	DECEMBER	SEPTEMBER	DECEMBER
Week Ending						
Number Employed						

CERTIFICATION

If you answered yes to Question 1 in Section II and if this organizational change involves companies with any commonality in ownership, management and/or control, you must proceed to Section IV. If not, please complete the certification below.

Massachusetts law provides for civil fines and criminal penalties for misrepresentation, evasion, willful nondisclosure, and failure or refusal to furnish reports or requested information to this agency. Both the employer of record or the agent, who knowingly advises in such a way that results in a violation of these provisions, shall be subject to said penalties. (MGL Ch 151A, Section 14N). Failure to comply with all reporting and payment requirements under MGL Chapter 151A may result in loss of your organization's right to operate or renew your license by the Commonwealth of Massachusetts.

THIS REPORT MUST BE SIGNED BY THE OWNER, PARTNER, OR CORPORATE OFFICER

CERTIFICATION

I certify, under penalties of law, that all statements made hereon are true to the best of my knowledge and belief.

Name of Employing unit: __Make My Day, Inc.__   Date: __03/31/07__

Signature: _____   Title: __President__

Name: (Print) __Tough Guy__

PREDECESSOR CERTIFICATION

I hereby certify that all information submitted by the successor is true in accordance with the transfer.

Name of Predecessor Company: _____   Date _____

Signature: _____   Title _____

Name: (Print) _____

DO NOT COMPLETE COMMON OWNERSHIP SECTION UNLESS TRANSFERS OCCURRED ON OR AFTER JANUARY 1, 2006.

SECTION IV	PART A	COMMON OWNERSHIP

To be completed by the TRANSFEREE employer initiating the change. Please note that by signing this document the transferring employer must attest to these answers.

(Transferee employer- one to whom a conveyance of title or property is made; a person/entity to whom something is transferred or conveyed. Example, Company B acquires part or all of the business of Company A. In this example Company B is the transferee employer and Company A is the transferring employer or transferor).

Is the transferee employer the Parent Company or a subsidiary of the transferring employer? ☐ Yes ☐ No

If yes, please list the name of the Parent Company and FEIN#

Name: _____ FEIN: _____

If yes, are the transferee employer and the transferring employer subsidiaries of the same Parent Company? ☐ Yes ☐ No

If yes, please list the name of the Parent Company and FEIN#

Name: _____ FEIN: _____

PLEASE CHECK OFF WHICH ORGANIZATIONAL TYPE BEST DESCRIBES YOUR BUSINESS AND ANSWER THE QUESTIONS LISTED FOLLOWING THAT ORGANIZATION TYPE:

1. **ORGANIZATIONAL TYPE**

   ☐ CORPORATION
   (includes Limited Liability Companies (LLC) organized as a corporation)

   Is there a person, corporation or other legal entity that serves in the capacity of Chief Financial Officer (CFO), Chief Executive Officer (CEO) or other similar authority for the transferring employer who also serves as the CFO or CEO or other person holding similar authority for the transferee employer?

   ☐ Yes ☐ No   *If yes, list the name/entity, SS#/FEIN and title below*

   Name _____ SS# _____ Title _____

   If Entity acts as CFO/CEO:

   Company Name: _____ FEIN# _____

   Does either the transferee or the transferring employer exercise power indirectly or directly through one or more persons of over 25% or more of any voting securities of BOTH the transferring employer and the transferee?

   ☐ Yes ☐ No   *If yes, list the name/entity, FEIN and the percentage of ownership*

   Name/Entity _____ % of ownership _____ SS# _____ FEIN# _____

   Does the CFO, CEO or other person holding similar authority for the transferring employer have a familial relationship with the CFO, CEO or other person holding a position of similar authority for the transferee employer?

   ☐ Yes ☐ No   *If yes, please list name, SS#, (title and relationship)*

   Name _____ SS# _____ Title _____ Relationship _____
   Name _____ SS# _____ Title _____ Relationship _____

2. ☐ SOLE PROPRIETOR
   (includes LLCs organized as a single member)

   Does the transferee employer's sole proprietor/owner have a familial relationship to the transferring employer's sole proprietor/owner?

   (Family member is defined but not limited to spouse, child, parent, sister, brother, sister-in-law, brother-in-law, aunt, uncle, niece, nephew, and first cousin.)

   ☐ Yes ☐ No   *If yes, please list name, SS# and relationship*

   Name _____ SS# _____ Relationship _____
   Name _____ SS# _____ Relationship _____

3. ☐ PARTNERSHIPS, JOINT VENTURES
(includes LLP, LLC organized as a partnership)

Is there a person, corporation or other legal entity that serves in the capacity of a managing partner in both the transferring employer and the transferee employer?

☐ Yes ☐ No   *If yes, please list name/entity, SS# /FEIN# and title*

Name _____ SS# _____ Title _____

If Entity acts as Managing Partner:

Company Name: _____ FEIN# _____

Does a partner for the transferring employer have a familial relationship to any partner, member or other person holding a position of authority for the transferee employer?

☐ Yes ☐ No   *If yes please list name, SS#, title and relationship*

Name _____ SS# _____ Title _____

Relationship _____

4. ☐ TRUST

Does one person, corporation or other legal entity serve as a trustee of the transferring trust, either directly or through an intermediary, and also serve as a trustee in the transferee trust, or as a beneficiary of the trust?

☐ Yes ☐ No

Name _____ SS# _____ Title _____

If Entity serves as trustee:

Company Name: _____ FEIN# _____

If you answered yes to any of the above questions, please complete Section IV Part B

SECTION IV	PART B	COMMON OWNERSHIP

Complete the following:

1. The business address of your corporate HQ: _____

2. Name of business transferred: _____

3. Transferor's DUA account number: _____

4. Transferor's business location: _____

5. Date of transfer: _____

6. Number of workers employed by transferor in Massachusetts just before the sale _____

   after the sale _____

7. Number of workers employed by you, the transferee, in Massachusetts just before the sale _____

   after the sale _____

8. How many of the transferor workers have you continued to employ? _____

   have you NOT continued to employ? _____

You must complete Section IV Part C if you took over part of another business operating in Massachusetts

SECTION IV	PART C	PART SUCCESSIONS

9. Is the transferor still doing business in MA?   ☐ Yes ☐ No ☐ Unknown

   If yes what business activities are continued? _____

(Note: Transferee may become liable for some or all of any DUA delinquency of the transferor)

This application must be accompanied by a schedule showing the name and social security number of each individual associated with that portion of the business being transferred, regardless of whether or not they are actually transferred to the transferee employer.

PLEASE SUMMARIZE ALL WAGE INFORMATION IN CHARTS A AND B ON THIS FORM. DO NOT JUST ATTACH PREVIOUSLY FILED FORMS 1. IN ADDITION, PLEASE COMPLETE EVERY APPLICABLE ITEM ON THIS FORM. FAILURE TO DO SO COMPLETELY, ACCURATELY, AND IN A TIMELY MANNER MAY RESULT IN PENALTIES FOR FAILURE TO COMPLY WITH THE LAW, AS PROVIDED FOR UNDER MGL, CH 151A, SECTION 14N.

Please provide, in Chart A, the transferring employer's entire payroll for the last 4 completed quarters prior to the transfer date.
In Chart B, provide the transferring employer's payroll for that portion acquired for the last 4 completed quarters prior to the transfer date.
Please provide dates of quarters (mo, day, yr) to which you are referring in the charts below.

EXAMPLE

Date transfer took place: 04/01/06

Chart A

*PLEASE PROVIDE **TOTAL** WAGES FOR ALL EMPLOYEES OF THE TRANSFERRING EMPLOYER FOR THE LAST 4 COMPLETED QUARTERS PRIOR TO THE TRANSFER DATE.*

PLEASE START WITH THE MOST RECENT QUARTER AND WORK BACK IN TIME.

Quarter dates	(1/01/06-3/31/06)	(10/01/05-12/31/05)	(7/01/05-9/30/05)	(4/01/05 -6/30/05)	12 Month Summary
Total Wages	$ 60,000	$ 75,500	$ 67,500	$ 67,500	$ 270,500
Excess Wages	$ 0.00	$ 67,500	$ 61,000	$ 8,000	$ 136,500
(wages over $14,000 wage base per employee)					
Taxable Wages	$ 60,000	$ 7,500	$ 6,500	$ 59,500	$ 133,500
Number of employees	8, 8, 8	10, 10, 10	9, 9, 9	9, 9, 9	

who worked during or received pay for the payroll period which includes the **12th** day of the month.

Chart B

*PLEASE PROVIDE WAGE DETAIL FOR **THAT PORTION ACQUIRED** OF THE TRANSFERRING EMPLOYER'S PAYROLL FOR THE LAST 4 COMPLETED QUARTERS PRIOR TO THE TRANSFER DATE.*

PLEASE START WITH THE MOST RECENT QUARTER AND WORK BACK IN TIME.

Quarter dates	(1/01/06-3/31/06)	(10/01/05-12/31/05)	(7/01/05-9/30/05)	(4/01/05 -6/30/05)	12 Month Summary
Total Wages	$ 37,500	$ 30,000	$ 37,500	$ 37,500	$ 142,500
Excess Wages	$ 0.00	$ 30,000	$ 37,500	$ 5,000	$ 72,500
(wages over $14,000 wage base per employee)					
Taxable Wages	$ 37,500	$ 0.00	$ 0.00	$ 32,500	$ 70,000
Number of employees	4, 4, 4	5, 5, 5	5, 5, 5	6, 6, 6	

who worked during or received pay for the payroll period which includes the **12th** day of the month..

Chart A

Date transfer took place: _____

*PLEASE PROVIDE **TOTAL** WAGES FOR ALL EMPLOYEES OF THE TRANSFERRING EMPLOYER FOR THE LAST 4 COMPLETED QUARTERS PRIOR TO THE TRANSFER DATE.*

PLEASE START WITH THE MOST RECENT QUARTER AND WORK BACK IN TIME.

Quarter dates	(-)	(-)	(-)	(-)	12 Month Summary
Total Wages	$_____	$_____	$_____	$_____	$_____
Excess Wages	$_____	$_____	$_____	$_____	$_____
(wages over $14,000 wage base per employee)					
Taxable Wages	$_____	$_____	$_____	$_____	$_____
Number of employees	_____	_____	_____	_____	

who worked during or received pay for the payroll period which includes the **12th** day of the month.

Chart B

*PLEASE PROVIDE WAGE DETAIL FOR **THAT PORTION ACQUIRED** OF THE TRANSFERRING EMPLOYER'S PAYROLL FOR THE LAST 4 COMPLETED QUARTERS PRIOR TO THE TRANSFER DATE.*

PLEASE START WITH THE MOST RECENT QUARTER AND WORK BACK IN TIME.

Quarter dates	(-)	(-)	(-)	(-)	12 Month Summary
Total Wages	$_____	$_____	$_____	$_____	$_____
Excess Wages	$_____	$_____	$_____	$_____	$_____
(wages over $14,000 wage base per employee)					
Taxable Wages	$_____	$_____	$_____	$_____	$_____
Number of employees	_____	_____	_____	_____	

who worked during or received pay for the payroll period which includes the **12th** day of the month.

CERTIFICATION

Massachusetts law provides for civil fines and criminal penalties for misrepresentation, evasion, willful nondisclosure, and failure or refusal to furnish reports or requested information to this agency. Both the employer of record or the agent, who knowingly advises in such a way that results in a violation of these provisions, shall be subject to said penalties. (MGL Ch 151A, Section 14N). Failure to comply with all reporting and payment requirements under MGL Chapter 151A may result in loss of your organization's right to operate or renew your license by the Commonwealth of Massachusetts.

THIS REPORT MUST BE SIGNED BY THE OWNER, PARTNER, OR CORPORATE OFFICER AUTHORIZED TO BIND THE CORPORATION.

SUCCESSOR CERTIFICATION

I certify, under penalties of law, that all statements made here on are true to the best of my knowledge and belief.

Name of Employing unit; _____ Date: _____

Signature: _____ Title: _____

Name (Print): _____

PREDECESSOR CERTIFICATION

I hereby certify that all information submitted by the successor is true in accordance with the transfer.

Name of Predecessor Company: _____ Date _____

Signature: _____ Title _____

Name: (Print) _____

Form NHR
New Hire and Independent
Contractor Reporting Form

Rev. 03/07
Massachusetts
Department of
Revenue

TO ENSURE ACCURACY, PRINT (OR TYPE) NEATLY IN UPPER-CASE LETTERS AND NUMBERS, USING A DARK, BALLPOINT PEN.

Employee Information

FIRST NAME*

Cheryl

MI

LAST NAME*

Haley

SOCIAL SECURITY NUMBER*

123 - 45 - 6789

DATE OF HIRE OR REINSTATEMENT*

11 / 01 / 2007

ADDRESS*

3 Pleasant Street

CITY/TOWN*

Natick

STATE*

MA

ZIP*

22222

+4 (OPTIONAL)

IT'S THE LAW! - Massachusetts regulations requires employers with 25 or more employees to report their new hires and independent contractors electronically.

For more information, go to www.mass.gov/dor and select the **Report New Hires** link located in the **Online Services** section.

Employer Information

EMPLOYER IDENTIFICATION NUMBER*

20 - 9999999

CORPORATE NAME*

Myboss, Inc.

PAYROLL ADDRESS TO WHICH THE INCOME WITHHOLDING ORDER WILL BE SENT*

2 River Street

PAYROLL ADDRESS (Continued)

CITY/TOWN*

Wellesley

STATE*

MA

ZIP*

00000

+4 (OPTIONAL)

NOTE: All fields on this form with an * are mandatory fields. Please ensure all information entered is legible and accurate prior to submitting the form to DOR.

Helpful Hint: Once you have completed your employer information, you may copy this form to save time when reporting future new hires and independent contractors.

Send Completed Form NHR to:
Massachusetts Department of Revenue, PO Box 55141, Boston, MA 02205-5141 or,
you may fax the completed form to 617-376-3262.

This page intentionally blank

Appendix B: Tax Timetable and Ready-to-Use Forms

The following forms may be photocopied or removed from this book and used immediately. Some of the tax forms explained in this book are not included here because you should use original returns provided by the IRS (940, 941) or the Massachusetts Department of Revenue (quarterly unemployment compensation form). Be sure to check with the proper authorities in case there are any additional requirements.

There are also several forms available to fill out online for free at:

The Offical Website of the Commonwealth of Massachusetts
www.mass.gov

This government website provides free official forms for you to form your business, reserve your business name, obtain a Federal Employee Identification Number, and obtain a Certificate of Good Standing. Some of them are also included here.

FORM 1: TAX TIMETABLE 227

FORM 2: APPLICATION OF RESERVATION OF NAME
If a corporation wants to reserve a corporate name before legally incorporating, this form needs to be filed. 229

FORM 3: CERTIFICATE STATING REAL NAME
    OF PERSON TRANSACTING BUSINESS 231

FORM 4: TRADEMARK/SERVICE MARK APPLICATION 233

FORM 5: ARTICLES OF ORGANIZAITON
    A corporation does not legally exist until this form
    is filed with the state..................................... 237

FORM 6: STATEMENT OF APPOINTMENT OF REGISTERED AGENT
    Corporations must always maintain a registered office
    and registered agent in the state.......................... 241

FORM 7: EMPLOYMENT ELIGIBILITY VERIFICATION (FORM I-9).......... 243

FORM 8: APPLICATION FOR EMPLOYER IDENTIFICATION NUMBER
    (IRS FORM SS-4) 247

FORM 9: DETERMINATION OF WORKER STATUS
    (IRS FORM SS-8)... 249

FORM 10: EMPLOYEE'S WITHHOLDING ALLOWANCE CERTIFICATE
    (IRS FORM W-4).. 255

FORM 11: EMPLOYER STATUS REPORT (1110-A) 257

FORM 12: NEW HIRE AND INDEPENDENT CONTRACTOR
    REPORTING FORM (FORM NHR)............................. 265

MASSACHUSETTS TAX TIMETABLE

	SALES			WITHHOLDING			MEALS	CORPORATE EXCISE	UNEMPLOY. INSURANCE
	Monthly filers	Quarterly filers	Annual filers	Monthly filers	Quarterly filers	Annual filers		(Assumes Fiscal Yr. = Cal.Yr.)	
JAN.	20th	20th	20th	31st	31st	31st	20th		30th
FEB.	20th			15th			20th		
MAR.	20th			15th			20th	40% estimated 15th	
APR.	20th	20th		30th	30th		20th		30th
MAY	20th			15th			20th		
JUN.	20th			15th			20th	25% estimated 15th	
JUL.	20th			31st	31st		20th		30th
AUG.	20th			15th			20th		
SEP.	20th			15th			20th	25% estimated 15th	
OCT.	20th	20th		31st	31st		20th		30th
NOV.	20th			15th			20th		
DEC.	20th			15th			20th	10% estimated 15th	

FEDERAL TAX TIMETABLE

	ESTIMATED PAYMENT	ANNUAL RETURN	FORM 941*	MISC.
JAN.	15th		31st	31st 940 W-2 508 1099
FEB.				28th W-3
MAR.		15th Corp. & Partnership		30th 508
APR.	15th		30th	
MAY				
JUN.	15th	15th Personal		
JUL.			31st	31st 508
AUG.				
SEP.	15th			
OCT.			31st	31st 508
NOV.				
DEC.				

* In addition to form 941, deposits must be made regularly if withholding exceeds $500 in any month.

The Commonwealth of Massachusetts

William Francis Galvin

Secretary of the Commonwealth

One Ashburton Place, Boston, Massachusetts 02108-1512

FORM MUST BE TYPED   **Application of Reservation of Name**   FORM MUST BE TYPED

(General Laws, Chapter 156D, Section 4.02; 950 CMR 113.18)

Filing Fee: $30.00

(1) Name of applicant: _____

(2) Address of applicant: _____

(3) Name to be reserved: _____

Applicant Contact Information:

Telephone: _____

Email: _____

Check # : _____

THIS FORM MAY NOT BE SUBMITTED BY FAX. PLEASE SUBMIT IN PERSON OR BY MAIL.

This page intentionally blank

CITY OF _____
MASSACHUSETTS

Certificate Stating Real Name of Person Transacting Business

Date: _____

To the City Clerk:

In conformity with the provisions of MGL chapter 110, Section 5, Notice is hereby given that business is being conducted under the name of:

Business name: _____

Proposed Use (please describe): _____

Location of Business: _____

The nearest cross street: _____and_____

The full name and address of each person conducting such business:

Name: _____ Address: _____

Name: _____ Address: _____

Name: _____ Address: _____

Signed: _____

_____

_____

_____

_____, SS   Date: _____

Then personally appeared the above named: _____

(affix seal here)

_____

and made oath that the foregoing are true before me,

Signed: _____

Title: _____

Please indicate here if the business in a "home business": **YES/NO** (circle one)

PLEASE NOTE: If the proposed business is to be located in a residence you must first go to the Inspectional Services Department and fill out a "Home Business Affidavit" thereby acknowledging compliance with the Home Business Ordinance.

I hereby certify that the above business address is in the following zoning district, and is an allowed use in accordance with the Revised Zoning Ordinances of the City of _____.

Zoning District: _____   Attest: _____
                                                     Inspectional Services Dept.
                                                             Official

Received: Date: _____   Time: _____

and entered in Records of Business Titles in the City Clerk's Office in the City of _____.

Book: _____   Page: _____

_____

_____ City Clerk

TM
SM

The Commonwealth of Massachusetts
William Francis Galvin
Secretary of the Commonwealth
One Ashburton Place, Boston, Massachusetts 02108-1512

Filing Fee $50.00 per class
5 year registration period

FORM MUST BE TYPED

Trademark / Service Mark Application
(General Laws Chapter 110H, Section 3)

FORM MUST BE TYPED

All information must be completed or this document will not be accepted for filing.

(1) Applicant's name and business address:

a) Individual: _____

Last	*First*	*Middle*

Business address: _____

Number	*Street*

City	*State*	*Zip*

or

b) Business Organization:_____

Business address: _____

Number	*Street*

City	*State*	*Zip*

(2) If applicant is a business, identify type (check box), and if applicable, state and date of organization:

☐ corporation   ☐ limited liability company   ☐ limited partnership   ☐ partnership   ☐ sole proprietor

☐ other _____
(indicate entity type)

a) State of incorporation or organization: _____   b) Date of incorporation or organization: _____

(3) If applicant is a partnership, state the names of the general partners:

(4) Applicant is seeking to register (check box):

☐ Trademark   ☐ Service Mark

(5) The mark is (complete one of the following):

a) **Words only** - If the mark is only words, the words in the mark are (include type style if it is claimed as part of the mark):

b) **Design Only** - If the mark is a design only, describe the design (include colors if they are claimed as part of the mark):

c) **Words and Design** - State the words in the mark (include color and type style if they are claimed as part of the mark) and describe the design:

(6) Describe briefly the goods or services used in connection with the mark:

(7) For each class provide the number and class in which such goods or services fall (see attached classification schedule): *(An application may include multiple classes)*

(8) Describe briefly how the mark is used in connection with such goods or services:

a) The mark is used by displaying it (check box):

☐ on documents, wrappers, or articles delivered with the goods
☐ in advertisements of the services
☐ in connection with the services rendered
☐ other

b) If other, describe briefly how the mark is used:

(9) The trademark or service-mark has been used by the applicant, or the applicant's predecessor in business, since

_____ and in the Commonwealth of Massachusetts since_____ .

        (month, day, year)   *(month, day, year)*

(If first use of the mark anywhere was in Massachusetts, use the same date for both.).

(10) a) Has the applicant or predecessor in interest filed an application for the same mark or portions of the same mark with the U.S. Patent and Trademark Office? ☐ Yes ☐ No

    b) If yes, for each application, provide (using additional pages if necessary):

        Filing date _____ and serial number _____ .

                               (month, day, year)

    c) What is the status of the application (check box)?   ☐ awaiting examination   ☐ refusal (office action) issued

                                                          ☐ approved for publication   ☐ registered

                                                           ☐ abandoned/withdrawn

    d) If finally refused, or not resulted in a registration, give reason: _____

(11) Attach a sample showing the mark as actively used. The sample specimen may not be larger than 3" x 3".

The applicant is the owner of the mark. The mark is in use, and, to the knowledge of the person verifying the application, no other person has registered, either federally or in this state, or has the right to use such mark either in the identical form thereof or in such near resemblance thereto as to be likely, when applied to the goods or services of such other person, to cause confusion, or to cause mistake, or to deceive.

I, _____ , state that I am the applicant or a lawfully authorized

          (Name of Applicant / Authorized Representative)

representative of the applicant and declare under penalty of perjury that the foregoing application is true and correct.

Executed on: _____

                                   (Month, Day, Year)

Signature: _____

COMMONWEALTH OF MASSACHUSETTS

William Francis Galvin
Secretary of the Commonwealth
One Ashburton Place, Boston, Massachusetts 02108-1512

Trademark / Service Mark Application
(General Laws Chapter 110H, Section 3)

Registered with

WILLIAM FRANCIS GALVIN
Secretary of the Commonwealth

on:

_____ , 20 _____

Trademark Section
One Ashburton Place, Rm. 1717
Boston, MA 02108

Contact Information

_____
Name

_____
Mailing Address

_____
City/town   *State*   *ZIP*

_____
Telephone   *Email*

D

The Commonwealth of Massachusetts

William Francis Galvin
Secretary of the Commonwealth
One Ashburton Place, Boston, Massachusetts 02108-1512

Articles of Organization
(General Laws Chapter 156D, Section 2.02; 950 CMR 113.16)

ARTICLE I
The exact name of the corporation is:

ARTICLE II
Unless the articles of organization otherwise provide, all corporations formed pursuant to G.L. Chapter 156D have the purpose of engaging in any lawful business. Please specify if you want a more limited purpose:

ARTICLE III
State the total number of shares and par value, * if any, of each class of stock that the corporation is authorized to issue. All corporations must authorize stock. If only one class or series is authorized, it is not necessary to specify any particular designation.

WITHOUT PAR VALUE		WITH PAR VALUE		
TYPE	NUMBER OF SHARES	TYPE	NUMBER OF SHARES	PAR VALUE

*G.L. Chapter 156D eliminates the concept of par value, however a corporation may specify par value in Article III. See G.L. Chapter 156D, Section 6.21, and the comments relative thereto.

ARTICLE IV

Prior to the issuance of shares of any class or series, the articles of organization must set forth the preferences, limitations and relative rights of that class or series. The articles may also limit the type or specify the minimum amount of consideration for which shares of any class or series may be issued. Please set forth the preferences, limitations and relative rights of each class or series and, if desired, the required type and minimum amount of consideration to be received.

ARTICLE V

The restrictions, if any, imposed by the articles of organization upon the transfer of shares of any class or series of stock are:

ARTICLE VI

Other lawful provisions, and if there are no such provisions, this article may be left blank.

Note: The preceding six (6) articles are considered to be permanent and may be changed only by filing appropriate articles of amendment.

ARTICLE VII

The effective date of organization of the corporation is the date and time the articles were received for filing if the articles are not rejected within the time prescribed by law. If a later effective date is desired, specify such date, which may not be later than the 90th day after the articles are received for filing:

ARTICLE VIII

The information contained in this article is not a permanent part of the articles of organization.

    a.   The street address of the initial registered office of the corporation in the commonwealth:

    b.   The name of its initial registered agent at its registered office:

    c.   The names and street addresses of the individuals who will serve as the initial directors, president, treasurer and secretary of the corporation (an address need not be specified if the business address of the officer or director is the same as the principal office location):

President

Treasurer

Secretary

Director(s):

    d.   The fiscal year end of the corporation:

    e.   A brief description of the type of business in which the corporation intends to engage:

    f.   The street address of the principal office of the corporation:

    g.   The street address where the records of the corporation required to be kept in the commonwealth are located is:

_ , which is

(number, street, city or town, state, zip code)

☐ its principal office;
☐ an office of its transfer agent;
☐ an office of its secretary/assistant secretary;
☐ its registered office.

Signed this _____ day of _____ , _____ by the incorporator(s):

Signature: _____

Name:

Address:

COMMONWEALTH OF MASSACHUSETTS

William Francis Galvin
Secretary of the Commonwealth
One Ashburton Place, Boston, Massachusetts 02108-1512

Articles of Organization
(General Laws Chapter 156D, Section 2.02; 950 CMR 113.16)

I hereby certify that upon examination of these articles of organization, duly submitted to me, it appears that the provisions of the General Laws relative to the organization of corporations have been complied with, and I hereby approve said articles; and the filing fee in the amount of $_____ having been paid, said articles are deemed to have been filed with me this _____ day of _____, 20____, at _____ a.m./p.m.

time

Effective date: _____

(must be within 90 days of date submitted)

WILLIAM FRANCIS GALVIN
Secretary of the Commonwealth

_____
Examiner

_____
Name approval

_____
C

_____
M

Filing fee: $275 for up to 275,000 shares plus $100 for each additional 100,000 shares or any fraction thereof.

TO BE FILLED IN BY CORPORATION
Contact Information:

Telephone: _____

Email: _____

Upon filing, a copy of this filing will be available at www.sec.state.ma.us/cor.
If the document is rejected, a copy of the rejection sheet and rejected document will be available in the rejected queue.

D PC

The Commonwealth of Massachusetts
William Francis Galvin
Secretary of the Commonwealth
One Ashburton Place, Boston, Massachusetts 02108-1512

FORM MUST BE TYPED

Statement of Appointment
of Registered Agent
(General Law, Chapter 156D, Section 5.01; 950 CMR 113.20)

FORM MUST BE TYPED

Exact name of corporation: _____

Registered office address: _____

(number, street, city or town, state, zip code)

Appoints as registered agent: _____

(name of registered agent)

The street address of the registered office of the corporation and the business address of the registered agent are identical as required by G.L., Chapter 156D, Section 5.02.

This certificate is effective at the time and on the date approved by the Division, unless a later effective date not more than 90 days from the date of filing is specified: _____

Signed by: _____,

(signature of authorized individual)

☐ Chairman of the board of directors,

☐ President,

☐ Other officer,

☐ Court-appointed fiduciary,

on this _____ day of _____   ___, _____ ___

Consent of registered agent:

I, _____,
registered agent of the above corporation, consent to my appointment as registered agent pursuant to G.L. Chapter 156D, Section 5.02.*

or attach registered agent's consent hereto.

COMMONWEALTH OF MASSACHUSETTS

William Francis Galvin
Secretary of the Commonwealth
One Ashburton Place, Boston, Massachusetts 02108-1512

Statement of Appointment
of Registered Agent
(General Law, Chapter 156D, Section 5.01; 950 CMR 113.20)

I hereby certify that upon examination of this statement of appointment, duly submitted to me, it appears that the provisions of the General Laws relative to the organization of corporations have been complied with, and I hereby approve said statement; and the filing fee in the amount of $_____ having been paid, said statement is deemed to have been filed with me this _____ day of _____, 20_____ , at _____a.m./p.m.

time

Effective date:_____

(must be within 90 days of date submitted)

WILLIAM FRANCIS GALVIN
Secretary of the Commonwealth

Filing fee: $25 for paper or fax filings.
No fee if filed electronically.

TO BE FILLED IN BY CORPORATION
Contact Information:

Telephone: _____

Email: _____

Upon filing, a copy of this filing will be available at www.sec.state.ma.us/cor.
If the document is rejected, a copy of the rejection sheet and rejected document will be available in the rejected queue.

OMB No. 1615-0047; Expires 06/30/08

Department of Homeland Security
U.S. Citizenship and Immigration Services

Form I-9, Employment Eligibility Verification

Instructions
Please read all instructions carefully before completing this form.

Anti-Discrimination Notice. It is illegal to discriminate against any individual (other than an alien not authorized to work in the U.S.) in hiring, discharging, or recruiting or referring for a fee because of that individual's national origin or citizenship status. It is illegal to discriminate against work eligible individuals. Employers **CANNOT** specify which document(s) they will accept from an employee. The refusal to hire an individual because the documents presented have a future expiration date may also constitute illegal discrimination.

What Is the Purpose of This Form?

The purpose of this form is to document that each new employee (both citizen and non-citizen) hired after November 6, 1986 is authorized to work in the United States.

When Should the Form I-9 Be Used?

All employees, citizens and noncitizens, hired after November 6, 1986 and working in the United States must complete a Form I-9.

Filling Out the Form I-9

Section 1, Employee: This part of the form must be completed at the time of hire, which is the actual beginning of employment. Providing the Social Security number is voluntary, except for employees hired by employers participating in the USCIS Electronic Employment Eligibility Verification Program (E-Verify). **The employer is responsible for ensuring that Section 1 is timely and properly completed.**

Preparer/Translator Certification. The Preparer/Translator Certification must be completed if **Section 1** is prepared by a person other than the employee. A preparer/translator may be used only when the employee is unable to complete **Section 1** on his/her own. However, the employee must still sign **Section 1** personally.

Section 2, Employer: For the purpose of completing this form, the term "employer" means all employers including those recruiters and referrers for a fee who are agricultural associations, agricultural employers or farm labor contractors.

Employers must complete **Section 2** by examining evidence of identity and employment eligibility within three (3) business days of the date employment begins. If employees are authorized to work, but are unable to present the required document(s) within three business days, they must present a receipt for the application of the document(s) within three business days and the actual document(s) within ninety (90) days. However, if employers hire individuals for a duration of less than three business days, **Section 2** must be completed at the time employment begins. **Employers must record:**

1. Document title;
2. Issuing authority;
3. Document number;
4. Expiration date, if any; and
5. The date employment begins.

Employers must sign and date the certification. Employees must present original documents. Employers may, but are not required to, photocopy the document(s) presented. These photocopies may only be used for the verification process and must be retained with the Form I-9. **However, employers are still responsible for completing and retaining the Form I-9.**

Section 3, Updating and Reverification: Employers must complete **Section 3** when updating and/or reverifying the Form I-9. Employers must reverify employment eligibility of their employees on or before the expiration date recorded in **Section 1**. Employers **CANNOT** specify which document(s) they will accept from an employee.

A. If an employee's name has changed at the time this form is being updated/reverified, complete Block A.

B. If an employee is rehired within three (3) years of the date this form was originally completed and the employee is still eligible to be employed on the same basis as previously indicated on this form (updating), complete Block B and the signature block.

C. If an employee is rehired within three (3) years of the date this form was originally completed and the employee's work authorization has expired **or** if a current employee's work authorization is about to expire (reverification), complete Block B and:

　1. Examine any document that reflects that the employee is authorized to work in the U.S. (see List A **or** C);

　2. Record the document title, document number and expiration date (if any) in Block C, and

　3. Complete the signature block.

What Is the Filing Fee?

There is no associated filing fee for completing the Form I-9. This form is not filed with USCIS or any government agency. The Form I-9 must be retained by the employer and made available for inspection by U.S. Government officials as specified in the Privacy Act Notice below.

USCIS Forms and Information

To order USCIS forms, call our toll-free number at **1-800-870-3676**. Individuals can also get USCIS forms and information on immigration laws, regulations and procedures by telephoning our National Customer Service Center at **1-800-375-5283** or visiting our internet website at **www.uscis.gov**.

Photocopying and Retaining the Form I-9

A blank Form I-9 may be reproduced, provided both sides are copied. The Instructions must be available to all employees completing this form. Employers must retain completed Forms I-9 for three (3) years after the date of hire or one (1) year after the date employment ends, whichever is later.

The Form I-9 may be signed and retained electronically, as authorized in Department of Homeland Security regulations at 8 CFR § 274a.2.

Privacy Act Notice

The authority for collecting this information is the Immigration Reform and Control Act of 1986, Pub. L. 99-603 (8 USC 1324a).

This information is for employers to verify the eligibility of individuals for employment to preclude the unlawful hiring, or recruiting or referring for a fee, of aliens who are not authorized to work in the United States.

This information will be used by employers as a record of their basis for determining eligibility of an employee to work in the United States. The form will be kept by the employer and made available for inspection by officials of U.S. Immigration and Customs Enforcement, Department of Labor and Office of Special Counsel for Immigration Related Unfair Employment Practices.

Submission of the information required in this form is voluntary. However, an individual may not begin employment unless this form is completed, since employers are subject to civil or criminal penalties if they do not comply with the Immigration Reform and Control Act of 1986.

Paperwork Reduction Act

We try to create forms and instructions that are accurate, can be easily understood and which impose the least possible burden on you to provide us with information. Often this is difficult because some immigration laws are very complex. Accordingly, the reporting burden for this collection of information is computed as follows: **1)** learning about this form, and completing the form, 9 minutes; **2)** assembling and filing (recordkeeping) the form, 3 minutes, for an average of 12 minutes per response. If you have comments regarding the accuracy of this burden estimate, or suggestions for making this form simpler, you can write to: U.S. Citizenship and Immigration Services, Regulatory Management Division, 111 Massachusetts Avenue, N.W., 3rd Floor, Suite 3008, Washington, DC 20529. OMB No. 1615-0047.

OMB No. 1615-0047; Expires 06/30/08

Department of Homeland Security
U.S. Citizenship and Immigration Services

Form I-9, Employment Eligibility Verification

Please read instructions carefully before completing this form. The instructions must be available during completion of this form.

ANTI-DISCRIMINATION NOTICE: It is illegal to discriminate against work eligible individuals. Employers CANNOT specify which document(s) they will accept from an employee. The refusal to hire an individual because the documents have a future expiration date may also constitute illegal discrimination.

Section 1. Employee Information and Verification. To be completed and signed by employee at the time employment begins.

Print Name: Last	First	Middle Initial	Maiden Name
Address *(Street Name and Number)*		Apt. #	Date of Birth *(month/day/year)*
City	State	Zip Code	Social Security #

I am aware that federal law provides for imprisonment and/or fines for false statements or use of false documents in connection with the completion of this form.

I attest, under penalty of perjury, that I am (check one of the following):
- [ ] A citizen or national of the United States
- [ ] A lawful permanent resident (Alien #) ^ _____
- [ ] An alien authorized to work until _____
  (Alien # or Admission #) _____

Employee's Signature	Date *(month/day/year)*

Preparer and/or Translator Certification. *(To be completed and signed if Section 1 is prepared by a person other than the employee.) I attest, under penalty of perjury, that I have assisted in the completion of this form and that to the best of my knowledge the information is true and correct.*

Preparer's/Translator's Signature	Print Name
Address *(Street Name and Number, City, State, Zip Code)*	Date *(month/day/year)*

Section 2. Employer Review and Verification. To be completed and signed by employer. Examine one document from List A OR examine one document from List B and one from List C, as listed on the reverse of this form, and record the title, number and expiration date, if any, of the document(s).

List A	OR	List B	AND	List C
Document title: _____		_____		_____
Issuing authority: _____		_____		_____
Document #: _____		_____		_____
Expiration Date *(if any):* _____		_____		_____
Document #: _____				
Expiration Date *(if any):* _____				

CERTIFICATION - I attest, under penalty of perjury, that I have examined the document(s) presented by the above-named employee, that the above-listed document(s) appear to be genuine and to relate to the employee named, that the employee began employment on *(month/day/year)* _____ **and that to the best of my knowledge the employee is eligible to work in the United States.   (State employment agencies may omit the date the employee began employment.)**

Signature of Employer or Authorized Representative	Print Name	Title
Business or Organization Name and Address *(Street Name and Number, City, State, Zip Code)*		Date *(month/day/year)*

Section 3. Updating and Reverification. To be completed and signed by employer.

A. New Name *(if applicable)*	B. Date of Rehire *(month/day/year) (if applicable)*

C. If employee's previous grant of work authorization has expired, provide the information below for the document that establishes current employment eligibility.

Document Title: _____	Document #: _____	Expiration Date (if any): _____

I attest, under penalty of perjury, that to the best of my knowledge, this employee is eligible to work in the United States, and if the employee presented document(s), the document(s) I have examined appear to be genuine and to relate to the individual.

Signature of Employer or Authorized Representative	Date *(month/day/year)*

Form I-9 (Rev. 06/05/07) N

LISTS OF ACCEPTABLE DOCUMENTS

LIST A		LIST B		LIST C
Documents that Establish Both Identity and Employment Eligibility	**OR**	**Documents that Establish Identity**	**AND**	**Documents that Establish Employment Eligibility**

LIST A	LIST B	LIST C
1. U.S. Passport (unexpired or expired)	1. Driver's license or ID card issued by a state or outlying possession of the United States provided it contains a photograph or information such as name, date of birth, gender, height, eye color and address	1. U.S. Social Security card issued by the Social Security Administration *(other than a card stating it is not valid for employment)*
2. Permanent Resident Card or Alien Registration Receipt Card (Form I-551)	2. ID card issued by federal, state or local government agencies or entities, provided it contains a photograph or information such as name, date of birth, gender, height, eye color and address	2. Certification of Birth Abroad issued by the Department of State *(Form FS-545 or Form DS-1350)*
3. An unexpired foreign passport with a temporary I-551 stamp	3. School ID card with a photograph	3. Original or certified copy of a birth certificate issued by a state, county, municipal authority or outlying possession of the United States bearing an official seal
4. An unexpired Employment Authorization Document that contains a photograph (Form I-766, I-688, I-688A, I-688B)	4. Voter's registration card	4. Native American tribal document
	5. U.S. Military card or draft record	5. U.S. Citizen ID Card *(Form I-197)*
5. An unexpired foreign passport with an unexpired Arrival-Departure Record, Form I-94, bearing the same name as the passport and containing an endorsement of the alien's nonimmigrant status, if that status authorizes the alien to work for the employer	6. Military dependent's ID card	6. ID Card for use of Resident Citizen in the United States *(Form I-179)*
	7. U.S. Coast Guard Merchant Mariner Card	
	8. Native American tribal document	7. Unexpired employment authorization document issued by DHS *(other than those listed under List A)*
	9. Driver's license issued by a Canadian government authority	
	For persons under age 18 who are unable to present a document listed above:	
	10. School record or report card	
	11. Clinic, doctor or hospital record	
	12. Day-care or nursery school record	

Illustrations of many of these documents appear in Part 8 of the Handbook for Employers (M-274)

Form **SS-4**
(Rev. July 2007)
Department of the Treasury
Internal Revenue Service

Application for Employer Identification Number

(For use by employers, corporations, partnerships, trusts, estates, churches,
government agencies, Indian tribal entities, certain individuals, and others.)

▶ See separate instructions for each line.   ▶ Keep a copy for your records.

OMB No. 1545-0003

EIN

Type or print clearly.

1	Legal name of entity (or individual) for whom the EIN is being requested

2	Trade name of business (if different from name on line 1)	3	Executor, administrator, trustee, "care of" name

4a	Mailing address (room, apt., suite no. and street, or P.O. box)	5a	Street address (if different) (Do not enter a P.O. box.)
4b	City, state, and ZIP code (if foreign, see instructions)	5b	City, state, and ZIP code (if foreign, see instructions)

6	County and state where principal business is located

7a	Name of principal officer, general partner, grantor, owner, or trustor	7b	SSN, ITIN, or EIN

8a	Is this application for a limited liability company (LLC) (or a foreign equivalent)? . . . . ☐ **Yes** ☐ **No**	8b	If 8a is "Yes," enter the number of LLC members . . . . ▶

8c If 8a is "Yes," was the LLC organized in the United States? . . . . ☐ **Yes** ☐ **No**

9a **Type of entity** (check only one box). **Caution.** If 8a is "Yes," see the instructions for the correct box to check.

☐ Sole proprietor (SSN) _____
☐ Partnership
☐ Corporation (enter form number to be filed) ▶_____
☐ Personal service corporation
☐ Church or church-controlled organization
☐ Other nonprofit organization (specify) ▶_____
☐ Other (specify) ▶

☐ Estate (SSN of decedent) _____
☐ Plan administrator (TIN) _____
☐ Trust (TIN of grantor) _____
☐ National Guard   ☐ State/local government
☐ Farmers' cooperative   ☐ Federal government/military
☐ REMIC   ☐ Indian tribal governments/enterprises
Group Exemption Number (GEN) if any ▶

9b	If a corporation, name the state or foreign country (if applicable) where incorporated	State	Foreign country

10 **Reason for applying** (check only one box)

☐ Started new business (specify type) ▶ _____
_____
☐ Hired employees (Check the box and see line 13.)
☐ Compliance with IRS withholding regulations
☐ Other (specify) ▶

☐ Banking purpose (specify purpose) ▶_____
☐ Changed type of organization (specify new type) ▶_____
☐ Purchased going business
☐ Created a trust (specify type) ▶ _____
☐ Created a pension plan (specify type) ▶ _____

11	Date business started or acquired (month, day, year). See instructions.	12	Closing month of accounting year

13	Highest number of employees expected in the next 12 months (enter -0- if none).	**14** Do you expect your employment tax liability to be $1,000 or less in a full calendar year? ☐ **Yes** ☐ **No** (If you expect to pay $4,000 or less in total wages in a full calendar year, you can mark "Yes.")
	Agricultural Household Other	

15 First date wages or annuities were paid (month, day, year). **Note.** If applicant is a withholding agent, enter date income will first be paid to nonresident alien (month, day, year) . . . . ▶

16 Check **one** box that best describes the principal activity of your business.
☐ Construction ☐ Rental & leasing ☐ Transportation & warehousing
☐ Real estate ☐ Manufacturing ☐ Finance & insurance
☐ Health care & social assistance ☐ Wholesale-agent/broker
☐ Accommodation & food service ☐ Wholesale-other ☐ Retail
☐ Other (specify)

17 Indicate principal line of merchandise sold, specific construction work done, products produced, or services provided.

18 Has the applicant entity shown on line 1 ever applied for and received an EIN? ☐ **Yes** ☐ **No**
If "Yes," write previous EIN here ▶

Third Party Designee	Complete this section **only** if you want to authorize the named individual to receive the entity's EIN and answer questions about the completion of this form.	
	Designee's name	Designee's telephone number (include area code) ( )
	Address and ZIP code	Designee's fax number (include area code) ( )

Under penalties of perjury, I declare that I have examined this application, and to the best of my knowledge and belief, it is true, correct, and complete.

Name and title (type or print clearly) ▶

Applicant's telephone number (include area code)
(   )

Applicant's fax number (include area code)
(   )

Signature ▶   Date ▶

For Privacy Act and Paperwork Reduction Act Notice, see separate instructions.   Cat. No. 16055N   Form **SS-4** (Rev. 7-2007)

Do I Need an EIN?

File Form SS-4 if the applicant entity does not already have an EIN but is required to show an EIN on any return, statement, or other document.[1] See also the separate instructions for each line on Form SS-4.

IF the applicant...	AND...	THEN...
Started a new business	Does not currently have (nor expect to have) employees	Complete lines 1, 2, 4a–8a, 8b–c (if applicable), 9a, 9b (if applicable), and 10–14 and 16–18.
Hired (or will hire) employees, including household employees	Does not already have an EIN	Complete lines 1, 2, 4a–6, 7a–b (if applicable), 8a, 8b–c (if applicable), 9a, 9b (if applicable), 10–18.
Opened a bank account	Needs an EIN for banking purposes only	Complete lines 1–5b, 7a–b (if applicable), 8a, 8b–c (if applicable), 9a, 9b (if applicable), 10, and 18.
Changed type of organization	Either the legal character of the organization or its ownership changed (for example, you incorporate a sole proprietorship or form a partnership)[2]	Complete lines 1–18 (as applicable).
Purchased a going business[3]	Does not already have an EIN	Complete lines 1–18 (as applicable).
Created a trust	The trust is other than a grantor trust or an IRA trust[4]	Complete lines 1–18 (as applicable).
Created a pension plan as a plan administrator[5]	Needs an EIN for reporting purposes	Complete lines 1, 3, 4a–5b, 9a, 10, and 18.
Is a foreign person needing an EIN to comply with IRS withholding regulations	Needs an EIN to complete a Form W-8 (other than Form W-8ECI), avoid withholding on portfolio assets, or claim tax treaty benefits[6]	Complete lines 1–5b, 7a–b (SSN or ITIN optional), 8a, 8b–c (if applicable), 9a, 9b (if applicable), 10, and 18.
Is administering an estate	Needs an EIN to report estate income on Form 1041	Complete lines 1–6, 9a, 10–12, 13–17 (if applicable), and 18.
Is a withholding agent for taxes on non-wage income paid to an alien (i.e., individual, corporation, or partnership, etc.)	Is an agent, broker, fiduciary, manager, tenant, or spouse who is required to file Form 1042, Annual Withholding Tax Return for U.S. Source Income of Foreign Persons	Complete lines 1, 2, 3 (if applicable), 4a–5b, 7a–b (if applicable), 8a, 8b–c (if applicable), 9a, 9b (if applicable), 10 and 18.
Is a state or local agency	Serves as a tax reporting agent for public assistance recipients under Rev. Proc. 80-4, 1980-1 C.B. 581[7]	Complete lines 1, 2, 4a–5b, 9a, 10 and 18.
Is a single-member LLC	Needs an EIN to file Form 8832, Classification Election, for filing employment tax returns, or for state reporting purposes[8]	Complete lines 1–18 (as applicable).
Is an S corporation	Needs an EIN to file Form 2553, Election by a Small Business Corporation[9]	Complete lines 1–18 (as applicable).

[1] For example, a sole proprietorship or self-employed farmer who establishes a qualified retirement plan, or is required to file excise, employment, alcohol, tobacco, or firearms returns, must have an EIN. A partnership, corporation, REMIC (real estate mortgage investment conduit), nonprofit organization (church, club, etc.), or farmers' cooperative must use an EIN for any tax-related purpose even if the entity does not have employees.

[2] However, do not apply for a new EIN if the existing entity only (a) changed its business name, (b) elected on Form 8832 to change the way it is taxed (or is covered by the default rules), or (c) terminated its partnership status because at least 50% of the total interests in partnership capital and profits were sold or exchanged within a 12-month period. The EIN of the terminated partnership should continue to be used. See Regulations section 301.6109-1(d)(2)(iii).

[3] Do not use the EIN of the prior business unless you became the "owner" of a corporation by acquiring its stock.

[4] However, grantor trusts that do not file using Optional Method 1 and IRA trusts that are required to file Form 990-T, Exempt Organization Business Income Tax Return, must have an EIN. For more information on grantor trusts, see the Instructions for Form 1041.

[5] A plan administrator is the person or group of persons specified as the administrator by the instrument under which the plan is operated.

[6] Entities applying to be a Qualified Intermediary (QI) need a QI-EIN even if they already have an EIN. See Rev. Proc. 2000-12.

[7] See also Household employer on page 4 of the instructions. **Note.** State or local agencies may need an EIN for other reasons, for example, hired employees.

[8] Most LLCs do not need to file Form 8832. See Limited liability company (LLC) on page 4 of the instructions for details on completing Form SS-4 for an LLC.

[9] An existing corporation that is electing or revoking S corporation status should use its previously-assigned EIN.

Form SS-8
(Rev. November 2006)
Department of the Treasury
Internal Revenue Service

Determination of Worker Status
for Purposes of Federal Employment Taxes
and Income Tax Withholding

OMB No. 1545-0004

Name of firm (or person) for whom the worker performed services	Worker's name

Firm's address (include street address, apt. or suite no., city, state, and ZIP code)	Worker's address (include street address, apt. or suite no., city, state, and ZIP code)

Trade name	Daytime telephone number ( )	Worker's social security number

Telephone number (include area code) ( )	Firm's employer identification number	Worker's employer identification number (if any)

Note. If the worker is paid by a firm other than the one listed on this form for these services, enter the name, address, and employer identification number of the payer.

Disclosure of Information

The information provided on Form SS-8 may be disclosed to the firm, worker, or payer named above to assist the IRS in the determination process. For example, if you are a worker, we may disclose the information you provide on Form SS-8 to the firm or payer named above. The information can only be disclosed to assist with the determination process. If you provide incomplete information, we may not be able to process your request. See *Privacy Act and Paperwork Reduction Act Notice* on page 5 for more information. **If you do not want this information disclosed to other parties, do not file Form SS-8.**

Parts I–V. All filers of Form SS-8 must complete all questions in Parts I–IV. Part V must be completed if the worker provides a service directly to customers or is a salesperson. If you cannot answer a question, enter "Unknown" or "Does not apply." If you need more space for a question, attach another sheet with the part and question number clearly identified.

Part I	**General Information**

1 This form is being completed by: ☐ Firm ☐ Worker; for services performed _____ to _____ .
(beginning date)   (ending date)

2 Explain your reason(s) for filing this form (for example, you received a bill from the IRS, you believe you erroneously received a Form 1099 or Form W-2, you are unable to get worker's compensation benefits, or you were audited or are being audited by the IRS). ....
....
....

3 Total number of workers who performed or are performing the same or similar services _____ .

4 How did the worker obtain the job? ☐ Application   ☐ Bid   ☐ Employment Agency   ☐ Other (specify) _____

5 Attach copies of all supporting documentation (contracts, invoices, memos, Forms W-2 or Forms 1099-MISC issued or received, IRS closing agreements, IRS rulings, etc.). In addition, please inform us of any current or past litigation concerning the worker's status. If no income reporting forms (Form 1099-MISC or W-2) were furnished to the worker, enter the amount of income earned for the year(s) at issue $ _____ .

If both Form W-2 and Form 1099-MISC were issued or received, explain why. ....
....

6 Describe the firm's business. ....
....

7 Describe the work done by the worker and provide the worker's job title. ....
....

8 Explain why you believe the worker is an employee or an independent contractor. ....
....
....

9 Did the worker perform services for the firm in any capacity before providing the services that are the subject of this determination request?
☐ Yes   ☐ No   ☐ N/A

If "Yes," what were the dates of the prior service? ....

If "Yes," explain the differences, if any, between the current and prior service. ....
....

10 If the work is done under a written agreement between the firm and the worker, attach a copy (preferably signed by both parties). Describe the terms and conditions of the work arrangement. ....
....

For Privacy Act and Paperwork Reduction Act Notice, see page 5.   Cat. No. 16106T   Form **SS-8** (Rev. 11-2006)

Part II **Behavioral Control**

1   What specific training and/or instruction is the worker given by the firm? ....

2   How does the worker receive work assignments? ....

3   Who determines the methods by which the assignments are performed? ....

4   Who is the worker required to contact if problems or complaints arise and who is responsible for their resolution? ....

5   What types of reports are required from the worker? Attach examples. ....

6   Describe the worker's daily routine such as, schedule, hours, etc. ....

7   At what location(s) does the worker perform services (e.g., firm's premises, own shop or office, home, customer's location, etc.)? Indicate
    the appropriate percentage of time the worker spends in each location, if more than one. ....

8   Describe any meetings the worker is required to attend and any penalties for not attending (e.g., sales meetings, monthly meetings, staff
    meetings, etc.). ....

9   Is the worker required to provide the services personally? . . . . ☐ **Yes** ☐ **No**

10 If substitutes or helpers are needed, who hires them? ....

11 If the worker hires the substitutes or helpers, is approval required? . . . . ☐ **Yes** ☐ **No**
    If "Yes," by whom? ....

12 Who pays the substitutes or helpers? ....

13 Is the worker reimbursed if the worker pays the substitutes or helpers? . . . . ☐ **Yes** ☐ **No**
    If "Yes," by whom?

Part III **Financial Control**

1   List the supplies, equipment, materials, and property provided by each party:
    The firm ....
    The worker ....
    Other party ....

2   Does the worker lease equipment? . . . . ☐ **Yes** ☐ **No**
    If "Yes," what are the terms of the lease? (Attach a copy or explanatory statement.) ....

3   What expenses are incurred by the worker in the performance of services for the firm? ....

4   Specify which, if any, expenses are reimbursed by:
    The firm ....
    Other party ....

5   Type of pay the worker receives: ☐ Salary   ☐ Commission   ☐ Hourly Wage   ☐ Piece Work
    ☐ Lump Sum   ☐ Other (specify) ....
    If type of pay is commission, and the firm guarantees a minimum amount of pay, specify amount $ _____ .

6   Is the worker allowed a drawing account for advances? . . . . ☐ **Yes** ☐ **No**
    If "Yes," how often? ....
    Specify any restrictions. ....

7   Whom does the customer pay? . . . . ☐ Firm   ☐ Worker
    If worker, does the worker pay the total amount to the firm? ☐ **Yes** ☐ **No** If "No," explain. ....

8   Does the firm carry worker's compensation insurance on the worker? . . . . ☐ **Yes** ☐ **No**

9   What economic loss or financial risk, if any, can the worker incur beyond the normal loss of salary (e.g., loss or damage of equipment,
    material, etc.)? ....

Part IV   **Relationship of the Worker and Firm**

1   List the benefits available to the worker (e.g., paid vacations, sick pay, pensions, bonuses, paid holidays, personal days, insurance benefits). ------

2   Can the relationship be terminated by either party without incurring liability or penalty?   ☐ **Yes**   ☐ **No**
If "No," explain your answer. ------

3   Did the worker perform similar services for others during the same time period?   ☐ **Yes**   ☐ **No**
If "Yes," is the worker required to get approval from the firm?   ☐ **Yes**   ☐ **No**

4   Describe any agreements prohibiting competition between the worker and the firm while the worker is performing services or during any later period. Attach any available documentation. ------

5   Is the worker a member of a union?   ☐ **Yes**   ☐ **No**

6   What type of advertising, if any, does the worker do (e.g., a business listing in a directory, business cards, etc.)? Provide copies, if applicable. ------

7   If the worker assembles or processes a product at home, who provides the materials and instructions or pattern? ------

8   What does the worker do with the finished product (e.g., return it to the firm, provide it to another party, or sell it)? ------

9   How does the firm represent the worker to its customers (e.g., employee, partner, representative, or contractor)? ------

10   If the worker no longer performs services for the firm, how did the relationship end (e.g., worker quit or was fired, job completed, contract ended, firm or worker went out of business)? ------

Part V   **For Service Providers or Salespersons.** Complete this part if the worker provided a service directly to customers or is a salesperson.

1   What are the worker's responsibilities in soliciting new customers? ------

2   Who provides the worker with leads to prospective customers? ------
3   Describe any reporting requirements pertaining to the leads. ------

4   What terms and conditions of sale, if any, are required by the firm? ------
5   Are orders submitted to and subject to approval by the firm?   ☐ **Yes**   ☐ **No**
6   Who determines the worker's territory? ------
7   Did the worker pay for the privilege of serving customers on the route or in the territory?   ☐ **Yes**   ☐ **No**
If "Yes," whom did the worker pay? ------
If "Yes," how much did the worker pay? $ _____
8   Where does the worker sell the product (e.g., in a home, retail establishment, etc.)? ------

9   List the product and/or services distributed by the worker (e.g., meat, vegetables, fruit, bakery products, beverages, or laundry or dry cleaning services). If more than one type of product and/or service is distributed, specify the principal one. ------

10   Does the worker sell life insurance full time?   ☐ **Yes**   ☐ **No**
11   Does the worker sell other types of insurance for the firm?   ☐ **Yes**   ☐ **No**
If "Yes," enter the percentage of the worker's total working time spent in selling other types of insurance   _____%
12   If the worker solicits orders from wholesalers, retailers, contractors, or operators of hotels, restaurants, or other similar establishments, enter the percentage of the worker's time spent in the solicitation   _____%
13   Is the merchandise purchased by the customers for resale or use in their business operations?   ☐ **Yes**   ☐ **No**
Describe the merchandise and state whether it is equipment installed on the customers' premises. ------

Sign Here

Under penalties of perjury, I declare that I have examined this request, including accompanying documents, and to the best of my knowledge and belief, the facts presented are true, correct, and complete.

_____ Title _____ Date _____
Type or print name below signature.

General Instructions

Section references are to the Internal Revenue Code unless otherwise noted.

Purpose

Firms and workers file Form SS-8 to request a determination of the status of a worker for purposes of federal employment taxes and income tax withholding.

A Form SS-8 determination may be requested only in order to resolve federal tax matters. If Form SS-8 is submitted for a tax year for which the statute of limitations on the tax return has expired, a determination letter will not be issued. The statute of limitations expires 3 years from the due date of the tax return or the date filed, whichever is later.

The IRS does not issue a determination letter for proposed transactions or on hypothetical situations. We may, however, issue an information letter when it is considered appropriate.

Definition

Firm. For the purposes of this form, the term "firm" means any individual, business enterprise, organization, state, or other entity for which a worker has performed services. The firm may or may not have paid the worker directly for these services.

 If the firm was not responsible for payment for services, be sure to enter the name, address, and employer identification number of the payer on the first page of Form SS-8, below the identifying information for the firm and the worker.

The SS-8 Determination Process

The IRS will acknowledge the receipt of your Form SS-8. Because there are usually two (or more) parties who could be affected by a determination of employment status, the IRS attempts to get information from all parties involved by sending those parties blank Forms SS-8 for completion. Some or all of the information provided on this Form SS-8 may be shared with the other parties listed on page 1. The case will be assigned to a technician who will review the facts, apply the law, and render a decision. The technician may ask for additional information from the requestor, from other involved parties, or from third parties that could help clarify the work relationship before rendering a decision. The IRS will generally issue a formal determination to the firm or payer (if that is a different entity), and will send a copy to the worker. A determination letter applies only to a worker (or a class of workers) requesting it, and the decision is binding on the IRS. In certain cases, a formal determination will not be issued. Instead, an information letter may be issued. Although an information letter is advisory only and is not binding on the IRS, it may be used to assist the worker to fulfill his or her federal tax obligations.

Neither the SS-8 determination process nor the review of any records in connection with the determination constitutes an examination (audit) of any federal tax return. If the periods under consideration have previously been examined, the SS-8 determination process will not constitute a reexamination under IRS reopening procedures. Because this is not an examination of any federal tax return, the appeal rights available in connection with an examination do not apply to an SS-8 determination. However, if you disagree with a determination and you have additional information concerning the work relationship that you believe was not previously considered, you may request that the determining office reconsider the determination.

Completing Form SS-8

Answer all questions as completely as possible. Attach additional sheets if you need more space. Provide information for all years the worker provided services for the firm. Determinations are based on the entire relationship between the firm and the worker. Also indicate if there were any significant changes in the work relationship over the service term.

Additional copies of this form may be obtained by calling 1-800-829-4933 or from the IRS website at *www.irs.gov.*

Fee

There is no fee for requesting an SS-8 determination letter.

Signature

Form SS-8 must be signed and dated by the taxpayer. A stamped signature will not be accepted.

The person who signs for a corporation must be an officer of the corporation who has personal knowledge of the facts. If the corporation is a member of an affiliated group filing a consolidated return, it must be signed by an officer of the common parent of the group.

The person signing for a trust, partnership, or limited liability company must be, respectively, a trustee, general partner, or member-manager who has personal knowledge of the facts.

Where To File

Send the completed Form SS-8 to the address listed below for the firm's location. However, only for cases involving federal agencies, send Form SS-8 to the Internal Revenue Service, Attn: CC:CORP:T:C, Ben Franklin Station, P.O. Box 7604, Washington, DC 20044.

Firm's location:	Send to:
Alaska, Arizona, Arkansas, California, Colorado, Hawaii, Idaho, Illinois, Iowa, Kansas, Minnesota, Missouri, Montana, Nebraska, Nevada, New Mexico, North Dakota, Oklahoma, Oregon, South Dakota, Texas, Utah, Washington, Wisconsin, Wyoming, American Samoa, Guam, Puerto Rico, U.S. Virgin Islands	Internal Revenue Service SS-8 Determinations P.O. Box 630 Stop 631 Holtsville, NY 11742-0630
Alabama, Connecticut, Delaware, District of Columbia, Florida, Georgia, Indiana, Kentucky, Louisiana, Maine, Maryland, Massachusetts, Michigan, Mississippi, New Hampshire, New Jersey, New York, North Carolina, Ohio, Pennsylvania, Rhode Island, South Carolina, Tennessee, Vermont, Virginia, West Virginia, all other locations not listed	Internal Revenue Service SS-8 Determinations 40 Lakemont Road Newport, VT 05855-1555

Instructions for Workers

If you are requesting a determination for more than one firm, complete a separate Form SS-8 for each firm.

 Form SS-8 is not a claim for refund of social security and Medicare taxes or federal income tax withholding.

If the IRS determines that you are an employee, you are responsible for filing an amended return for any corrections related to this decision. A determination that a worker is an employee does not necessarily reduce any current or prior tax liability. For more information, call 1-800-829-1040.

Time for filing a claim for refund. Generally, you must file your claim for a credit or refund within 3 years from the date your original return was filed or within 2 years from the date the tax was paid, whichever is later.

Filing Form SS-8 does not prevent the expiration of the time in which a claim for a refund must be filed. If you are concerned about a refund, and the statute of limitations for filing a claim for refund for the year(s) at issue has not yet expired, you should file Form 1040X, Amended U.S. Individual Income Tax Return, to protect your statute of limitations. File a separate Form 1040X for each year.

On the Form 1040X you file, do not complete lines 1 through 24 on the form. Write "Protective Claim" at the top of the form, sign and date it. In addition, you should enter the following statement in Part II, Explanation of Changes: "Filed Form SS-8 with the Internal Revenue Service Office in (Holtsville, NY; Newport, VT; or Washington, DC; as appropriate). By filing this protective claim, I reserve the right to file a claim for any refund that may be due after a determination of my employment tax status has been completed."

Filing Form SS-8 does not alter the requirement to timely file an income tax return. Do not delay filing your tax return in anticipation of an answer to your SS-8 request. In addition, if applicable, do not delay in responding to a request for payment while waiting for a determination of your worker status.

Instructions for Firms

If a **worker** has requested a determination of his or her status while working for you, you will receive a request from the IRS to complete a Form SS-8. In cases of this type, the IRS usually gives each party an opportunity to present a statement of the facts because any decision will affect the employment tax status of the parties. Failure to respond to this request will not prevent the IRS from issuing a determination letter based on the information he or she has made available so that the worker may fulfill his or her federal tax obligations. However, the information that you provide is extremely valuable in determining the status of the worker.

If you are requesting a determination for a particular class of worker, complete the form for one individual who is representative of the class of workers whose status is in question. If you want a written determination for more than one class of workers, complete a separate Form SS-8 for one worker from each class whose status is typical of that class. A written determination for any worker will apply to other workers of the same class if the facts are not materially different for these workers. Please provide a list of names and addresses of all workers potentially affected by this determination.

If you have a reasonable basis for not treating a worker as an employee, you may be relieved from having to pay employment taxes for that worker under section 530 of the 1978 Revenue Act. However, this relief provision cannot be considered in conjunction with a Form SS-8 determination because the determination does not constitute an examination of any tax return. For more information regarding section 530 of the 1978 Revenue Act and to determine if you qualify for relief under this section, you may visit the IRS website at *www.irs.gov*.

Privacy Act and Paperwork Reduction Act Notice. We ask for the information on this form to carry out the Internal Revenue laws of the United States. This information will be used to determine the employment status of the worker(s) described on the form. Subtitle C, Employment Taxes, of the Internal Revenue Code imposes employment taxes on wages. Sections 3121(d), 3306(a), and 3401(c) and (d) and the related regulations define employee and employer for purposes of employment taxes imposed under Subtitle C. Section 6001 authorizes the IRS to request information needed to determine if a worker(s) or firm is subject to these taxes. Section 6109 requires you to provide your taxpayer identification number. Neither workers nor firms are required to request a status determination, but if you choose to do so, you must provide the information requested on this form. Failure to provide the requested information may prevent us from making a status determination. If any worker or the firm has requested a status determination and you are being asked to provide information for use in that determination, you are not required to provide the requested information. However, failure to provide such information will prevent the IRS from considering it in making the status determination. Providing false or fraudulent information may subject you to penalties. Routine uses of this information include providing it to the Department of Justice for use in civil and criminal litigation, to the Social Security Administration for the administration of social security programs, and to cities, states, and the District of Columbia for the administration of their tax laws. We may also disclose this information to other countries under a tax treaty, to federal and state agencies to enforce federal nontax criminal laws, or to federal law enforcement and intelligence agencies to combat terrorism. We may provide this information to the affected worker(s), the firm, or payer as part of the status determination process.

You are not required to provide the information requested on a form that is subject to the Paperwork Reduction Act unless the form displays a valid OMB control number. Books or records relating to a form or its instructions must be retained as long as their contents may become material in the administration of any Internal Revenue law. Generally, tax returns and return information are confidential, as required by section 6103.

The time needed to complete and file this form will vary depending on individual circumstances. The estimated average time is: Recordkeeping, 22 hrs.; Learning about the law or the form, 47 min.; and Preparing and sending the form to the IRS, 1 hr., 11 min. If you have comments concerning the accuracy of these time estimates or suggestions for making this form simpler, we would be happy to hear from you. You can write to the Internal Revenue Service, Tax Products Coordinating Committee, SE:W:CAR:MP:T:T:SP, 1111 Constitution Ave. NW, IR-6406, Washington, DC 20224. Do not send the tax form to this address. Instead, see *Where To File* on page 4.

This page intentionally blank

Form W-4 (2007)

Purpose. Complete Form W-4 so that your employer can withhold the correct federal income tax from your pay. Because your tax situation may change, you may want to refigure your withholding each year.

Exemption from withholding. If you are exempt, complete **only** lines 1, 2, 3, 4, and 7 and sign the form to validate it. Your exemption for 2007 expires February 16, 2008. See Pub. 505, Tax Withholding and Estimated Tax.

Note. You cannot claim exemption from withholding if (a) your income exceeds $850 and includes more than $300 of unearned income (for example, interest and dividends) and (b) another person can claim you as a dependent on their tax return.

Basic instructions. If you are not exempt, complete the **Personal Allowances Worksheet** below. The worksheets on page 2 adjust your withholding allowances based on itemized deductions, certain credits, adjustments to income, or two-earner/multiple job situations. Complete all worksheets that apply. However, you may claim fewer (or zero) allowances.

Head of household. Generally, you may claim head of household filing status on your tax return only if you are unmarried and pay more than 50% of the costs of keeping up a home for yourself and your dependent(s) or other qualifying individuals.

Tax credits. You can take projected tax credits into account in figuring your allowable number of withholding allowances. Credits for child or dependent care expenses and the child tax credit may be claimed using the **Personal Allowances Worksheet** below. See Pub. 919, How Do I Adjust My Tax Withholding, for information on converting your other credits into withholding allowances.

Nonwage income. If you have a large amount of nonwage income, such as interest or dividends, consider making estimated tax payments using Form 1040-ES, Estimated Tax for Individuals. Otherwise, you may owe additional tax. If you have pension or annuity income, see Pub. 919 to find out if you should adjust your withholding on Form W-4 or W-4P.

Two earners/Multiple jobs. If you have a working spouse or more than one job, figure the total number of allowances you are entitled to claim on all jobs using worksheets from only one Form W-4. Your withholding usually will be most accurate when all allowances are claimed on the Form W-4 for the highest paying job and zero allowances are claimed on the others.

Nonresident alien. If you are a nonresident alien, see the Instructions for Form 8233 before completing this Form W-4.

Check your withholding. After your Form W-4 takes effect, use Pub. 919 to see how the dollar amount you are having withheld compares to your projected total tax for 2007. See Pub. 919, especially if your earnings exceed $130,000 (Single) or $180,000 (Married).

Personal Allowances Worksheet (Keep for your records.)

A Enter "1" for **yourself** if no one else can claim you as a dependent . . . . **A** _____

B Enter "1" if: { You are single and have only one job; or
You are married, have only one job, and your spouse does not work; or
Your wages from a second job or your spouse's wages (or the total of both) are $1,000 or less. } . . **B** _____

C Enter "1" for your **spouse**. But, you may choose to enter "-0-" if you are married and have either a working spouse or more than one job. (Entering "-0-" may help you avoid having too little tax withheld.) . . . . **C** _____

D Enter number of **dependents** (other than your spouse or yourself) you will claim on your tax return . . . . . . **D** _____

E Enter "1" if you will file as **head of household** on your tax return (see conditions under **Head of household** above) . **E** _____

F Enter "1" if you have at least $1,500 of **child or dependent care expenses** for which you plan to claim a credit . . **F** _____
(**Note.** Do **not** include child support payments. See Pub. 503, Child and Dependent Care Expenses, for details.)

G **Child Tax Credit** (including additional child tax credit). See Pub 972, Child Tax Credit, for more information.
• If your total income will be less than $57,000 ($85,000 if married), enter "2" for each eligible child.
• If your total income will be between $57,000 and $84,000 ($85,000 and $119,000 if married), enter "1" for each eligible child plus "1" **additional** if you have 4 or more eligible children. **G** _____

H Add lines A through G and enter total here. (**Note.** This may be different from the number of exemptions you claim on your tax return.) . **H** _____

For accuracy, complete all worksheets that apply. {
• If you plan to **itemize or claim adjustments to income** and want to reduce your withholding, see the **Deductions and Adjustments Worksheet** on page 2.
• If you have **more than one job** or are **married and you and your spouse both work** and the combined earnings from all jobs exceed $40,000 ($25,000 if married) see the **Two-Earners/Multiple Jobs Worksheet** on page 2 to avoid having too little tax withheld.
• If **neither** of the above situations applies, **stop here** and enter the number from line H on line 5 of Form W-4 below.

- **Cut here and give Form W-4 to your employer. Keep the top part for your records.** -

Form **W-4**	**Employee's Withholding Allowance Certificate**	OMB No. 1545-0074
Department of the Treasury Internal Revenue Service	**Whether you are entitled to claim a certain number of allowances or exemption from withholding is subject to review by the IRS. Your employer may be required to send a copy of this form to the IRS.**	20**07**

1 Type or print your first name and middle initial.	Last name	2 Your social security number

Home address (number and street or rural route)

3 ☐ Single ☐ Married ☐ Married, but withhold at higher Single rate.
Note. If married, but legally separated, or spouse is a nonresident alien, check the "Single" box.

City or town, state, and ZIP code

4 If your last name differs from that shown on your social security card, check here. You must call 1-800-772-1213 for a replacement card. ☐

5 Total number of allowances you are claiming (from line **H** above **or** from the applicable worksheet on page 2) | **5** |_____

6 Additional amount, if any, you want withheld from each paycheck . . . . | **6** | $ _____

7 I claim exemption from withholding for 2007, and I certify that I meet **both** of the following conditions for exemption.
• Last year I had a right to a refund of **all** federal income tax withheld because I had **no** tax liability **and**
• This year I expect a refund of **all** federal income tax withheld because I expect to have **no** tax liability.
If you meet both conditions, write "Exempt" here . . . . | **7** |_____

Under penalties of perjury, I declare that I have examined this certificate and to the best of my knowledge and belief, it is true, correct, and complete.

Employee's signature
(Form is not valid unless you sign it.) ▶ _____ **Date** ▶ _____

8 Employer's name and address (Employer: Complete lines 8 and 10 only if sending to the IRS.)	9 Office code (optional)	10 Employer identification number (EIN)

Cat. No. 10220Q   Form **W-4** (2007)

Deductions and Adjustments Worksheet

Note. Use this worksheet *only* if you plan to itemize deductions, claim certain credits, or claim adjustments to income on your 2007 tax return

1   Enter an estimate of your 2007 itemized deductions. These include qualifying home mortgage interest, charitable contributions, state and local taxes, medical expenses in excess of 7.5% of your income, and miscellaneous deductions. (For 2007, you may have to reduce your itemized deductions if your income is over $156,400 ($78,200 if married filing separately). See *Worksheet 2* in Pub. 919 for details.) . .   **1** $ _____

2   Enter: { $10,700 if married filing jointly or qualifying widow(er)
$ 7,850 if head of household
$ 5,350 if single or married filing separately }   . . . .   **2** $ _____

3   **Subtract** line 2 from line 1. If zero or less, enter "-0-" . . . .   **3** $ _____

4   Enter an estimate of your 2007 adjustments to income, including alimony, deductible IRA contributions, and student loan interest   **4** $ _____

5   **Add** lines 3 and 4 and enter the total. (Include any amount for credits from *Worksheet 8* in Pub. 919) .   **5** $ _____

6   Enter an estimate of your 2007 nonwage income (such as dividends or interest) . . . .   **6** $ _____

7   **Subtract** line 6 from line 5. If zero or less, enter "-0-" . . . .   **7** $ _____

8   **Divide** the amount on line 7 by $3,400 and enter the result here. Drop any fraction . . . . .   **8** _____

9   Enter the number from the **Personal Allowances Worksheet,** line H, page 1 . . . .   **9** _____

10 **Add** lines 8 and 9 and enter the total here. If you plan to use the **Two-Earners/Multiple Jobs Worksheet,** also enter this total on line 1 below. Otherwise, **stop here** and enter this total on Form W-4, line 5, page 1   **10** _____

Two-Earners/Multiple Jobs Worksheet (See *Two earners/multiple jobs* on page 1.)

Note. Use this worksheet *only* if the instructions under line H on page 1 direct you here.

1   Enter the number from line H, page 1 (or from line 10 above if you used the **Deductions and Adjustments Worksheet**)   **1** _____

2   Find the number in **Table 1** below that applies to the **LOWEST** paying job and enter it here. **However, if** you are married filing jointly and wages from the highest paying job are $50,000 or less, do not enter more than "3." . . . .   **2** _____

3   If line 1 is **more than or equal to** line 2, subtract line 2 from line 1. Enter the result here (if zero, enter "-0-") and on Form W-4, line 5, page 1. **Do not** use the rest of this worksheet . . . .   **3** _____

Note. If line 1 is *less than* line 2, enter "-0-" on Form W-4, line 5, page 1. Complete lines 4–9 below to calculate the additional withholding amount necessary to avoid a year-end tax bill.

4   Enter the number from line 2 of this worksheet . . . .   **4** _____

5   Enter the number from line 1 of this worksheet . . . .   **5** _____

6   **Subtract** line 5 from line 4 . . . .   **6** _____

7   Find the amount in **Table 2** below that applies to the **HIGHEST** paying job and enter it here . . . .   **7** $ _____

8   **Multiply** line 7 by line 6 and enter the result here. This is the additional annual withholding needed . .   **8** $ _____

9   Divide line 8 by the number of pay periods remaining in 2007. For example, divide by 26 if you are paid every two weeks and you complete this form in December 2006. Enter the result here and on Form W-4, line 6, page 1. This is the additional amount to be withheld from each paycheck . . . .   **9** $ _____

Table 1

Married Filing Jointly		All Others	
If wages from **LOWEST** paying job are—	Enter on line 2 above	If wages from **LOWEST** paying job are—	Enter on line 2 above
$0 - $4,500	0	$0 - $6,000	0
4,501 - 9,000	1	6,001 - 12,000	1
9,001 - 18,000	2	12,001 - 19,000	2
18,001 - 22,000	3	19,001 - 26,000	3
22,001 - 26,000	4	26,001 - 35,000	4
26,001 - 32,000	5	35,001 - 50,000	5
32,001 - 38,000	6	50,001 - 65,000	6
38,001 - 46,000	7	65,001 - 80,000	7
46,001 - 55,000	8	80,001 - 90,000	8
55,001 - 60,000	9	90,001 - 120,000	9
60,001 - 65,000	10	120,001 and over	10
65,001 - 75,000	11		
75,001 - 95,000	12		
95,001 - 105,000	13		
105,001 - 120,000	14		
120,001 and over	15		

Table 2

Married Filing Jointly		All Others	
If wages from **HIGHEST** paying job are—	Enter on line 7 above	If wages from **HIGHEST** paying job are—	Enter on line 7 above
$0 - $65,000	$510	$0 - $35,000	$510
65,001 - 120,000	850	35,001 - 80,000	850
120,001 - 170,000	950	80,001 - 150,000	950
170,001 - 300,000	1,120	150,001 - 340,000	1,120
300,001 and over	1,190	340,001 and over	1,190

Massachusetts Department of

Workforce
Development
Division of Unemployment Assistance

EMPLOYER STATUS REPORT

Complete And Return This Form Within 10 days To:
Division of Unemployment Assistance
Status Department - 5ᵗʰ Floor
19 Staniford Street
Boston, MA 02114-2589

PLEASE TYPE OR PRINT CLEARLY IN INK.

CALL (617) 626-5075 FOR ASSISTANCE.

Fax: (617) 727-8221

**THIS FORM IS FOR USE
BY NEW AND EXISTING EMPLOYERS**

FOR DIVISION USE ONLY

Emp. No.: _____ Subj. Date: _____

Reason: _____ Qtr.: _____ 13th Wk.: _____

No. Employees: _____ Area: _____

Rate Yr: _____ NAICS: _____ Aux: _____

Org.: _____ % Transfer _____

Deter. By: _____

Pred. No.: _____

Pred. Date: _____

Pred. Cd.: _____

ESR Status: _____

Leasing Code: _____

Employer Type: _____

	Workforce Training Yr./Rate	Contribution Yr./Rate
1.		1.
2.		2.
3.		3.
4.		4.
5.		5.

SECTION I   ALL FIELDS REQUIRED

1. Name of employing unit: _____ 2. Trade name: _____

3. List **ALL** business locations in Massachusetts. If more than one, attach a separate sheet.

No. _____ Street (do not use P.O. box number) _____ City _____ State _____ Zip Code

4. Mailing address: _____ 5. Payroll Records Address: _____

6. Business phone: _____ 7. Federal Identification #: _____

8. Owner, partners or officers:

Name (Required)	S.S.A. No. (Required)	Home address	Title	Are officers compensated for their services?
				☐ Yes ☐ No
				☐ Yes ☐ No
				☐ Yes ☐ No

9. Type of organization: ☐ Sole Proprietor   ☐ Partnership   ☐ Corporation   ☐ Other (specify)_____
                           ☐ Trust   ☐ LLC (single member)   ☐ LLC (corp.)   ☐ LLC (partnership)

   If corporation: date incorporated _____ state incorporated _____

10. First date of employment in Massachusetts: _____ 11. Describe nature of your company's business/industry: _____

12. Name your principle commodity, product or service _____

13. Are you a client of an employee leasing company?   ☐ Yes   ☐ No
    Please attach a copy of your contract.   If Yes Name and Address of Leasing Company: _____
    _____

14. Are you liable for federal unemployment tax?   ☐ Yes   ☐ No   First date of liability : _____

15. If your main activity in Massachusetts is to provide support services to other locations of your company, please check appropriate box:

    ☐ Headquarters   ☐ Research   ☐ Warehouse   ☐ Computer Center   ☐ Other (specify) _____

16. Do you hold an exemption from federal income taxes as a non-profit organization described under section 501 (c)(3) of the
    Internal Revenue Code?   ☐ Yes   ☐ No   If Yes, please attach a copy of your exemption with this report.

17. Have you previously been subject to the Massachusetts Unemployment Insurance Law?   ☐ Yes   ☐ No

    If yes, give DUA Account Number _____ Name _____

SECTION II   PLEASE REFER TO INSTRUCTIONS TO COMPLETE THIS FORM

*You must answer **"yes"** if any of the following apply: You acquired **All** or **Part** of another business or organization operating in MA; you were part of a merger with (or consolidation of) a business operating in MA; you changed your Federal Identification Number; you have had a relationship with or are a "spin-off" of a company registered with MA DUA; you changed organizational structure. This includes any changes from one business type to another (examples include—but not limited to—changes from a sole proprietorship to corporation, LLC, LLP, etc., or from a corporation to a sole proprietor, partnership, LLP Trust, etc).*

1. Have you undergone any type of organizational change? ☐ Yes ☐ No If no proceed to Section III

2. What was the nature of the organizational change in Massachusetts?
   ☐ Acquisition ☐ Merger ☐ Consolidation ☐ Transfer of Employees only
   ☐ Other (please explain) _____

3. What is the date of the business transfer or organizational change? (mm/dd/yy) _____

4. Predecessor DUA account number: _____ 5. Predecessor FEIN _____

6. Name of predecessor: _____

7. Did you acquire the assets of the predecessor's business? ☐ Yes ☐ No

8. Did you acquire all or part of the predecessor's business? ☐ All ☐ Part

   If part, please explain: _____

9. Please check major assets acquired:

   ☐ Place of business   ☐ Workforce   ☐ License

   ☐ Customers   ☐ Goodwill   ☐ Franchise rights

   ☐ Trade name   ☐ Stock   ☐ Other

   ☐ Accounts receivable   ☐ Tools, fixtures, equipment, furniture

10. Did you continue the operation of business that you acquired? ☐ Yes ☐ No

11. Brief summary of business reason(s) for this acquisition _____

12. Will the predecessor remain in business in Massachusetts?

   ☐ Yes   If yes, list the present Massachusetts location of the predecessor. _____

       If yes, state the number of employees to remain with predecessor in Massachusetts after the date of succession. _____

   ☐ No   If no, please give the date of the predecessor's final payroll. (mm/dd/yy) _____

13. Has the predecessor employer filed all quarterly reports and paid all contributions, interest, and penalties due to this Agency?

   ☐ Yes   ☐ No   ☐ Unknown

SECTION III   PLEASE SELECT WHICH EMPLOYMENT TYPE LISTED BELOW BEST DESCRIBES YOUR BUSINESS

1. **DOMESTIC EMPLOYERS** (Services performed in the home such as: gardener, personal care attendant, baby sitter, housekeeper, etc.)

   Did you pay $1,000 or more in cash remuneration in any calendar quarter during the current or preceding calendar year for domestic services? ☐ Yes ☐ No

2. **AGRICULTURAL EMPLOYERS** (Services performed on a farm including stock, dairy, poultry, fruit, fur bearing animals, and truck farms, plantations, ranches, nurseries, ranges, orchards, greenhouses, and other similar structures that are used primarily for raising of agricultural and horticultural commodities.)

   Did you pay $20,000 or more in cash remuneration for agricultural services during any calendar quarter of the current or preceding calendar year? ☐ Yes ☐ No

   Did you employ 10 or more individuals on some day in each of 20 calendar weeks, not necessarily consecutive, in either the current or preceding calendar year? ☐ Yes ☐ No

   If you do not meet the agricultural requirements but have a farm-based retail operation that includes the sale of items other than those produced on your farm, you are <u>not</u> an agricultural employer. Please proceed to question #3 (all other employers).

3. ALL OTHER MASSACHUSETTS EMPLOYERS

Did you pay wages of $1,500 or more in any calendar quarter in either the current or preceding calendar year? ☐ Yes ☐ No

Did you employ one or more individuals on some day in each of 13 weeks, not necessarily consecutive, in either the current or preceding calendar quarter? ☐ Yes ☐ No

4. OUT-OF-STATE EMPLOYERS

Did you have a MASSACHUSETTS payroll in excess of $200? ☐ Yes ☐ No

5. PLEASE DO NOT SUBMIT UNTIL YOU ARE ABLE TO DOCUMENT ACTUAL GROSS WAGES PAID PER THE ABOVE REPORTING CRITERIA

List below the number of individuals in your employment in Massachusetts within each calendar week. Include full and part-time employees, also paid officers, if corporation. An individual sole proprietor or a partner should not be counted as an employee. Show total Massachusetts payroll for each calendar quarter.

This application cannot be processed with estimated or anticipated future wages. If this application is not completed in full it will be returned to you for the required information (i.e.: number of employees, dates of employment, gross wages).

RECORD OF MASSACHUSETTS EMPLOYMENT

	CURRENT CALENDAR YEAR		PRECEDING CALENDAR YEAR		PRECEDING CALENDAR YEAR	
	Enter Year _____ Total Wages 1st QTR _____ 2nd QTR _____		Enter Year _____ Total Wages 1st QTR _____ 2nd QTR _____		Enter Year _____ Total Wages 1st QTR _____ 2nd QTR _____	
	JANUARY	APRIL	JANUARY	APRIL	JANUARY	APRIL
Week Ending						
Number Employed						
	FEBRUARY	MAY	FEBRUARY	MAY	FEBRUARY	MAY
Week Ending						
Number Employed						
	MARCH	JUNE	MARCH	JUNE	MARCH	JUNE
Week Ending						
Number Employed						
	Total Wages _____ 3rd QTR _____ 4th QTR _____		Total Wages _____ 3rd QTR _____ 4th QTR _____		Total Wages _____ 3rd QTR _____ 4th QTR _____	
	JULY	OCTOBER	JULY	OCTOBER	JULY	OCTOBER
Week Ending						
Number Employed						
	AUGUST	NOVEMBER	AUGUST	NOVEMBER	AUGUST	NOVEMBER
Week Ending						
Number Employed						
	SEPTEMBER	DECEMBER	SEPTEMBER	DECEMBER	SEPTEMBER	DECEMBER
Week Ending						
Number Employed						

CERTIFICATION

If you answered yes to Question 1 in Section II and if this organizational change involves companies with any commonality in ownership, management and/or control, you must proceed to Section IV. If not, please complete the certification below.

Massachusetts law provides for civil fines and criminal penalties for misrepresentation, evasion, willful nondisclosure, and failure or refusal to furnish reports or requested information to this agency. Both the employer of record or the agent, who knowingly advises in such a way that results in a violation of these provisions, shall be subject to said penalties. (MGL Ch 151A, Section 14N). Failure to comply with all reporting and payment requirements under MGL Chapter 151A may result in loss of your organization's right to operate or renew your license by the Commonwealth of Massachusetts.

THIS REPORT MUST BE SIGNED BY THE OWNER, PARTNER, OR CORPORATE OFFICER

CERTIFICATION

I certify, under penalties of law, that all statements made hereon are true to the best of my knowledge and belief.

Name of Employing unit: _____ Date: _____

Signature: _____ Title: _____

Name: (Print) _____

PREDECESSOR CERTIFICATION

I hereby certify that all information submitted by the successor is true in accordance with the transfer.

Name of Predecessor Company: _____ Date _____

Signature: _____ Title _____

Name: (Print) _____

DO NOT COMPLETE COMMON OWNERSHIP SECTION UNLESS TRANSFERS OCCURRED ON OR AFTER JANUARY 1, 2006.

SECTION IV	**PART A**	**COMMON OWNERSHIP**

To be completed by the TRANSFEREE employer initiating the change. Please note that by signing this document the transferring employer must attest to these answers.

> *(Transferee employer- one to whom a conveyance of title or property is made; a person/entity to whom something is transferred or conveyed. Example, Company B acquires part or all of the business of Company A. In this example Company B is the transferee employer and Company A is the transferring employer or transferor).*

Is the transferee employer the Parent Company or a subsidiary of the transferring employer?   ☐ Yes   ☐ No

If yes, please list the name of the Parent Company and FEIN#

Name: _____   FEIN: _____

If yes, are the transferee employer and the transferring employer subsidiaries of the same Parent Company?   ☐ Yes   ☐ No

If yes, please list the name of the Parent Company and FEIN#

Name: _____   FEIN: _____

PLEASE CHECK OFF WHICH ORGANIZATIONAL TYPE BEST DESCRIBES YOUR BUSINESS AND ANSWER THE QUESTIONS LISTED FOLLOWING THAT ORGANIZATION TYPE:

1. ORGANIZATIONAL TYPE

☐ CORPORATION
(includes Limited Liability Companies (LLC) organized as a corporation)

Is there a person, corporation or other legal entity that serves in the capacity of Chief Financial Officer (CFO), Chief Executive Officer (CEO) or other similar authority for the transferring employer who also serves as the CFO or CEO or other person holding similar authority for the transferee employer?

☐ Yes   ☐ No   *If yes, list the name/entity, SS#/FEIN and title below*

Name _____   SS# _____   Title _____

If Entity acts as CFO/CEO:

Company Name: _____   FEIN# _____

Does either the transferee or the transferring employer exercise power indirectly or directly through one or more persons of over 25% or more of any voting securities of BOTH the transferring employer and the transferee?

☐ Yes   ☐ No   *If yes, list the name/entity, FEIN and the percentage of ownership*

Name/Entity _____   % of ownership _____   SS# _____   FEIN# _____

Does the CFO, CEO or other person holding similar authority for the transferring employer have a familial relationship with the CFO, CEO or other person holding a position of similar authority for the transferee employer?

☐ Yes   ☐ No   *If yes, please list name, SS#, (title and relationship)*

Name _____   SS# _____   Title _____   Relationship _____

Name _____   SS# _____   Title _____   Relationship _____

2. ☐ SOLE PROPRIETOR
(includes LLCs organized as a single member)

Does the transferee employer's sole proprietor/owner have a familial relationship to the transferring employer's sole proprietor/owner?

(Family member is defined but not limited to spouse, child, parent, sister, brother, sister-in-law, brother-in-law, aunt, uncle, niece, nephew, and first cousin.)

☐ Yes   ☐ No   *If yes, please list name, SS# and relationship*

Name _____   SS# _____   Relationship _____

Name _____   SS# _____   Relationship _____

3. ☐ PARTNERSHIPS, JOINT VENTURES
(includes LLP, LLC organized as a partnership)

Is there a person, corporation or other legal entity that serves in the capacity of a managing partner in both the transferring employer and the transferee employer?

☐ Yes   ☐ No   *If yes, please list name/entity, SS# /FEIN# and title*

Name ———————————— SS# ———————————— Title ————————————————

If Entity acts as Managing Partner:

Company Name: ———————————————   FEIN# ————————————————

Does a partner for the transferring employer have a familial relationship to any partner, member or other person holding a position of authority for the transferee employer?

☐ Yes   ☐ No   *If yes please list name, SS#, title and relationship*

Name ———————————— SS# ———————————— Title ————————————————

Relationship ——

4. ☐ TRUST

Does one person, corporation or other legal entity serve as a trustee of the transferring trust, either directly or through an intermediary, and also serve as a trustee in the transferee trust, or as a beneficiary of the trust?

☐ Yes   ☐ No

Name ———————————— SS# ———————————— Title ————————————————

If Entity serves as trustee:

Company Name: ———————————————   FEIN# ————————————————

If you answered yes to any of the above questions, please complete Section IV Part B

SECTION IV   PART B   COMMON OWNERSHIP

Complete the following:

1. The business address of your corporate HQ: ————————————————————————

2. Name of business transferred: ————————————————————————————————

3. Transferor's DUA account number: ————————————————————————————

4. Transferor's business location: ————————————————————————————————

5. Date of transfer: ——

6. Number of workers employed by transferor in Massachusetts just before the sale ————————————

   after the sale ————————————————

7. Number of workers employed by you, the transferee, in Massachusetts just before the sale ————————

   after the sale ————————————————

8. How many of the transferor workers have you continued to employ?   ————————————————

   have you NOT continued to employ? ————————————————

You must complete Section IV Part C if you took over part of another business operating in Massachusetts

SECTION IV   PART C   PART SUCCESSIONS

9. Is the transferor still doing business in MA?   ☐ Yes   ☐ No   ☐ Unknown

   If yes what business activities are continued? ————————————————————————

(Note: Transferee may become liable for some or all of any DUA delinquency of the transferor)

This application must be accompanied by a schedule showing the name and social security number of each individual associated with that portion of the business being transferred, regardless of whether or not they are actually transferred to the transferee employer.

PLEASE SUMMARIZE ALL WAGE INFORMATION IN CHARTS A AND B ON THIS FORM. DO NOT JUST ATTACH PREVIOUSLY FILED FORMS 1. IN ADDITION, PLEASE COMPLETE EVERY APPLICABLE ITEM ON THIS FORM. FAILURE TO DO SO COMPLETELY, ACCURATELY, AND IN A TIMELY MANNER MAY RESULT IN PENALTIES FOR FAILURE TO COMPLY WITH THE LAW, AS PROVIDED FOR UNDER MGL, CH 151A, SECTION 14N.

Please provide, in Chart A, the transferring employer's entire payroll for the last 4 completed quarters prior to the transfer date.
In Chart B, provide the transferring employer's payroll for that portion acquired for the last 4 completed quarters prior to the transfer date.
Please provide dates of quarters (mo, day, yr) to which you are referring in the charts below.

EXAMPLE

Date transfer took place: 04/01/06

Chart A

*PLEASE PROVIDE **TOTAL** WAGES FOR ALL EMPLOYEES OF THE TRANSFERRING EMPLOYER FOR THE LAST 4 COMPLETED QUARTERS PRIOR TO THE TRANSFER DATE.*

PLEASE START WITH THE MOST RECENT QUARTER AND WORK BACK IN TIME.

Quarter dates	(1/01/06-3/31/06)	(10/01/05-12/31/05)	(7/01/05-9/30/05)	(4/01/05 -6/30/05)	12 Month Summary
Total Wages	$ 60,000	$ 75,500	$ 67,500	$ 67,500	$ 270,500
Excess Wages (wages over $14,000 wage base per employee)	$ 0.00	$ 67,500	$ 61,000	$ 8,000	$ 136,500
Taxable Wages	$ 60,000	$ 7,500	$ 6,500	$ 59,500	$ 133,500
Number of employees	8, 8, 8	10, 10, 10	9, 9, 9	9, 9, 9	

who worked during or received pay for the payroll period which includes the **12th** day of the month.

Chart B

*PLEASE PROVIDE WAGE DETAIL FOR **THAT PORTION ACQUIRED** OF THE TRANSFERRING EMPLOYER'S PAYROLL FOR THE LAST 4 COMPLETED QUARTERS PRIOR TO THE TRANSFER DATE.*

PLEASE START WITH THE MOST RECENT QUARTER AND WORK BACK IN TIME.

Quarter dates	(1/01/06-3/31/06)	(10/01/05-12/31/05)	(7/01/05-9/30/05)	(4/01/05 -6/30/05)	12 Month Summary
Total Wages	$ 37,500	$ 30,000	$ 37,500	$ 37,500	$ 142,500
Excess Wages (wages over $14,000 wage base per employee)	$ 0.00	$ 30,000	$ 37,500	$ 5,000	$ 72,500
Taxable Wages	$ 37,500	$ 0.00	$ 0.00	$ 32,500	$ 70,000
Number of employees	4, 4, 4	5, 5, 5	5, 5, 5	6, 6, 6	

who worked during or received pay for the payroll period which includes the **12th** day of the month..

Chart A

Date transfer took place: _____

*PLEASE PROVIDE **TOTAL** WAGES FOR ALL EMPLOYEES OF THE TRANSFERRING EMPLOYER FOR THE LAST 4 COMPLETED QUARTERS PRIOR TO THE TRANSFER DATE.*

PLEASE START WITH THE MOST RECENT QUARTER AND WORK BACK IN TIME.

Quarter dates	(-)	(-)	(-)	(-)	12 Month Summary
Total Wages	$	$	$	$	$
Excess Wages (wages over $14,000 wage base per employee)	$	$	$	$	$
Taxable Wages	$	$	$	$	$
Number of employees					

who worked during or received pay for the payroll period which includes the **12th** day of the month.

Chart B

*PLEASE PROVIDE WAGE DETAIL FOR **THAT PORTION ACQUIRED** OF THE TRANSFERRING EMPLOYER'S PAYROLL FOR THE LAST 4 COMPLETED QUARTERS PRIOR TO THE TRANSFER DATE.*

PLEASE START WITH THE MOST RECENT QUARTER AND WORK BACK IN TIME.

Quarter dates	(-)	(-)	(-)	(-)	12 Month Summary
Total Wages	$	$	$	$	$
Excess Wages (wages over $14,000 wage base per employee)	$	$	$	$	$
Taxable Wages	$	$	$	$	$
Number of employees					

who worked during or received pay for the payroll period which includes the **12th** day of the month.

CERTIFICATION

Massachusetts law provides for civil fines and criminal penalties for misrepresentation, evasion, willful nondisclosure, and failure or refusal to furnish reports or requested information to this agency. Both the employer of record or the agent, who knowingly advises in such a way that results in a violation of these provisions, shall be subject to said penalties. (MGL Ch 151A, Section 14N). Failure to comply with all reporting and payment requirements under MGL Chapter 151A may result in loss of your organization's right to operate or renew your license by the Commonwealth of Massachusetts.

THIS REPORT MUST BE SIGNED BY THE OWNER, PARTNER, OR CORPORATE OFFICER AUTHORIZED TO BIND THE CORPORATION.

SUCCESSOR CERTIFICATION

I certify, under penalties of law, that all statements made here on are true to the best of my knowledge and belief.

Name of Employing unit: _____ Date: _____

Signature: _____ Title: _____

Name (Print): _____

PREDECESSOR CERTIFICATION

I hereby certify that all information submitted by the successor is true in accordance with the transfer.

Name of Predecessor Company: _____ Date _____

Signature: _____ Title _____

Name: (Print) _____

Form NHR
New Hire and Independent
Contractor Reporting Form

Rev. 03/07
Massachusetts
Department of
Revenue

TO ENSURE ACCURACY, PRINT (OR TYPE) NEATLY IN UPPER-CASE LETTERS AND NUMBERS, USING A DARK, BALLPOINT PEN.

Employee Information

FIRST NAME*   MI   LAST NAME*

SOCIAL SECURITY NUMBER*   DATE OF HIRE OR REINSTATEMENT*

          -          -   /   /

ADDRESS*

CITY/TOWN*   STATE*   ZIP*   +4 (OPTIONAL)

IT'S THE LAW! - Massachusetts regulations requires employers with 25 or more employees to report their new hires and independent contractors electronically.

For more information, go to www.mass.gov/dor and select the **Report New Hires** link located in the **Online Services** section.

Employer Information

EMPLOYER IDENTIFICATION NUMBER*   -

CORPORATE NAME*

PAYROLL ADDRESS TO WHICH THE INCOME WITHHOLDING ORDER WILL BE SENT*

PAYROLL ADDRESS (Continued)

CITY/TOWN*   STATE*   ZIP*   +4 (OPTIONAL)

NOTE: All fields on this form with an * are mandatory fields. Please ensure all information entered is legible and accurate prior to submitting the form to DOR.

Helpful Hint: Once you have completed your employer information, you may copy this form to save time when reporting future new hires and independent contractors.

Send Completed Form NHR to:
Massachusetts Department of Revenue, PO Box 55141, Boston, MA 02205-5141 or,
you may fax the completed form to 617-376-3262.

Index

A

accountant, 12, 51, 72, 154, 178, 183, 185
accounting, 3, 44, 51, 137, 177, 178, 180
advertisement, 78, 128, 155, 176
advertising, 3, 30, 36, 40, 41, 43, 46, 48–51, 69, 81, 125–130, 132–136, 144, 151, 152, 157, 158, 167, 168, 175, 176, 187
affirmative action, 122
Americans with Disabilities Act (ADA), 65, 68, 99, 106, 107
Anti-Cybersquatting Consumer Protection Act, 162
Application for Employer Identification Number (IRS Form SS-4), 183
Application for Registration of a Trademark, 31
articles of organization, 10, 11, 16, 18, 20

attorney, 14, 19, 29, 60, 61, 73, 77, 82, 85, 122, 141, 142, 170, 172, 187
automatic dialing, 133

B

bait and switch laws, 78
bonding, 40, 87
bookkeeping, 23, 177, 178, 180
borrowing money, 57
Boston Entrepreneurs' Network, 7
business plan, 39–49, 51, 103
Business Resource Center, 4
buy-sell agreement, 59

C

C corporation, 11, 178, 182

Cambridge Business Development Center, 8

capital, 13, 23, 52, 55, 56, 59–61, 140, 163

cash, 33, 57–59, 121, 137, 138

Certificate of Formation, 19, 21

Certificate of Limited Partnership, 19, 20

Certificate Stating Real Name of Person Transacting Business, 27

chamber of commerce, 5, 7, 45

check, 23, 25, 26, 28, 67–69, 74, 85, 86, 98, 105, 115, 117, 119, 120, 125, 137, 138, 153, 155, 165, 170, 174, 178, 185

child labor law, 117

Children Online Privacy Protection Act of 1998 (COPPA), 172

Code of Federal Regulations (C.F.R.), 90, 92, 117, 125–127, 140, 142, 150

Commonwealth Corporation, 6

Consumer Product Safety Commission (CPSC), 91, 92

contract, 16, 19, 47, 77–82, 91, 100, 104, 105, 120–123, 126, 129–131, 169, 174

Controlling the Assault of Nonsolicited Pornography and Marketing Act of 2003 (CANSPAM), 135

copyright, 146, 147, 164, 170, 171, 173

corporate veil, 15, 19

corporation, 6, 7, 9–22, 26–29, 40, 55, 59, 66, 67, 79, 80, 85, 86, 140, 142, 154, 158, 162, 163, 172, 177–180, 182, 183, 185, 189

counteroffer, 79

court, 20, 25, 60, 70, 78–80, 82, 100, 104, 109, 111, 112, 144, 162, 169

credit card, 23, 58, 137–141, 173, 174

customer, 3, 10, 30, 40, 42–49, 51, 56, 64, 65, 77–79, 82, 85, 89, 128, 133, 138, 139, 141, 167, 168, 172, 174, 192

D

Davis-Bacon Act, 121

debt, 9, 12, 13, 15, 18, 81, 142, 155

Department of Employment and Training (D.E.T.), 84

Department of Revenue, 99, 189–192

Determination of Worker Status (IRS Form SS-8), 102

discrimination, 104, 105, 107, 110, 111, 123, 141, 144, 155, 158

domain name, 29, 161–163, 165

E

email, 28, 135, 167, 168, 171, 174

email advertising, 135, 167

employee, 1–4, 6, 10, 12, 26, 44, 47, 48, 51, 56, 65, 70, 83–87, 89, 90, 94, 97–117, 119–124, 132, 149, 156, 163, 179, 183–186, 188, 189, 191

Employee Polygraph Protection Act, 98

Employee Retirement Income Security Act (ERISA), 115

employee theft, 87

Employee's Withholding Allowance Certificate (IRS Form W-4), 183

employer, 84, 89, 98–100, 102, 105–114, 116, 117, 120, 122–124, 156, 183, 184, 186, 188, 189

Employers Status Report, 189

Employment Eligibility Verification (form I-9), 119

Encyclopedia of Associations, 41

Enterprise Center at Salem State College, 8

entrepreneur, 1, 7, 8, 55, 59

Environmental Protection Agency (EPA), 90

Equal Employment Opportunity Commission (EEOC), 105, 108, 123

Equal Pay Act, 105

equity, 14, 17, 39, 56, 67

Executive Office of Housing and Economic Development (EOHED), 5

exemption, 60, 111, 188

F

Fair Credit Billing Act, 140

Fair Debt Collection Practices Act of 1977, 142

Fair Labor Standards Act (FLSA), 111, 112, 117

Family and Medical Leave Act of 1993 (FEML), 115, 116

Federal Trade Commission (FTC), 125–127, 129, 132, 135, 142, 144, 150, 168, 174–176

fictitious name, 9, 18, 23, 25, 27–29, 69, 70

financing law, 140

firing, 97, 104, 105, 107

Food and Drug Administration (FDA), 74, 91, 127

Foundation for Continuing Education, 8

fraud, 80, 176

G

government, 5, 6, 60, 68, 70, 89, 99, 102, 114, 121–123, 125, 137, 140, 142, 144, 149, 153, 183, 185, 192, 193

H

hazardous material, 91

hiring, 2, 3, 10, 23, 40, 48, 97–101, 103, 105, 107, 117, 119–122, 163, 165, 167, 173, 178

home business, 63, 69, 70, 86

I

immigration, 119–121

income, 11–15, 17, 41, 50, 51, 55–57, 70, 114, 115, 137, 141, 177–182, 184, 185, 188, 189, 192

independent contractor, 2, 44, 84, 101–103, 106, 120, 184

individual retirement account (IRA), 114, 115

insurance, 23, 36, 40, 41, 44, 49, 63, 83–88, 97, 102, 103, 121, 151, 156

insurance, automobile, 86

insurance, hazard, 85

insurance, health, 49, 86

insurance, home business, 86

insurance, liability, 85

insurance, unemployment, 84, 97

insurance, workers' compensation, 83, 84, 102

intellectual property, 145

Internal Revenue Service (IRS), 11, 17, 101, 102, 107, 137, 138, 177, 178, 181–186
Interstate Commerce Commission, 150
investor, 39, 42, 44, 59, 60

L

lawyer. *See* attorney.
layoff, 122
leasing, 10, 65–67, 69, 81, 131
lender, 39, 56, 73
liability, 9, 10, 12–15, 18–23, 29, 59, 83, 85, 86, 102, 109, 121, 156, 161, 170, 172, 182, 188, 189
libel, 170
license, 18, 19, 23, 69, 70, 74
limited liability company (LLC), 9, 13, 14, 19, 29, 59, 172
limited liability partnership (LLP), 9, 14, 15, 19, 20, 178, 182
LLC, 13–18, 20, 26, 46, 178, 182
loan, 23, 55, 57, 58, 60

M

marketing, 4, 23, 42–44, 48, 52, 135, 147, 167, 175, 176
Massachusetts Alliance for Economic Development, 7
Massachusetts Classification of Goods and Services, 31
Massachusetts Department of Business and Technology, 6

Massachusetts Office of Business Development, 6
Massachusetts Small Business Development Centers, 7
Massachusetts Technology Development Corporation, 6
McNamara-O'Hara Service Contract Act, 122
Medicare, 101, 102, 179, 183, 184
merger, 11

N

National Association for the Self-Employed, 4
National Labor Relations Act of 1935, 122
networking, 7, 48
new hire reporting, 99
nonprofit organization, 6–8, 12, 13, 20, 22, 161
Nutritional Labeling Education Act of 1990, 127

O

Occupational Safety and Health Administration (OSHA), 89, 90
off the books, 121
operating agreement, 16, 59

P

partner, 2, 10, 13, 18, 19, 22, 27, 58, 59, 181, 184
partnership, 9, 10, 13–15, 18–22, 27, 29, 157, 158, 177, 178, 181–183
patent, 26, 29, 31, 134, 145–147
Personal Responsibility and Work Opportunity Reconciliation Act of 1996 (PRWORA), 99
poster law, 122
product, 2, 3, 35, 36, 41–44, 46, 56, 64, 85, 91–93, 97, 101, 122, 126–128, 133–135, 139, 144–146, 151–155, 157, 158, 163, 164, 167, 169, 171, 174–176, 180, 188
professional corporation, 12, 20, 29, 158
profit, 2, 9–11, 23, 39–41, 44, 50, 51, 55, 60, 82, 93, 140, 177, 179, 181, 182
property ownership, 67
proprietor, 9, 181, 183, 184
proprietorship, 9, 14, 18, 22, 86, 177, 178, 181, 183
publicity, 3, 23, 25, 68, 161, 163, 165, 167
Pure Food and Drug Act of 1906, 91

R

registration, 18–21, 27, 30, 31, 60, 74, 158, 162, 163, 187, 188
Regulation Z (Reg. Z), 140, 141
resources, 2, 4, 7, 8, 57, 61, 127
retail, 40, 42, 64, 81, 94, 125, 139, 141, 152, 158, 175, 187
right of rescission, 129
Robinson-Patman Act of 1936, 144

S

S corporation, 11–18, 178, 179, 182, 189
Secretary of State, 15, 18, 19, 25, 26, 28–30
securities, 19, 20, 60, 61, 74, 141
self-employment, 17
Service Corps of Retired Executives (SCORE), 4, 5, 45
service mark, 29, 146
sexual harassment, 100, 108–111
shareholders, 10–12, 17–19, 22, 59, 182
shareholders' agreement, 59
Sherman Antitrust Act of 1890, 144
Small Business Administration (SBA), 4, 58, 61
smoking, 93, 189
Social Security, 99, 101, 102, 179, 181, 183, 184
sole proprietor, 183, 184
sole proprietorship, 14, 18, 86, 178
solicitation, home, 129
solicitation, telephone, 132
start-up kit, 41
State Office of Minority and Women's Business Assistance (SOMWBA), 6
statute, 12, 14, 16, 17, 71, 80, 99, 116, 134, 143
statute of frauds, 80
stock, 11, 13, 15–18, 59, 60, 67, 180
subleasing, 66

T

tax, 8, 9, 11–18, 22, 23, 41, 44, 49, 56, 60, 68, 94, 101–103, 107, 113, 114, 121, 127, 137, 177–192 trade association, 41, 82, 93

Trade Names Directory, 26

trade secret, 100, 146, 147, 159

trademark, 23, 25, 26, 29–31, 146, 147, 162, 167

Truth in Lending Act, 140

U

umbrella policy, 85

unemployment compensation, 97, 98, 159, 189

Unfair Debt Collection Practices Law, 142

Unfair Sales Act, 144

Uniform Commercial Code (UCC), 143

union, 122

United States Patent and Trademark Office (USPTO), 26, 29, 31, 146

usury, 141

V

volunteer, 4, 124

W

wage, 44, 84, 101, 107, 111, 112, 121–123, 154, 155, 157, 160, 182–184, 186, 188, 189

Walsh-Healey Public Contracts Act, 122

Worcester Regional Chamber of Commerce, 5, 7

work, full-time, 49, 55, 103, 113, 122, 191

work, part-time, 51, 55, 83, 84, 97, 114

Worker Adjustment and Retraining Notification Act, 122

Worker Protection Standard for Agricultural Pesticides, 90

worker, seasonal, 83

worker, temporary, 103, 104

workers' compensation, 83, 84, 102, 106, 160

worker, illegal, 83

working conditions, 123

Z

zoning, 23, 65, 67, 69, 70